A
DEMOCRATIC
CATHOLIC CHURCH

A DEMOCRATIC CATHOLIC CHURCH

The Reconstruction
of
Roman Catholicism

EDITED BY

EUGENE C. BIANCHI

AND

ROSEMARY RADFORD RUETHER

CROSSROAD • NEW YORK

1992

The Crossroad Publishing Company
370 Lexington Avenue, New York, NY 10017

Copyright © 1992 by Eugene C. Bianchi and Rosemary Radford Ruether

Printed in the United States of America

Library of Congress Cataloging-in-Publication Data

A democratic Catholic Church : the reconstruction of Roman Catholicism
/ Eugene C. Bianchi and Rosemary Radford Ruether, editors.
    p. cm.
  ISBN 0-8245-1186-7
  1. Catholic Church—Government. 2. Democracy—Religious aspects—
Catholic Church. I. Bianchi, Eugene C. II. Ruether, Rosemary
Radford.
BX1802.D46 1992
262'.02—dc20   92-7920
                                                                        CIP

Contents

Introduction

Whenever groups of Catholics attempt to assert rights of popular decision making in the church, it is common for bishops to declare "the church is not a democracy." While this may be an accurate factual statement about the church today, the assumption that it is either a comprehensive historical statement or a biblically and theologically normative statement needs to be challenged. The essential question is "why shouldn't the church be democratic?"

Those who make such statements assume that the Roman Catholic Church historically has always possessed a centralized monarchical and hierarchical form of government and that this government was given to it by Jesus Christ. It is therefore divinely mandated and unchangeable. It is the intention of this book to challenge this set of assumptions, to show that democratic elements have always existed in the past in certain aspects of church government, and that democratic polity suits the theological meaning of the church as redemptive society better than does monarchical hierarchy.

The issue of a democratic Catholic Church is not merely an academic debate. Rather it is a crucial hinge for opening the door to further reforms in the spirit of Vatican II. The quarter century since the council has been a long lesson in how needed change in the church can be derailed for lack of participational, democratic structures. As Walter Goddijn's chapter shows, ecclesiastical monarchy in the Vatican operates without democratic checks and balances and without public discourse or deliberation. In this institutional situation, the most creative reforms attempted by local and national churches can be and are impeded at the will or whim of the monarch and his curia.

Renewal-minded Catholics need to understand that the question of ecclesial structures will be at the heart of church reform in the twenty-first century. Moreover, Catholics must shake off the intellectual lethargy that, for too long, has allowed them to acquiesce in the view that the present church structure is divinely mandated for all time. They must begin to ask the hard questions about the relationship between historical realities and theological and ethical norms.

In her chapter on the New Testament, Elisabeth Schüssler Fiorenza makes clear that the Christian Scriptures not only do not provide proof for a monarchical hierarchy as Christ's intention for church government, but they actually witness to an opposite vision: the church as "discipleship of equals." This was expressed in a church primarily ordered on the congregational level. Local congregations chose their own leadership through a combination of election and discernment of gifts. Any governance above the congregational level was loose, primarily based on a sense of spiritual communion between local churches and also special relationships with itinerant founding apostles.

Although the Catholic Church in the second century moved toward patriarchal ordering of the local congregation and then an increasing approximation of the hierarchical system of imperial bureaucracy, local control on the metropolitan and provincial level remained the norm well into the Middle Ages. Election of bishops by local clergy and popular acclamation by the laity, validated by assembled bishops of a region, were typical. Indeed the election of the pope by the college of cardinals itself is a descendent of this practice, since the college of cardinals was originally not a worldwide body, but simply the clergy of the "cardinal" churches of the diocese of Rome, a concept that persists today in the appointment of all cardinals as titular priests of Roman churches.

Although Latin Christianity from the fourth to the sixth centuries moved increasingly toward elevating the bishop of Rome as the primal see, papal primacy was no part of the tradition of Eastern Christianity and has never been accepted by it. Eastern Christianity rests on a collegiality of patriarchal sees, of which Rome is seen as one among others, perhaps with a primacy of honor, but not of jurisdiction. Moreover, in practice papal primacy in the West until the late nineteenth century remained limited by a variety of other authorities: princes and kings and synods of local clergy designated by local priests and bishops. Universal jurisdiction might have been a claim made by popes of the high Middle Ages, but the effort to actually practice it in a thoroughgoing manner is a modern phenomenon dating from Vatican I.

Monastic communities, despite their paternalism, had a basically congregational form and assumed election of abbots and abbesses, as they still do today. As Eugene Bianchi has pointed out, the late Middle Ages saw the rise of parliamentary government in society, with its church counterpart in conciliarism. Universal church councils in the patristic church were called by emperors, not popes. Late medieval conciliarism sought to make the pope a constitutional monarch, subordinate to the council as parliament of the Western church.

Parliamentary government itself is rooted in medieval Christian concepts of the state in which the three orders of clergy, aristocracy, and "commons" were each represented. This is still reflected in English parliamentary government with its House of Lords, which includes Lords spiritual (bishops) and Lords temporal, and the Commons. More radical concepts of democracy that challenged the divine right of kings and the privileged status of the nobility arose from the revival of congregational forms of church government among radical Puritans. The concept of society as a "social contract" based on the rights of the governed arises from the practice of the Christian congregation as a covenantal community.

Nor were such ideas totally foreign among Roman Catholics. As Jay Dolan, historian of American Catholicism, shows in his chapter, many European Catholics who immigrated to North America in the eighteenth and nineteenth centuries brought with them traditions in which local lay leaders administered church property and appointed the priest. They sought to widen this practice in the United States to a congregational form of government based on parish councils.

These remnants of participatory government on the parish, diocesan, and national church levels were stifled in the late nineteenth century when the Vatican I doctrine of universal papal jurisdiction became the rule for centralized monarchical control from Rome. Yet, even in the late twentieth century, in many national churches the role that the national clergy has traditionally played in designating bishops clashes with the efforts of John Paul II to assert the Vatican I principle of universal direct jurisdiction. The pope today advances this principle, not only against concepts of collegiality unleashed by the Second Vatican Council, but also against these more ancient customs.

It should be clear from the above account that papal monarchical government not only is not based on Scripture, but also has never been uncontested in church history. The basic forms of papal monarchy and episcopal hierarchy did not arise from the Christian message itself, but mirror the political, social forms of the various societies that have shaped the Catholic Church.

Roman imperial bureaucracy provided the major model for papal government, which, in a certain sense, replaced it when the Roman emperor disappeared in the West in the early fifth century. Many terms of papal government, such as "Pontifex Maximus" (the title of the head of the Roman pagan priesthood) and "curia" derive from the bureaucracy of the Roman emperor. "Diocese" was the name for the new provincial units of the reformed Diocletian empire of the late third century.

Medieval feudalism provided the theory and imagery for the ecclesiastical hierarchy, while the theory of papal absolutism both borrowed from and reenforced the growing absolute monarchies of early modern European national kings. Today the church is once again adapting itself to contemporary organizational models in adopting the patterns of the multinational banking corporation. None of these models has been unchangeable or distinct from the historical context in which the church was shaped. Rather, the evolution of church government offers us a picture of continuous historical adaptation to theories and models of society prevalent at the time.

The fact that the church has continually shaped its institutional life according to contemporary social models is in itself not the problem. The problem lies in the effort to deny this fact and to impose upon the identity of the church an unhistorical theory of a church structure that is unchanging and derived from outside history. This unhistorical concept of church order itself reflects a premodern view of the cosmos as an unchanging hierarchy of being and social order as a sacral reflection of this hierarchical cosmic order. Since the eighteenth century modern society has increasingly recognized that forms of social, political, and economic organization are human artifacts, created by humans and open to revision.

When democratic secular concepts of social organization were put forward in the eighteenth and nineteenth centuries, Roman Catholicism resisted them, attempting to buttress sacral kingship and aristocracy as the normative Christian society. Only with the Second Vatican Council was Roman Catholicism reconciled with democratic society, adopting its theories of human rights and consent of the governed for secular society. But it has refused a similar revision of its own structure. This means that its own concept of sacral monarchy is left hanging in the air. The Vatican attempts to justify this political structure as "supernatural," denying its actual historical origins.

This means not only that the Catholic bureaucracy, particularly the Vatican, behaves in a highly repressive manner similar to totalitarian societies, without accountability for its own actions, consultation with constituencies, or consent of the governed, but it also veils these forms of operation in a cloak of secrecy and deceptive rhetoric. No disputed issue, whether moral, doctrinal, or organizational can be discussed in a straightforward manner. Every issue must be manipulated to appear to fit into an a priori theory of immutable omniscience and right order.

This false theory of church order and power makes the Catholic church in its hierarchical structure a particularly egregious "zone of untruth," as Charles Davis noted in *A Question of Conscience* in 1967. Its clerical paternalism is expressed in an effort to keep all those whom it rules, from bishops to priests to nuns to laity, in a state of moral and intellectual immaturity, dependent on outside authority and daring not to think and act as moral agents in their own right.

This volume seeks to provide the basis for challenging this concept of the church by gathering together highly qualified scholars who argue for democratic restructuring of the church from many different contexts and points of view. In addition to the contributors mentioned above, John Beal underscores the role of canon law as providing historical precedents for a more democratic church. Hans Küng reinforces Beal's chapter in developing the theological and historical foundations for participation of the people, specifically the laity, in church governance. Charles Curran calls on the church to apply the principles of subsidiarity and justice, so clearly enunciated in Catholic social teaching for secular society, to the life of the church itself.

Ribeiro de Oliveira focuses on the growth of base communities in Brazil as the practical, as well as theological, base for a more participatory church, while Phillip Berryman details the Central American experience and the ambiguity of concepts of democracy in the relationships of church and society there. Much also can be learned about the democratizing process, Sister Marie Augusta Neal shows, by studying the struggles and experimentation in participatory polity among American sisterhoods since Vatican II. Rosemary Ruether describes several grassroots peace and justice and feminist movements in the Chicago area as case studies in the development of democratic movements within the church as community, but outside hierarchical control. Dale Dunlap provides an ecumenical perspective by depicting the various forms of democratic ordering of the Protestant churches. Finally, sociologist John Coleman ponders various strategies for actually changing Catholicism from an imperial to a democratic church.

The historical and theological arguments for a democratic church in this book can help Catholics to see that the effort of Vatican I to reify papal monarchy as an unchangeable divine order is a form of idolatry of the church institution, a heresy that manifests itself in the bad fruits of untruth, abusive relationships, corruption, and lovelessness. Any effort to open up the question of reform of the institutional structures of Roman Catholicism in the direction of more participatory forms of government must face a double critique.

First, the effort to fix the existing monarchical and hierarchical forms of church government as transhistorical, divinely mandated, and unchangeable must be rejected not only as an error, but an error made idolatrous by the effort to put it beyond question. Second, once the relativity and historicity of all forms of church government is recognized, one has to ask what norms should guide the discussion of the optimum forms of church order.

The discussion of the second question of what would be "good" forms of church government seems to us not fundamentally different from the question of what would be "good" forms of social and political order generally. This is a theological and not simply a secular claim. It is based on the premise that the God who is revealed in Jesus Christ is not other than the God who created the world. The church as redemptive society does not witness to some "other world," but witnesses to the redemption of this world. The church should witness to what is most redemptive in human relations: just, loving, and truthful relationality that fosters mutual respect. A church that has become a paradigm of the opposite of all these traits falls below, rather than rises above, the "world" to which it is sent to speak God's saving word.

Thus democratic church reform is not simply a new adaptation to forms of society prevalent today, although it is partly this. It is also based on normative premises:

1. the recognition that all forms of social structure are human creations, partial, historical, and open to revision, is a view truer to historical reality than the belief that social and church order should reflect an unchanging hierarchical cosmos;

2. democratic, participatory forms of government are more appropriate for the expression of respect for persons and safeguarding against abusive relationships than hierarchical and monarchical systems of government that treat the governed as rightless dependents.

This by no means assumes that every form of government today that claims the name "democratic" is in fact just and respectful of persons equally. Much of what is called democracy in American society and elsewhere is simply a way of covering up political and economic oligarchy with a façade of electoral politics. The American ideology of "democracy" virtually identifies it with free market capitalism of a form that is generating vast injustice between a small elite of wealthy people and a vast underclass of impoverished people. It is this confusion of democracy with American-style capitalism which has given the word a "bad name" in much of Latin America.

Thus if we are to discuss democracy in the church, Americans and Christians throughout the world have to return to the roots of modern democratic theory, which sought to create more just societies based on the consent of the governed. We have to ask anew how just societies that respect the rights of all persons equally can best be ordered. How can accountability of leadership be structured into our political systems? What is the relationship between democratic political power and just distribution of wealth and social services? In short, democratic theory and its failures in practice need themselves to be examined.

One then needs to ask in a fresh way what is the relation of the church to society as witness to redemption in Christ. Once we have an idea of a good democratic political system, does that mean the church should simply reduplicate such a system in its institutional governance? This notion is based on the assumption that the church should be a total institution, a kind of counterstate. But this patterning of the church after the state as a kind of ecclesiastical state needs to be questioned. In what way does such an ecclesiastical organization really promote redemptive relations in society and to what extent does it simply become an institution seeking its own power and prestige?

Perhaps a much simpler structure, in which the church takes primarily the form of intentional communities gathered amid a variety of social relations (and not just in the domestic sector), needs to be imaged. Such communities scattered across all sectors of society could then become ways of deepening relationships and witnessing against unjust and abusive power in many different contexts, economic, political, and environmental, as well as familial. Simple forms of networking, linking such communities together in a sense of a common identity as the Christian church, while retaining pluriformity of organization and cultural expression, might be more appropriate than a vast state-like superstructure.

In short, the discussion of democratic church reform opens up the fundamental questions of what is the church. What is its basic message and ministry to society? How can the basic insight that the church is both a community in its own right commissioned to keep alive and live out of the message of redemption in Christ, and yet has as its object, not its own promotion, but the redemption of creation, be best expressed in social ordering of church and society?

What does redemption mean on the level of social relationships? What kind of social ordering of human relationships best approximates, even if always imperfectly, redemptive relationality? How can the very process of continual repentance and renewal, as the way of keeping ourselves open to the Spirit alive in our midst, be itself built into our understanding of social order in church and society? These are some of the questions that need to be probed as Catholics shake off the myth of sacral hierarchy and examine the meaning of church renewal, not simply as theological theory or as personal spirituality, but as reform of structures.

A
DEMOCRATIC
CATHOLIC CHURCH

ELISABETH SCHÜSSLER FIORENZA

–1–
A Discipleship of Equals:
Ekklesial Democracy and Patriarchy
in Biblical Perspective

Democratic movements around the globe have struggled in the past years to reclaim the "power of the people" in the face of military dictatorship, terrorism, political trials, torture, and execution. In her 1989 Harvard Commencement address, the former prime minister of Pakistan, Benazir Bhutto, therefore, identified "democracy" as "the most powerful political idea" in the world today. She called for the creation of an Association of Democratic Nations that could promote the universal values of democracy. Members of this democratic alliance should then cooperate in the protection of human rights, principles of justice, and due process.

Acknowledging the influence of Western democratic institutions, Benazir Bhutto also asserted that in her country the love of freedom and human rights "arises fundamentally from the strong egalitarian spirit that pervades Islamic traditions." She pointed to herself, a Muslim woman and prime minister of millions of Muslims, as the living refutation of the argument that a country cannot be democratic because it is Muslim. Islamic religion and its strong democratic ethos, she insisted, have inspired and provided sustenance to democratic struggles, as well as faith in the righteousness of just causes and in the Islamic teaching "that tyranny cannot long endure." In light of this conviction, she proposes the progress of women as a practical criterion for judging the progress of a society or religion. The criterion for measuring whether a religion is democratic and liberating consists in the practical test of whether it allows for the full participation and leadership of women.

In light of the spreading democratic movements around the globe, official Roman Catholic warnings that the church should not be mistaken as a democratic community have strongly ironical overtones. This anti-democratic argument of Rome is two-pronged: On the one hand, it insists

17

that the church is a hierarchical and not a democratic institution. Until very recently official church documents have asserted that the democratic form of government is not compatible with biblical teaching because the Bible clearly proclaims G–d,[1] Christ, and the kingdom of G–d in monarchical terms.[2] More recent statements argue that in distinction to society the church is not a democracy but a hierarchical institution[3] that is bound by the founding intentions of Christ and the apostles canonized in Scripture.

On the other hand, the Vatican argues that women do not have the right to be ordained to church office.[4] In the past, official church teaching has asserted that woman's Christian calling was not to the work place but to motherhood and home. More recent statements still insist that women's essential potential is motherhood[5] but they also argue that women have "in domestic and in public life, the rights and duties that befit a human person."[6] At the same time, official church teaching argues that women cannot fully participate in the leadership of the church because Christ and the apostles did not "ordain" women. Such an argument does not mention that — as far as we know — Christ did not "ordain" anyone.[7] It also ignores that women like Mary of Magdala or Junia were not only followers of Jesus but also were counted among the apostles.[8]

In light of Bhutto's statement, this interconnection between the shift in ecclesiastical arguments with respect to democracy and the similar shift with regard to women's place and role seems not accidental. These shifts in argument both against democracy and against women's full participation in the church seem to prove the maxim that official anti-democratic arguments and the prohibition of women from full participation in the church are intertwined. The questions of women's ordination and of whether the church has not only monarchic-hierarchic but also democratic biblical roots are therefore not just of intra-ecclesial significance. Rather, their resolve indicates whether or not Catholicism can contribute to the global struggles for a more democratic world order. These questions are intrinsically intertwined with the power of the gospel for salvation and well-being in a global context.

Therefore, a critical feminist theology of liberation[9] claims the diverse democratic struggles to overcome patriarchal oppression structured by racism, class-exploitation, sexism, and colonialist militarism[10] as the political-ecclesial site from where to speak. Since its aim is to recover Bible, history, and theology as memory and heritage of the *ekklesia* of women, such a critical theology of liberation seeks to retrieve Christian history and theology not just as the memory of the suffering and victimization of all women and marginalized men. It also seeks to repossess this heritage as the memory of those women and men who have shaped Christian history as religious interlocutors, agents of change, and survivors in the struggles against patriarchal domination.

However, one would be ill-advised to approach in an apologetic fashion the question of whether Scripture supports democratic structures and the full participation of women and other marginalized people in public ecclesial government. For it is not methodologically possible to "prove" that the Scriptures advocate egalitarian democracy rather than patriarchal monarchy since both forms of social organization have shaped the socio-symbolic universe of biblical writings. Rather, one has to become aware that sociohistorical models informing the reconstruction of biblical history and community are shaped by the interests of the biblical historian or theologian or general biblical reader just as much as they elaborate historical realities.[11] For our experience functions as what Clifford Geertz calls "a model" of reality.[12] Without such "common sense" models we would have no basis for comprehending the past that requires interpretation. In other words, those biblical interpreters whose polity resembles a "free-church" model will emphasize the democratic elements inscribed in biblical texts and those whose polity favors a "hierarchical" model of church will stress the patriarchal-monarchical aspects advocated by biblical writers. They can do so, however, because variations of both models of church are inscribed in the biblical traditions and available as models of reality today.

This tension between the democratic-charismatic and the patriarchal-hierarchical models of church comes to the fore in the linguistic notion of the word "church." The Greek word *ekklesia* is translated as "church," although the English word "church" derives from the Greek word *kyriake*, i.e., belonging to the Lord/Master. However, the original meaning of *ekklesia* would be best rendered as "public assembly of the political community" or "democratic assembly of full citizens."[13]

> This original meaning of "church" is still found in Origen, who compares the civil assemblies in Athens, Corinth, and Alexandria with the Christian assemblies: God ... caused churches [assemblies] to exist in opposition to the assemblies of superstitious, licentious and unrighteous men. For such is the character of the crowds who constitute the assemblies of the cities. And the "assemblies of God" which have been taught by Christ, when compared with the assemblies of the people where they live, are as "lights in the world." (*Contra Celsum* 3.29)

The translation process that transformed *ekklesia*/assembly into *kyriake*/church indicates a historical development that has privileged the patriarchal/hierarchical form of church. Thus the same word "church" in English entails two contradictory meanings: one derived from the patriarchal model of the household in antiquity, which is governed by the lord/master of the house to whom freeborn women, freeborn dependents, clients, and workers as well as slaves, both women and men, were subordinated. The other meaning of "church" understands the equality of its members in terms of siblings in a family and in terms of friendship.[14] This meaning of "church" derives from the classical institution of democracy that promised freedom and equality to all its citizens.

Ekklesia: Equality in the Power of the Spirit[15]

The traces of democratic structures and visions that surface as "dangerous memory" in a critical democratic reading of the Pauline letters still indicate that the two key terms for the self-understanding of the early missionary communities in the Greco-Roman cities were political: *soma*, or body/corporation of Christ, and *ekklesia*, the democratic assembly.[16] The meaning of the metaphor of Christ's *soma* should not be derived from the anthropological discourse[17] but is best contextualized within the popular political discourse of antiquity that understood the *polis*, or city state, as a "body politic" in which all members were interdependent.[18] This metaphor circumscribes the reality of being "in Christ."

> For just as the *soma* is one and has many members, and all the members of the body, though many, are one *soma*, so is it with Christ. For by one Spirit we were all baptized into one *soma* — Jews or Greeks, slaves or free [both women and men] — and all were made to drink of one Spirit. (1 Cor 12:12–13)

In the *soma/polis* of Christ, all have equal access to the gifts of the Spirit. This equality in the Spirit does not mean that all are the same. Rather, the gifts of the members vary and their individual functions are irreplaceable. No one can claim to have a superior function because all functions are necessary and must be equally honored for the building up of the "corporation." Solidarity and collaboration are the "civic" virtues in the *politeuma* of Christ, which is best characterized as a pneumatic or charismatic democracy.

"In Christ," i.e., in the body politic, the power sphere of Christ, all socioreligious status inequalities were abolished including those between priest and laity, between officials and ordinary members of the community, as well as between especially holy or religious people dedicated to the sacred and the common people who are immersed in profane matters of everyday life. Equally, social status distinctions and privileges between Jews and Gentiles, Greeks and barbarians, slave and free — both women and men — were abolished among those who were "in Christ" (Gal. 3:28).[19]

They understood themselves as equally gifted and called to freedom. G–d's Spirit was poured out upon all, sons and daughters, old and young, slaves and free, both women and men (see Acts 2:17–18). Those who have been "baptized into Christ" live by the Spirit (Gal. 5:25). They are pneumatics, i.e., spirit-filled people (Gal. 6:1). They are a "new creation" (2 Cor. 5:17). Those who have entered into the "force-field" of the Resurrected One have been set free from "the law of sin and death" in order to share "in the glorious freedom of the children of G–d" (Rom. 8:21).

As siblings, they are all equal because they share in the Spirit as G–d's power for salvation. They are all called, elect, and holy, adopted children of G–d.[20] All without exception: Jews, pagans, slaves, free, poor, rich, both women and men, those with high status and those who are "nothing" in the eyes of the world. Their equality in the Spirit is expressed in alternating leadership[21] and partnership,[22] in equal access for everyone, Greeks, Jews, barbarians, slaves, free, rich, poor, both women and men. They, therefore, name their assembly with the democratic term *ekklesia*.

The full decision-making assembly of Christians, who were exiles and resident aliens in their societies (1 Pet. 2:11)[23] and constituted a different *politeuma* (Phil. 3:20), met in private houses. The house-churches were crucial factors in the missionary movements insofar as they provided space and actual leadership. They supplied space for the preaching of the gospel, for worship as well as for social and eucharistic table sharing.[24] Theologically, the community that assembled in houses is called the "household of faith" (Gal. 6:10), the new temple in which the Spirit dwells.[25] These house-assemblies did not take over the structures of the patriarchal household but were patterned after those of private associations. Women played a decisive role in the founding, sustaining, and shaping of such house-assemblies. They could do so, because the classic division between private and public spheres was abolished in the *ekklesia* that assembled in the "house." In the Christian *ekklesia* the private realm of the house constituted the public of the church.

Christians were neither the first nor the only group who gathered together in house-assemblies. Religious cults, voluntary associations, professional clubs, funeral societies as well as the Jewish synagogue gathered in private houses. However, these groups did not adopt the structures of the patriarchal household, but utilized rules and offices of the democratic assembly of the *polis*. Such assemblies were often socially stratified but conceded an equal share in the life of the association to all their members.

Advocacy of Patriarchal Adaptation[26]

Like other private associations, however, the Christian *ekklesia* was considered with suspicion and as potentially subversive to the hegemonic patriarchal-imperial order of Rome. Insofar as Christians admitted individual converts as equals independently of their status in the patriarchal household, membership in the Christian *ekklesia* stood often in tension to the patriarchal structures of the household. The early Christian texts advocating adaptation to the Greco-Roman patriarchal structures of household and state seek to lessen this tension.[27]

Patriarchal hegemonic structures were legitimated in the first century especially by Neo-Platonic and Aristotelian political philosophy. Such patriarchal legitimizations found their way into Christian Scriptures in the form of the patriarchal injunctions to submission. Whereas 1 Corinthians 11:2–16, for example, argues on scriptural grounds for women's subordination in terms of the Neo-Platonic chain of the hierarchy of beings,[28] the First Epistle of Peter, for instance, utilizes the Neo-Aristotelian pattern of patriarchal submission. 1 Peter admonishes Christians who are servants to be submissive even to brutal masters (2:18–25) and instructs wives to subordinate themselves to their husbands, even to those who are not Christians (3:1–6). Simultaneously it entreats Christians to be subject and give honor to the emperor as well as to his governors (2:13–17).[29]

This conflict and contradiction between Greco-Roman sociopolitical structures of domination and the democratic vision of G–d's *ekklesia* as the "alternative democratic community" and "new [social] creation" has engendered the need for apologetic legitimization. Freeborn women like artisans or slaves (women and men) belonged to a submerged group in antiquity. They could develop leadership in the emergent Christian movements because these movements stood in conflict with the dominant patriarchal ethos of the Greco-Roman world. The struggle of freeborn women and slaves (women and men) to maintain their authority and freedom in the Christian *ekklesia*, therefore, is to be seen as an integral part of the struggle between the emerging Christian movement and its vision of equality and freedom, on the one hand, and the hegemonic patriarchal ethos of the Greco-Roman world on the other. In this struggle, the ecclesial leadership of freeborn women and slaves (women and men) in the *ekklesia* as a charismatic democracy was submerged again, transformed or pushed to the fringes of mainstream churches.[30]

However, the egalitarian currents of early Christianity have never been eliminated. Neither fourth- nor sixteenth- nor twentieth-century ecclesial struggles can be understood if one does not take this democratic undercurrent into account. This democratic vision of church inscribed in biblical writings has again and again spawned ecclesial movements of reformation and renewal in protest against the hierarchical/monarchical form of church. These ecclesial reform movements have appealed in the past — and still do so today — to the traditions of freedom, equality, and dignity of all the people of G–d that have shaped the sociosymbolic universes of biblical writings. They can do so because Scripture still allows us to glimpse the "dangerous memory" of a movement and community of radical equality in the power of the Spirit.

In short, I argue, the patriarchal rhetorics of early Christian writings must be read as an attempt to adjust Christian community to its Greco-Roman sociopolitical environment. By using a reconstructive model that reads androcentric biblical texts in terms of the early Christian struggles and arguments about the politics and rhetorics of "equality in the Spirit" and "patriarchal submission" one can situate the cultural dependencies and effects generated by the early Christian debates and struggles.[31]

Such a rhetorical model for the reconstruction of the early Christian movements, which I have proposed in *In Memory of Her*, should however not be misread as an apologetic search for the "true," pristine, orthodox democratic origins of Christianity that have been corrupted very quickly by early Catholicism or gnostic heresy; nor should it be seen as an argument for a patriarchal-hierarchical institutionalization that was absolutely necessary for the survival of Christianity. The model of historical reconstruction suggested here is that of social interaction and religious transformation, of struggle between *ekklesia* as the discipleship of equals and church as the patriarchal household of G–d promulgating the "politics" of subordination and domination in Western societies.

Greco-Roman Patriarchal Democracy

Although this "patriarchal politics of submission" was inscribed in and mediated by Christian Scriptures, it did not originate with them. It was not invented by Christian theology but was first articulated in the context of the Greek city-state.[32] In ancient Greece the notion of democracy was not constructed in abstract and universal terms but was seen as rooted in a concrete sociopolitical situation. Greek patriarchal democracy constituted itself by excluding the "others" who did not have a share in the land but whose labor sustained society. Freedom and citizenship were not only measured over and against slavery but were also restricted in terms of gender. Moreover, the socioeconomic realities in the Greek city-state were such that only a few select freeborn, propertied, elite, male heads of households could actually exercise democratic government. The attempt to equalize the situation by paying male citizens who did not have sufficient wealth on their own for participating in the government could not balance out the existing tension between equality and community in the Greek city-state.[33]

According to the theoretical vision, but not the historical realization, of democracy, all those living in the *polis* should be equal citizens, able to participate in government. In theory, all citizens of the *polis* are equal in rights, speech, and power. As the assembly of free citizens the *ekklesia* should come together to deliberate and decide the best course of action for achieving its own well-being and for securing the welfare of the *polis*. Democratic political practice was not to be disengaged and detached. On the contrary, by engaging in the rhetorical deliberation of the *ekklesia* citizens were to be the arbiters of their fate and to promote the well-being of all.

However, the socioeconomic realities in the Greek city-state were such that only a very few freeborn, propertied, educated, male heads of households actually exercised democratic government. Active participation in government was conditional not only upon citizenship but also upon the combined privilege of property, education, and freeborn male family status. As Page DuBois has succinctly pointed out: "The ancient democracy must be mapped as an absence. We have only aristocratic, hostile representations of it. . . . The *demos*, the people themselves, have no voice in history; they exist only figured by others."[34]

It was this contradiction and tension between the ideal of democracy and actual sociopolitical patriarchal structures that produced the kyrio-centric (master-centered)[35] ideology of "natural differences" between elite men and women, between freeborn and slaves, between property own-ers and farmers or artisans, between Athenian-born citizens and other residents, between Greeks and barbarians, between the civilized and the uncivilized world.

Feminist theorists have shown that Plato and Aristotle, who were crit-ics of the democratic Athenian city-state, articulated their philosophy of patriarchal democracy in order to argue why certain groups of people, such as freeborn women or slave women and men, were not capable of participating in democratic government.[36] These groups of people were not fit to rule or to govern, they argued, on grounds of their deficient natural powers of reasoning. Such an explicit ideological justification al-ways becomes necessary at points in history when democratic notions are introduced into patriarchal society. Philosophical rationalizations in antiquity and in modern times for the exclusion of certain people from gov-ernment were engendered by this contradiction between the democratic self-definition of the city-state and its actual patriarchal socioeconomic structures.

The early Christian injunctions to patriarchal submission, therefore, are best understood as a part of this patriarchal cultural rhetoric that seeks to adapt the egalitarian and therefore subversive Christian movement to its Greco-Roman patriarchal society and culture. They would not have been necessary if from its inception Christian community and faith had existed as a patriarchal formation. The Greek paradigm of patriarchal submission encoded in Christian Scriptures and that of the monarchical episcopate, which closely resembles the Roman imperial pyramid in Christian terms, developed hierarchical cultic structures in the second and third centuries and determined the post-Constantinian Roman church.[37]

Although the Greek aristocratic/oligarchic and the Roman imperial/ colonialist forms of patriarchy have been modified under changing socio-economic and political conditions, they seem to have been the two prevail-ing forms of patriarchy in the history of Western Christianity. For instance, the hierarchical institutions of Roman Catholicism tend to resemble the imperial patriarchal pyramid of Rome, since like the Roman emperor the pope is called *pater patrum*, who represents G–d on earth. In contrast, some churches of the Reformation tend to conform to the classical Greek form of patriarchy insofar as they have adopted institutional forms resembling those inscribed in the Pastoral Epistles.

In the first two centuries of Roman imperial rule traditional at-tributed status based on aristocratic or national elite prerogatives was undermined by the "pax Romana," which created new possibilities and prospects for status achievement through economic or political change. Whereas Roman imperial rule produced oppressive conditions for rural and slave populations, threatened the old local elites whose lands could be confiscated, and undermined both Rome's republican and the Greek cities' democratic systems and alliances, it made honor and status accessible to whoever could generate wealth and influence. Artisans, traders, freed people, well-placed slaves, and women from all walks of life could improve their status by meeting the rising demand for goods and services.

Elite freeborn Greco-Roman women or those whose cultural traditions accorded women political influence and status, as was the case in the traditional societies of Asia Minor, and who experienced status inconsistency under imperial Roman patriarchy gained influence and status in the more democratically structured private organizations and religious cults. In particular, well-educated women with independent financial resources could develop patronage and leadership in these house "assemblies" even though they could not do so in Roman imperial society and hegemonic religion. Such experienced status dissonance compelled women to break through the traditional patriarchal patterns entrenched in law and custom. Not only upper-class freeborn women, but also freeborn of lower standing, freed-women, and slave women had the opportunity to follow their trade and accumulate some wealth of their own.[38]

Women were active in finance, trade, and commerce. Greco-Roman, Asian, and Jewish women used their capital for providing private and public patronage and gained recognition and public honor in return for their benevolence. Archeological evidence from Pompeii, for instance, indicates that women of this city were actively involved in business transactions as well as in civic and religious public projects during the last centuries of the city's existence. Eumachia, who lived in the beginning of the first century C.E., donated a local club center and held religious office surely facilitated by her wealth and business connections. A tomb inscription tells us that a Jewish woman by the name of Rufina was president of the synagogue of Smyrna in Asia Minor in the second or third century.[39]

Since Hellenistic culture allowed them to assume important positions in civic life and religious institutions, free women in the Greco-Roman world who converted to Christianity must have expected to have the same opportunities within the Christian *ekklesia* as within their wider socio-cultural context. Slave women in turn were most probably attracted to the Christian message of freedom and equality. Whereas joining the Christian *ekklesia* brought increased status and bettered the situation of women from all walks of life living in the Roman empire, it meant civic and religious status loss for freeborn elite men. Their anxiety to align themselves with the traditional patriarchal status quo engendered the theological injunctions to submission and obedience for all women as well as for marginalized men.

The *Basileia:* G–d's Intended World and Society

The Roman form of imperial domination also determined the world and experience of Jesus and his first followers, but in a different way. Whereas the *pax romana* created new opportunity for people in the cities of the empire, it intensified the colonial oppression of the rural population.[40] The colonial situation of first-century rural Palestine, which is the sociopolitical context of Jesus' ministry, was characterized by the tension between the urban ruling elites aligned with the Roman occupation and the 90 percent of the rural population whom they exploited through heavy taxation. The context of the Jesus traditions is a situation of colonial oppression existing between the Herodian and Roman elite and the bulk of the people. This situation of oppression is eloquently depicted by the Jewish scholar Ellis Rivkin:

> The Roman emperor held the life or death of the Jewish people in the palm of his hand; the governor's sword was always at the ready; the high priest's eyes were always penetrating and his ears were always keen; the soldiery was always eager for the slaughter. . . . The emperor sought to govern an empire; the governor sought to hold anarchy in check; the high priest sought to hold on to his office; the members of the high priest's Sanhedrin sought to spare the people the dangerous consequences of a charismatic's innocent visions of the Kingdom of God, which they themselves believed was not really at hand. . . . For he had taught and preached that the Kingdom of God was near at hand, a kingdom which were it to come, would displace the kingdom of Rome. By creating the impression that he . . . would usher in the Kingdom of God . . . he had readied the people for riotous behavior. The fact that the charismatic of charismatics had taught no violence, had preached no revolution, and lifted up no arms against Rome's authority would have been utterly irrelevant. The High Priest Caiaphas and the Prefector Pontius Pilate cared not a whit how or by whom the Kingdom of God would be ushered in, but only that the Roman Emperor and his instruments would not reign over it.[41]

Jesus and his first followers, women and men, stood in a long line of Sophia's prophets and witnesses.[42] Standing in the prophetic wisdom tradition Jesus and his followers took the side of the majority, the exploited and poor population of Palestine, and indicted the elites. They sought the renewal and well-being of Israel as the people of G–d, a kingdom of priests and a holy nation. They threatened the temple, the symbolic as well as economic center of the Jewish social world, and criticized the high-priestly establishment that abused the temple as an "instrument of imperial legitimation and control of a subjected people."[43] They announced the *basileia*, the empire of G–d, as an alternative vision to the imperial utopia of Rome. The *basileia* message of Jesus found acceptance among the poor, the despised, the ill, and possessed, the outcast, the prostitutes, and sinners — both women and men. In distinction to patriarchal Greek democracy, the *basileia* movement initiated by Jesus did not secure its identity by drawing exclusive boundaries but by welcoming all the people of G–d, even tax collectors and sinners.[44]

The term *basileia* belongs to a royal-monarchical context of meaning that has as its sociopolitical referent the Roman empire. *Basileia* is however also a tensive symbol of ancestral range,[45] which appeals to Israelite traditions. These traditions, which are located in the prophetic milieu of the North, assert a democratic countermeaning to the royal meaning of the term. According to these Northern traditions Yahweh saved the children of Israel from Egypt (Josh. 24:7) and made a covenant with the people (e.g., Exod. 3:9–13), who are called "a kingdom of priests and a holy nation" (Exod. 19:4–6). These traditions are critical of kingship and monarchy (see the Jotham fable in Judg. 9:8–15) and regard human monarchy, which engenders militarism, economic exploitation, and slavery, as a rejection of G–d's kingship (1 Sam. 8:1–22). Israel's great sin and wickedness consists in asking for a human king (1 Sam. 12:16–20). For in doing so, they have rejected G–d, who delivered them from "all the kingdoms that have oppressed" and "saved [them] from all their misery and distress" (1 Sam. 10:17–27:18f.; Hos 8:4; 9:15). Kingship in Israel is not a divine but a human institution dependent on the people and their prophetic leaders.[46]

However, Jesus' proclamation of the *basileia* of G–d[47] alluded not only to a range of ancestral democratic-religious traditions that proclaimed G–d's kingship and power of salvation. It was also an anti-imperial political symbol that appealed to the oppositional imagination of the Jewish people victimized by the Roman imperial system. The gospel of the *basileia* envisioned an alternative world free of hunger, poverty, and domination.

Jesus and his first disciples announced the *basileia* of G–d to the common people in the villages and small towns of Israel. They promised the *basileia* to the impoverished, to those who were hungry in the present time, and to those who groaned under oppressive conditions (Luke 6:20–21). They summoned the people in the local villages, the sinners, tax collectors, debtors, beggars, prostitutes, and all those exploited and marginalized, the lost "sheep" of the house of Israel (Matt. 15:24; 10:6) to recognize the presence of the *basileia* and to enter it. Its shalom, i.e., liberation and salvation, was already present in the healing and liberating practices of the Jesus movement, in its inclusive table-community, as well as in the domination-free kinship relations among the disciples.

In the face of the breakdown of traditional patriarchal authority as a consequence of the Roman domination of Palestinian Jewish society, they did not call for the restitution of traditional patriarchal authority but broke with it. Several Jesus sayings and traditions challenge the traditional patriarchal family and advocate its replacement with egalitarian familial kinship relations among the disciples. Their egalitarian community, the "new family" of Jesus, recognizes sisters, brothers, and mothers, but no fathers in the community of disciples, since G–d alone is their father. The paradigm for the "equality from below" that must be practiced in the discipleship of equals is the child/slave who in antiquity was totally powerless and at the mercy of the paterfamilias.

In the last third of the first century C.E., some writers in the Pauline tradition advocate the patriarchal pattern of submission not only for the household but also for the church in order to lessen the tensions with their dominant patriarchal society. At the same time, some of the gospel traditions acknowledge women's leadership in the Jesus movement[48] and insist on domination-free relations in the community of disciples even in the face of suffering and persecution.

For instance, Mark's position contrasts to that of the post-Pauline writers. These writers appropriate the power of the paterfamilias for the leadership of the community while appealing to Christ's suffering as a paradigm for the submission that slave women and men as well as freeborn women and young people should choose freely. Mark's Gospel, by contrast, makes it quite clear that suffering and persecution must not be avoided by adapting the structures of Christian leadership in the community to Greco-Roman structures of domination. The Gospel of Mark also stresses that women were the most faithful disciples of Jesus, ones who witnessed his ministry, execution, burial, and resurrection, whereas its portrayal of the leading male disciples is rather negative.[49]

The three predictions of Jesus' suffering, execution, and resurrection (8:31; 9:31; 10:33f.) form part of Mark's instruction on true discipleship (8:22–10:52). Whereas the first saying is an invitation to follow Jesus on the way to the cross even to the point of jeopardizing one's life, the latter two advocate domination-free leadership in the community.[50] Both stress that the greatest in the community must become the least. The third call to suffering discipleship makes the point most forcefully with respect to the leading male disciples. The sons of Zebedee, James and John, ask for the places of glory and power in Jesus' *basileia*. Jesus points out that they are not promised glory and power. Rather, while Greco-Roman leadership is based on power and domination of others, among Christians such patriarchal relations of dominance are prohibited.

This injunction is part of a sevenfold Synoptic tradition that variegates the saying of Jesus that "whoever does not receive the *basileia* of G–d like a child/slave, shall not enter it" (Mark 10:15) in order to apply it to various community situations.[51] The child/slave who occupies the lowest rank within patriarchal structures becomes the primary paradigm for leadership in the discipleship community of equals. The ecclesial process of interpretation applied a saying that originally advocated "equality from below" by calling the socially well-to-do to solidarity with the slaves and powerless in Israel, to its own relationships in the discipleship of equals.[52] It contrasts the political structures of domination with those required from the disciples. Structures of domination must not be tolerated in the discipleship community. Rather the social status of slaves and servants who have no power over others is to be paradoxically the social location of its "would be" great or first. Like Mark, Matthew does not acknowledge any status of being "great" or "first" in the discipleship community of equals. Luke, by contrast, accepts such leaders but requires that they orient themselves on the example of Jesus. In doing so he shifts from a rhetorical democratic construction of community that does not recognize structures of domination and status positions of preeminence to rhetorical moralist construction that admonishes those who are in power to serve.

In conclusion: Like that of the *basileia*, the democratic construction of the Christian *ekklesia* constitutes a partial reality and provides an enduring vision. This vision is realized again and again in the democratic practices of the *ekklesia*. The democratic construction of early Christian communal self-understanding is not simply a given fact nor just an ideal. Rather it is an active process[53] moving toward greater equality, freedom, and responsibility as well as toward communal relations free of domination. All women and those silenced and marginalized by patriarchal-hierarchical structures of domination are crucial in this ekklesial process of democratization that is inspired by the *basileia*-vision of a world free of exploitation, domination, and evil.

Notes

1. I have adopted this traditional Jewish spelling of the word "G–d" in order to indicate the brokenness and inadequacy of human language for naming the divine.

2. See Edward Schillebeeckx, *Ministry: A Case for Change* (London: SCM Press, 1981); idem, *Church: The Human Story of God* (New York: Crossroad, 1990), 200ff.

3. See P. Eicher, "Hierarchie," in *Neues Handbuch theologischer Grundbegriffe* (1984), 2:193f.

4. See especially the Vatican *Declaration on the Question of the Admission of Women to the Ministerial Priesthood*, 1976, and Pope John Paul II, *Mulieris Dignitatem*, 1988; see the discussion of the theological arguments in the Anglican, Methodist and Roman Catholic churches on women's ordination by Jaqueline Field-Bibb, *Women Toward Priesthood: Ministerial Politics and Feminist Praxis* (Cambridge: University Press, 1991), 7–200.

5. See Gregory Baum, "Bulletin: The Apostolic Letter Mulieris Dignitatem," in Anne Carr and Elisabeth Schüssler Fiorenza, eds., *Motherhood: Experience, Institution, Theology*, Concilium 206 (Edinburgh: T. & T. Clark, 1989), 144–49.

6. Pope John XXIII, *Pacem in Terris*, no. 41. See also Rosemary Radford Ruether, "Women's Difference and Equal Rights in the Church," in Anne Carr and Elisabeth Schüssler Fiorenza, eds., *The Special Nature of Women?*, Concilium 1991/6 (London: SCM Press, 1991), 11–18.

7. See the various exegetical-historical contributions in P. Hoffmann, ed., *Priesterkirche* (Düsseldorf: Patmos Verlag, 1987).

8. For documentation see my book *In Memory of Her: A Feminist Theological Reconstruction of Christian Origins* (New York: Crossroad, 1983). Although with

Rabanus Maurus and Thomas Aquinas Pope John Paul II calls Mary of Magdala "the apostle to the apostles," his insistence on the exclusion of women from ordination does not allow him to draw any consequences from this insight (*Mulieris Dignitatem*, no. 16).

9. Katie Geneva Cannon and Elisabeth Schüssler Fiorenza, eds., *Semeia* 47: *Interpretation for Liberation* (Atlanta: Scholars Press, 1989).

10. I do not understand "patriarchy" either in the sense of sexism and gender dualism or use it as an undefined label. Rather, I construe the term in the "narrow sense" as "father-right and father-might." I understand here "patriarchy"/ "patriarchal" to connote a complex systemic interstructuring of sexism, racism, classism, and cultural-religious imperialism that has produced the Western "politics of Otherness." Although patriarchy has adjusted throughout history, its Aristotelian articulation is still powerful today. For a review of the terminology see V. Beechey, "On Patriarchy," *Feminist Review* 3 (1979): 66–82; G. Lerner, *The Creation of Patriarchy* (New York: Oxford University Press, 1986), 231–41; C. Schaumberger, "Patriarchat als feministischer Begriff," in *Wörterbuch der feministischen Theologie* (Gütersloh: Mohn, 1991), 321–23 with literature.

11. For a fuller development of this hermeneutical approach see my forthcoming book *But She Said: Feminist Practices of Biblical Interpretation* (Boston: Beacon Press, 1992).

12. Clifford Geertz, "Religion as a Cultural System," in M. Banton, ed., *Anthropological Approaches to the Study of Religion* (London: Tavistock, 1966), 1–46.

13. This general classical meaning is found in Acts 19:21–41, where the town clerk of Ephesus, probably the chief civil officer in the city, urges silversmiths and people not to solve the issue at hand in the near-riotous *ekklesia* now in session but to bring the matter before the lawful *ekklesia* where such matters were decided (19:39–41).

14. See C. K. Schäfer, *Gemeinde als "Bruderschaft," Ein Beitrag zum Kirchenverständnis des Paulus* (Frankfurt: B. Lang, 1989); K. Treu, "Freundschaft," *Reallexikon für Antike und Christentum* 8:418–34; H. J. Klauck, "Brotherly Love in Plutarch and in 4 Maccabees," in *Greek, Romans and Christians,* Festschrift for A. Malherbe (Philadelphia: Trinity, 1990), 144–56; idem, "Kirche als Freundesgemeinschaft? Auf Spurensuche im Neuen Testament," *Münchener Theologische Zeitschrift* 42 (1991): 1–14. However, one must not overlook that just as democracy so also the notions of "friendship" and "brotherhood" have been masculine-defined in antiquity.

15. For this whole section see also the social world studies of R. A. Atkins, *Egalitarian Community: Ethnography and Exegesis* (Tuscaloosa: University of Alabama Press, 1991), 1–21 and 145–90; N. R. Petersen, *Rediscovering Paul: Philemon and the Sociology of Paul's Narrative World* (Philadelphia Fortress Press, 1985); and Antoinette Clark Wire, *The Corinthian Women Prophets: A Reconstruction through Paul's Rhetoric* (Minneapolis: Augsburg Fortress, 1990).

16. However, the terms do not totally overlap. See R. Banks, *Paul's Idea of Community: The Early House Churches in Their Historical Setting* (Grand Rapids: Eerdmans, 1980), 62–70.

17. See Ernst Käsemann, *Commentary on Romans* (Grand Rapids: Eerdmans, 1980), 139–58 and 331–42, who rejects the theories of "Jewish corporate person-

ality" and "gnostic redeemer myth" and categorically states: "Anthropology as such is not at issue" (143).

18. For extensive discussion of the literature see Margret M. Mitchell, *Paul and the Rhetoric of Reconciliation* (Tübingen: J. C. B. Mohr, 1991), 157–64.

19. See my article "Justified by All Her Children: Struggle, Memory, and Vision," in The Foundation of Concilium, eds., *On the Threshold of the Third Millennium* (London: SCM Press, 1990), 19–38, 32–35.

20. See also Reinhold Reck, *Kommunikation und Gemeindeaufbau Eine Studie zur Entstehung, Leben und Wachstum paulinischer Gemeinden in den Konmmunikationsstrukturen der Antike* (Stuttgart: Kath. Bibelwerk, 1991), 232–85.

21. It seems that it was Paul who introduced in 1 Corinthians 12:28–30 a ranking of spiritual gifts. The introduction of "hierarchical governance structure [is] another response to the divisions within the church . . . " (Mitchell, *Paul and the Rhetoric of Reconciliation*, 164). See also J. H. Neyrey, "Body Language in 1 Corinthians: The Use of Anthropological Models for Understanding Paul and His Opponents," *Semeia* 35 (1986): 129–64. For Paul's use of the rhetorics of power see Elizabeth Castelli, *Imitating Paul: A Discourse of Power* (Louisville: Westminster/John Knox, 1991).

22. For the understanding of *koinonia* as consensual *societas* and reciprocal partnership see J. P. Sampley, *Pauline Partnership in Christ: Christian Community and Commitment in Light of Roman Law* (Philadelphia: Fortress, 1980).

23. J. H. Elliott, *A Home for the Homeless: A Sociological Exegesis of 1 Peter, Its Situation and Strategy* (Philadelphia: Fortress, 1981).

24. For a discussion of the formation of the *ekklesia* see Wayne A. Meeks, *The First Urban Christians: The Social World of the Apostle Paul* (New Haven: Yale University Press, 1983), 74–110; H. J. Klauck, *Hausgemeinde und Hauskirche im frühen Christentum* (Stuttgart: Kath. Bibelwerk, 1981); idem, "Neuere Literatur zur urchristlichen Hausgemeinde," *Biblische Zeitschrift* 26 (1982): 288–94.

25. 2 Corinthians 6:14–7:1; 1 Corinthians 3:16; Ephesians 2:22; 1 Peter 2:4–10.

26. For discussion and literature to this section see my book *Bread Not Stone: The Challenge of Feminist Biblical Interpretation* (Boston: Beacon Press, 1984), 65–92.

27. See also Marlies Gielen, *Tradition und Theologie neutestamentlicher Haustafelethik: Ein Beitrag einer christlichen Auseinandersetzung mit gesellschaftlichen Normen*, Bonner biblische Beiträge 75 (Frankfurt: Anton Hain, 1990), especially 24–67. However, her discussion does not explicitly refer to the extensive work of David Balch on the Greco-Roman political context of these texts nor is it aware of feminist theory and exegetical work.

28. Page DuBois, *Centaurs and Amazons: Women and the Pre-History of the Great Chain of Being* (Ann Arbor: University of Michigan Press, 1982), 9–16.

29. D. L. Balch, *Let Wives Be Submissive: The Domestic Code in 1 Peter*, Society of Biblical Literature Monograph 26 (Chico, Calif.: Scholars Press, 1981).

30. For discussion and literature see my article "Die Anfänge von Kirche, Amt und Priestertum in feministisch-theologischer Sicht," in Hoffmann, ed., *Priesterkirche*, 62–95. For a Marxist reconstruction of the early Christian developments after the first century C.E. see Dimitris J. Kyrtatas, *The Social Structure of the Early Christian Communities* (London: Verso, 1987).

31. For a sociohistorical account along the reconstructive model of Max Weber see Margaret Y. Macdonald, *The Pauline Churches: A Socio-historical Study of Institutionalization in the Pauline and Deutero-Pauline Writings* (Cambridge: University Press, 1988).

32. See Susan Moller Okin, *Women in Western Political Thought* (Princeton: University Press, 1979), 15–98; Elizabeth V. Spelman, *Inessential Woman: Problems of Exclusion in Feminist Thought* (Boston: Beacon Press, 1988), 19–56.

33. For Roman patriarchal structures see W. K. Lacey, "Patria Potestas," in Beryl Rawson, *The Family in Ancient Rome: New Perspectives* (Ithaca: Cornell University Press, 1986), 121–44.

34. Page DuBois, *Torture and Truth* (New York: Routledge, 1991), 123; for Roman slavery see K. R. Bradley, *Slaves and Masters in the Roman Empire: A Study in Social Control* (New York: Oxford University Press, 1986); Dale B. Martin, *Slavery as Salvation: The Metaphor of Slavery in Pauline Christianity* (New Haven: Yale University Press, 1990), 1–49, paints a positive picture of slavery, probably in order to justify Paul's use of this metaphor.

35. By the term "kyriocentric" I mean to indicate that not all men dominate and exploit all women without difference but that elite, Western, educated, propertied Euro-American men have articulated and benefited from women's and other "unpersons'" exploitation. See my article "The Politics of Otherness: Biblical Interpretation as a Critical Praxis for Liberation," in Marc H. Ellis and Otto Maduro, *The Future of Liberation Theology: Essays in Honor of Gustavo Gutiérrez* (Maryknoll, N.Y.: Orbis, 1989), 311–25.

36. M. E. Hawkesworth, *Beyond Oppression: Feminist Theory and Political Strategy* (New York: Continuum, 1990); Hannelore Schröder, "Feministische Gesellschaftstheorie," in L. F. Pusch, ed., *Feminismus: Inspektion der Herrenkultur*, edition Suhrkamp NF 192 (Frankfurt, Suhrkamp 1983), 449–78.

37. See especially K. Thraede, "Zum historischen Hintergrund der 'Haustafeln' des Neuen Testaments," in *Pietas: Festschrift B. Kötting* (Münster: Aschendorff, 1980), 359–68; D. Lührmann, "Neutestamentliche Haustafeln und antike Ökonomie," *New Testament Studies* 27 (1980/81): 83–97.

38. See H. Moxnes, "Social Integration and the Problem of Gender in St. Paul's Letters," *Studia Theologica* 43 (1989): 99–113; H. Montgomery, "Women and Status in the Greco-Roman World," ibid., 115–24.

39. For documentation see B. Brooten, *Women Leaders in the Ancient Synagogue* (Chico, Calif.: Scholars Press, 1982).

40. See especially Richard Horsley and John S. Hanson, *Bandits, Prophets, and Messiahs: Popular Movements at the Time of Jesus* (Minneapolis: Winston, 1985).

41. Ellis Rivkin, "What Crucified Jesus," in James H. Charlesworth, ed., *Jesus' Jewishness: Exploring the Place of Jesus within Early Judaism* (New York: Crossroad, 1991), 226–57. This quotation p. 242.

42. For a discussion of the social reconstructions of the Jesus movement see M. Ebertz, *Das Charisma des Gekreuzigten: Zur Soziologie der Jesusbewegung* (Tübingen: Mohr, 1987), and especially Richard A. Horsley, *Sociology and the Jesus Movement* (New York: Crossroad, 1989).

43. See especially Richard Horsley, *Jesus and the Spiral of Violence* (San Francisco: Harper & Row, 1987), 287.

44. See Marcus J. Borg, "Portraits of Jesus in Contemporary North-American Scholarship," *Harvard Theological Review* 84 (1991): 1–22.

45. For this understanding see Norman Perrin, *Jesus and the Language of the Kingdom* (Philadelphia: Fortress Press, 1976), 15–88.

46. For a discussion of these traditions see my book *Priester für Gott: Studien zum Herrschafts — und Priestermotiv in der Apokalypse* (Münster: Aschendorff, 1972), 90–160, and the recent commentaries to Exodus, Samuel, and Hosea.

47. For a more recent review of the vast literature see H. Merkel, "Die Gottesherrschaft in der Verkündigung Jesu," in Martin Hengel and Anna Maria Schwemer, eds., *Königsherrschaft Gottes und himmlischer Kult im Judentum, Urchristentum, und in der hellenistischen Welt* (Tübingen: J. C. B. Mohr, 1991), 119–62.

48. See for instance Monika Fander, *Die Stellung der Frau im Markusevangelium: Unter besonderer Berücksichtigung kultur- und religionsgeschichtlicher Hintergründe* (Altenberge: Telos Verlag, 1989), and Elaine M. Wainwright, *Towards a Feminist Critical Reading of the Gospel according to Matthew* (Berlin: de Gruyter, 1991).

49. See the discussion of this question by Raymond E. Brown, Karl P. Donfried, and John Reumann, eds., *Peter in the New Testament* (Minneapolis: Augsburg, 1973), 57–73; building on my work L. Schottroff, "Maria Magdalena und die Frauen am Grabe," *Evangelische Theologie* 42 (1982): 3–25, has argued for the discipleship of women on social-historical grounds; against this interpretation W. Munro, "Women Disciples in Mark," *Catholic Biblical Quarterly* 44 (1982): 225–41, maintains that the women are not portrayed so as to discredit the leading male disciples but that the Markan redaction silences women. For the argument that women are the true disciples according to Mark see also Ched Myers, *Binding the Strong Man: A Political Reading of Mark's Story of Jesus* (Maryknoll, N.Y.: Orbis, 1988), 280–81, 396–98, against Munro but without reference to Schottroff or my own work. M. A. Tolbert, *Sowing the Gospel: Mark's World in Literary-Historical Perspective* (Fortress: Minneapolis, 1989), 296f., argues that the women characters have the literary function of underlining that the "authorial audience" represents the "true disciples." It seems that the feminist discussion divides along methodological lines of inquiry.

50. For discussion and literature on this whole section see *In Memory of Her*, 145–51.

51. Mark 10:42–45 par Matthew 20:26–27; Luke 22:24–27; Mark 9:33–37 par Matthew 18:1–4; Luke 9:48.

52. G. Lohfink, *Jesus and Community: The Social Dimensions of Christian Faith* (Philadelphia: Fortress, 1984), 115–22.

53. For this distinction see Anne Phillips, *Engendering Democracy* (University Park, Pa.: Pennsylvania State University Press, 1991), 162.

–2–
A Democratic Church:
Task for the Twenty-First Century

The greatest obstacle to deeper reform within the Roman Catholic Church is its patriarchal, monarchical structure. This realization is obscured in most of the contemporary debate over specific issues. Attention focuses on such questions as the ordination of women or married men, the second-class status of women in the church, the need for change in Catholic teaching on divorce, birth control, homosexuality, and other sexual matters. Or particular crises of governance arise: the Vatican silences theologians, investigates liberal bishops, neutralizes regional and national bishops' conferences, and demands orthodoxy oaths. Rome continues to appoint very conservative candidates to important episcopal sees. In light of all this, too many theologians still focus on single issues, seeing them as problems of competing theologies or of misusing power. But adequate theologies for these specific changes are already in place. It is not a matter of developing better theological arguments for individual topics. Nor does the solution lie in finding liberal leaders. We seem to be blind to a systemic difficulty in the church's structure. This structural problem can be seen as religious monarchy overwhelming the beginnings of religious democracy in the Catholic Church.

I contend that democratic structures and ideas are deeply rooted in the Catholic tradition from its earliest sources. Some of these sources have been ignored, suppressed, or forgotten. Since the Catholic heritage claims to honor tradition as it undertakes modern reforms, it is valuable to review church history, pointing out resources for the needed fundamental change in Catholic ecclesial structure: the movement from patriarchal monarchy to a complex, plural, democratic church institution. This reflection on *loci* for a democratic church will be representative, not exhaustive. Moreover, we should keep in mind that useful knowledge is not enough in itself to bring about change. The latter requires concerted action on many levels at once.

The word "democracy" in this inquiry deserves some reflection. I

34

disagree in principle with the popular reaction, "the church is not a democracy." When that statement is made, it usually implies that the monarchical order is divinely established and unchangeable. On the contrary, imperial ecclesiology came about in historical contexts and was quite understandable, even justifiable, in those historical circumstances. But what happened in history can and should be changed in history. Moreover, the "engine" for this change is not primarily the tradition of secular democracies since the Enlightenment, but rather a renewed theology of the Holy Spirit.

The broad sweep of historical *loci* discussed in this chapter is intended as a stimulus for further research on the democratic potential in Catholic ecclesiology. It is not hard to find democratic perspectives in the documents of Vatican II. For example, the notion of collegiality and people of God lend themselves to such thinking. Even before Vatican II, the Catholic concept of subsidiarity in social encyclicals is a democratic construct. But these doctrines flow from a historical stream, sometimes underground, sometimes dammed up or diverted, but never destroyed.

Yet is the term "democracy" appropriate for the new structures of Catholic ecclesiology? William Everett prefers "federal republic." He criticizes the symbol of "body" because it conceives of society as a single actor, whereas "community" is not inclusive enough.[1] He honors "democracy" for stressing individual equality and participation in decision making, but he finds that it does not sufficiently embrace plurality and complexity in fashioning the church. Everett ties his language of "God's federal republic" to a covenant theology in which we are called to participation in common purposes, to persuasion vs. coercion, and to seeking greater justice and pluralism. Yet it seems to me that all these positive qualities can be gathered within the term "democracy" or "democratic" without resort to the rather strange phrase "federal republic."

Everett argues persuasively that monarchy or kingship as symbols for church governance had certain positive consequences in earlier centuries. He speaks of the functions of kingship: survival and stability amid chaotic tendencies, the socialization of loyalties from family to wider society, the forming of systems of justice and reasoned discourse, and the gradual participation of some subjects in choosing the king.[2] In a more specifically Catholic context, J. M. Miller maintains in an extensive work on the "divine right of the papacy" that we can respect many aspects of past structures as religiously positive, while seeing the need to effect deep changes in our understanding and practice of "papal primacy."[3] Underlying this evolutionary approach to church structure is a theology of the Holy Spirit. The latter moves away from trying to use Scripture as a proof text for a divine-right-of-kings papacy. Rather, a Spirit theology accepts historical and personal factors as part of an ongoing process. In this outlook, God is immersed in the historical process, helping us continually to rethink and reform the shape of the church. Impelled by such a theology, we move ahead by also moving back. We look to the present and the future for signs of Spirit direction. But we also rework the past to discern neglected or repressed clues for crafting the church.

The evidence from the earliest New Testament communities points toward democratic structures in the fledgling churches. Again, I am using "democratic" in the broad sense of decentralized networks of communities bound together by a common faith and similar practices. Of course, there were leaders with special gifts like Paul who based the authenticity of his ministry on its provenance from apostolic origins. But in both the intra-community and intercommunity relations of the first centuries, we observe a powerful egalitarian dynamic at work. Elisabeth Schüssler Fiorenza calls it the "discipleship of equals."[4] It was much more than a matter of electing officials. A sense of profound equality was built into the baptismal sacrament. Baptismal egalitarianism and inclusivity constituted the revelational bedrock of the early Christian movements. The initiated were first and foremost members of God's people, the *laos*, before they assumed positions of leadership in the communities. The role of teacher in the ancient church was not commissioned by or identified with ecclesiastical hierarchy. The teacher could be a man or a woman, and the *Didache* reminds us that the place of teacher was of equal importance to that of prophet or priest.[5]

As sect movements (not distinguished from church in the Weberian sense, but against the wider society) early Christian communities were egalitarian rather than hierarchical groupings. They offered love and acceptance especially to marginal and outcast persons. In true Jewish fashion, they acknowledged God as Father. But this confession did not factor out into forms of patriarchal monarchy in the earliest centuries. On the contrary, since God was Father in a unique sense, all others on earth became basically equal. Schüssler Fiorenza sums up this egalitarian thrust in ancient Christianity:

> They are all equal, because they all share in the Spirit, God's power; they are all called elect and holy because they are adopted by God, all without exception: Jews, pagans, women, men, slaves, free, poor, rich, those with high status and those who are "nothing" in the eyes of the world.[6]

In her eloquent argument for a new consciousness of the "*ecclesia* of women" in early Christianity, Schüssler Fiorenza underscores the profoundly democratic nature of those communities. She sees the above paraphrase of Galatians 3:28 not as a specially Pauline understanding, but rather as the theological self-understanding of the whole Christian missionary movement.[7]

In his still seminal study of Pauline communities, Wayne Meeks describes these groupings as intense spiritual families over against the rigid hierarchical structures of Greco-Roman society.[8] He acknowledges the dialectic of structure and antistructure within the Pauline communities. But the main emphasis is horizontal, in various patterns of brothers and sisters expressing the gifts of the Spirit. Monarchical governance had little place in these groups. Rather, their inner cohesion rested on a lively mix of preaching, liturgies, mutual support, visits and letters from charismatic leaders, and a general environment of social intimacy. These communities attracted a variety of members who suffered a certain status inconsistency in the wider society: independent women, Jews of some wealth, and freedmen still blighted by their origins. Such persons frequently became leaders in communities that also welcomed more marginal persons. In this blend, there was a courage and desire to break out of given hierarchical patterns.[9]

A contemporary penchant in New Testament studies to explore the social setting of the earliest Christian communities continues to depict these small churches in more horizontal or democratic perspectives. Halvor Moxnes examines the economic situation of Lukan communities.[10] He finds a system of horizontal reciprocity that continues the "moral economy of the peasant."[11] This meant a pressure within these groups to share food, hospitality, and clothing. The sharing itself had a levelling influence in the social network of each community. They were expressing the communal rules of village solidarity in systems of horizontal reciprocity.[12] The almsgiving advocated by Jesus and enacted by the centurion Cornelius became essential for salvation. This system of wealth redistribution had political consequences. It tended to free indentured servants from complete dependency on their patrons. These Christian communities were proclaiming that all are clients before God who gives without expecting a return. Again, we find in the Lukan mentality a democratizing thrust in reaction to a stratified society of political and economic hierarchy.

Arianism, viewed from a different perspective, becomes instructive for appreciating democratic tendencies. It is useful to look again at such "historical losers" for insights too easily swept away in the polemical fervor of those ancient times. Over against the powerfully hierarchical, divine-nature theologies of a "winner" like Athanasius, the Arian teaching stressed the creaturely humanity of the Christ. The opponents of Arius thought that his adoptionistic view of Jesus as the Christ degraded the divinity of the Son. For Arius numbered him among creatures. Athanasius lashes out against the Arians for "denying the divinity of our saviour and proclaiming that he is equal to all."[13] But underneath these charges lie diverse theological anthropologies. Arius was not trying to denigrate the Christ's divinity, but rather to elevate the humanity of all. "Arius and his followers believed that God has and will have many sons.... Sharing in a single kind of sonship, Christ is one among many brothers."[14] Arian anthropology might be called optimistic about the excellence of the human creature. The Athanasian approach can be seen as pessimistic concerning the human, distancing humanity in its lowliness from participation in the divine.

At stake here are presuppositions bearing on how the church as well as civil society should be governed. If, according to Athanasius, humanity as such is abysmally removed from God, its path to salvation consists in obedience to a superior hierarchical order, imposed by a monarchical God and communicated by church leaders. The Arian approach stressed the possibility of moral development in both the Christ and other humans as the very orchestration of God's free will. What was done on the horizontal level of human interaction in history, although fraught with positive and negative potentials, became part of the salvific process for Arius and his followers. This outlook is much closer to a presupposition of democratic governance, namely, that the free and responsible action of the people advances the welfare of the whole society. Athanasius's dimmer view of human nature lends itself to a need for greater control in a divinely given, static, and monarchical system. The anti-Arian victors embraced the seeming security of hierarchical order, which would have its reflection in the Constantinian church.

The monastic movement of Pachomius in fourth-century Egypt manifested a more horizontal, less hierarchical orientation when compared with the subsequent Benedictine spirituality. Such a comparison, of course, is not completely symmetrical. Abba Pachomius founded one of the earliest coenobitic or communal forms of monasticism. The Pachomian *koinonia*, unlike the eremetical life of Anthony, drew monks and nuns into some of the first monastic communities along the banks of the Nile. The church itself was less centralized in the early fourth century than it would be in Benedict's Italy of the sixth century. Yet the comparison between Pachomius and Benedict reveals important differences.

Pachomian spirituality was to some extent paternal and hierarchical in that his followers chose to follow his rule toward God. But the emphasis of his rule was not obedience to himself as a form of obedience to God. Rather Pachomius urged his monastics to govern themselves interiorly and exteriorly.[15] They were not to imitate Pachomius but to mutually support one another in imitating the humanity of Christ. For them salvation lay not so much in participating in Christ's divine nature, but in following his truly human way of life. Pachomian spirituality stressed brotherhood in community rather than vertical hierarchy.[16] There is an interesting conjunction between a less hierarchical view of monasticism and a greater emphasis on the humanity of Christ. For Benedict, obedience to superiors in itself takes on soteriological overtones. Such obedience to hierarchy constitutes a primary means of demonstrating obedience to God. The Benedictine abbot takes Christ's place; he is responsible for the monks' obedience and must account at Judgment for his disciples' souls.[17] For the salvation of his soul, the monk must see "in him [the abbot] . . . Christ personified and, as it were, newly made incarnate in quasi-sacramental fashion."[18]

Of course, the Benedictine rule was not intended to divinize the abbot. But the language of "newly made incarnate in quasi-sacramental fashion" is a much more soteriological and vertical concept than that of Pachomius, the facilitator of his community's spiritual growth. Pachomius was followed because he was "an imitator of the saints,"[19] not because he was Christ "newly incarnate." Again, we should not expect to find ready-made democratic movements in church history, given different social structures and personal mentalities in past eras. Yet we can find in history incipient, and sometimes well-developed, institutions that incorporate the egalitarian, horizontal, and communal groundwork for shaping a democratic church. The later development of monasticism with Francis and Dominic is also revealing in this regard. Franciscan and Dominican orders came into being in the much more hierarchical church of the thirteenth century. But within these movements were the seeds of communal and participatory developments. The very egalitarian genius of Francis stood against the aristocratic and politicized church of his day. His mendicants were witnessing to a church of humble fellowship from the bottom up, as it were. And Dominic's monastic chapters were already a form of participatory democracy.

The metropolitan structure of early church government offers yet another locus of decentralization and pluralism, qualities often suppressed in the second millennium of Catholic history. From the fourth to the sixth centuries, metropolitan bishops had widespread jurisdiction over lesser dioceses in the same episcopal province or region. Rome was rarely consulted in important decision making. The bishop of Rome was preeminent in honor, as he occupied the see attributed to St. Peter, but the metropolitan bishop ran his own church. A doctrinal dispute might call for consultation or even a council beyond a particular region, but even these events were frequently handled without Rome's intervention. A recent study underscores the independence of metropolitans in Gaul of the fourth and fifth centuries. Mathisen points out:

> Before the 380s the Bishop of Rome made no obvious attempts to exercise ecclesiastical authority in Gaul: he did not order the convening of church councils, he did not become involved in the Gauls' internal affairs, and he was neither consulted nor informed about Gallic problems. The Gauls rather convened their own interprovincial councils on their own authority, and passed canons binding on themselves.[20]

This did not mean that metropolitans were completely independent in their provinces. Gallic bishops had little contact with Rome in the fourth century, but they cultivated close ties with the church of northern Italy, especially the see of Milan. The latter, as the imperial capital of the time, overshadowed Rome.[21] Bishop Ambrose of Milan, whose father had been Roman prefect in Gaul, had far more influence on the ancient see of Arles and on other Gallic bishops than did the bishop of Rome. This kind of regional independence continued well into the fifth century. Zosimus, bishop of Rome, was either rebuffed or ignored when he tried to exercise authority in Gaul. "The bishops of Rome learned not to intervene in Gaul unless they had the support of some party there."[22] The point of this discussion is not to claim that early metropolitan systems were democratic. The metropolitan bishop could have been an authoritarian in his mode of ruling. But he operated in a far more decentralized polity than we know today. He was elected by the priests and people of his province and he was subject to regional councils.

As is well known, the eleventh century saw the beginnings of medieval centralization in the church. Europe after Charlemagne fell increasingly into disorder, conflict, and decline. The Viking invasions led to great political fragmentation. The degenerate state of the church and the papacy called out for the reforms of Germanic kings like Henry III and churchmen like Gregory VII, Hildebrand. Yet when Hildebrand was attempting to reconstruct the hierarchy and remove it from the control of Italian groups, he invoked the long-traditional mode of electing bishops by the priests and people of their regions. The twelfth century saw the juridical reorganization of the church in Gratian's compendium of canon laws, echoing Roman law. Innocent II and Innocent III, both lawyers, were able to use this reorganization of church law to focus great ecclesiastical power in the papacy. Yet even while the papacy was rising to a pinnacle of temporal and sacral influence in Europe, the twelfth century witnessed important levelling or egalitarian movements. The Waldensians, or the Poor Men of Lyons, emphasized lay and even women preachers, and they tended to ignore the orders of the hierarchy.[23] Similar groups like the Fratricelli and the Humiliati spread through southern France and northern Italy seeking to live in lay form the simpler virtues of the gospels. Often enough the hierarchy accused such people of heterodoxy, especially in their views of Christ. The medieval church tended to associate denigration of its authority with Christological heresy.

In a time when one might expect a juridical understanding of the church among its leading theologians, Thomas Aquinas presented a powerfully theological view of ecclesiology. In Aquinas we find a particularly valuable theological vision as a source for a more pluralistic and democratic restructuring of the church today. The key point of Thomas's understanding of the institutional church is its subordinate and instrumental character.[24] Thomas justifies the place and necessity of a visible, institutional church. And he supports its papal and episcopal structure in the thirteenth-century form that he knew. But he also relativizes that very structure by making it secondary to his theological ecclesiology. His functional teaching about the institutional church means that it is a *ministerium*, a ministry of word and sacrament to help humans approach God. "This means that what is most essential and decisive about it is not so much speculation about its nature, [but] its nature and its very identity derive from its functionality."[25] Thomas's fundamentally teleological perspective undergirds this position. The church is not to be sacralized in itself, but rather its institutional structure must serve the Christological goals of helping people participate in God's grace. The church's function is to foster lives of faith, hope, and love in individuals and communities. If its structure impedes these goals, it should be changed.

Thomas's dominant conception of the church is *congregatio fidelium*. The stress is on the community of faith that links the believer to God through Christ. Within the *congregatio*, the ministry of word and sacrament energizes Christians to participate more fully in God's life of grace. Institution and hierarchy are secondary to, or better, ancillary (in the sense of servants of) the *congregatio*. His ecclesiology is encompassing and catholic. It bursts through the limits of the constituted church, through the juridical structures of the Catholic hierarchy to embrace a much wider constituency. Such were the implications of his distinction between the actual and the potential church, not understood as two different entities, but as one mystery of God reaching beyond the narrow systems and rules of any group of church leaders.

In the sixteenth century the Spanish bishop Bartolomé de Las Casas cited Thomas's *Summa* text (IIIa, q. 8, a. 3) to protect the Indians of Latin America from colonial persecution. He argued that Christ suffered in their sufferings; even as pagans they were already within the extended church.[26] However we might want to critique the implicit European triumphalism in such ideas of anonymous Christians, the important point here is Aquinas's sense of priorities. His theology relativizes any given structure of the church as fixed or permanent. His functional sense of the church "means that it is not absolute ... it is not there for its own sake, but for a function ... it always points beyond itself. Thus, the institutional church is essentially subordinate ... and provisional."[27] The institution in some visible form remains necessary as *congregatio fidelium*, but it is not necessary that its form be monarchical as we have inherited it from Western history.

Yet in Thomas's own century a controversy erupted between the defenders of an almost absolute papal power and those who claimed a type of ecclesiastical constitutionalism that included the decentralized power of the bishops. Innocent III had declared for himself the plenitude of power over the whole church. He made use of Gratian's *Decretum* to find legal techniques to bolster total papal sovereignty. It is ironical that he used some of this authority to approve the Franciscans and Dominicans, whose own inner structures expressed more egalitarian emphases. The Dominicans wrote into their constitutions the right to elect all superiors and to establish limited tenure in office. These democratic controls were devised to render superiors responsible for their administration. "Every attempt was made to guarantee freedom of elections and to ensure each voter the exercise of his right."[28]

But when Innocent sent these friars and preachers into the domains of other bishops without their permission, resistance arose. The quarrel reached its greatest intensity in the 1250s at the University of Paris. William of St. Amour defended the constitutional rights of the bishops that he saw being usurped by the pope. William cited both Scripture and Gratian's *De-cretum* to urge that "the other apostles received honor and power with Peter in equal fellowship."[29] The church was established as a whole constitutional order in which the pope's ruling power was limited by the authority of bishops and priests. Bonaventure held the opposing position that all ruling authority resided in the pope.

William of St. Amour's tenet of the church as a constitutional corporation lost out in the pragmatic struggle for power in the thirteenth century, but this does not minimize its importance. For it expressed a democratizing thrust in ecclesiology that was never far from the surface of medieval life. It would reemerge in the long conciliarist debate during the Western schism toward the end of the fourteenth and the beginning of the fifteenth centuries. Yet this theology of conciliarism should also be seen in the context of republican thought in northern Italy, best represented by Niccolo Machiavelli. This Florentine intellectual sought to reshape the Roman sense of republicanism for the welfare of Italian city states. He appealed not to monarchy, which kept citizens in dependency and immaturity, but to a mixed republic in which the prince and the aristocracy would be joined by an active citizenry in seeking the common good of the state. The prince was not to rule by coercion, invoking some God-anointed status. Rather he was to inspire the people to civic involvement and virtue that would protect the state against constant revolution and blind fortune. Machiavelli's interest was not religious salvation, but his greatly influential republicanism helped to mold an environment in which theologians in the conciliar controversies could muster their arguments from Christian tradition for a more democratic church.

The Avignon papacy after 1305 created a vast bureaucracy of patronage and profit. Bishops continued to be chosen by local secular rulers, but to assume office they had to be approved by the pope. The financial cost for such approval was high; bishoprics were seen largely as profit-making branches of the main office. As the church slid into ever greater scandal and eventually schism with two then three claimants to the papal throne, councils were called at Konstanz (1414–18) and Basle (1439–48) to find a remedy. In some of the leading thinkers of the conciliar movement, we discover a rich tapestry of democratic theologizing. Andrés Díaz de Escobar described the church in a remarkable statement:

> The church is a kind of mystical body, and a kind of republic of the Christian people... that most holy republic is the universal church... and therefore, it is a common affair of the Christian people.[30]

Conciliarists invoked a corporate sense of the church, stemming in part from medieval organic thinking and from the collegiate experience of the universities. The council was understood as a body inspired directly by the Holy Spirit. Not just the head but every organ of the body was permeated by the Spirit. In its democratic, participatory thrust, the council was seen as a microcosm of the whole church. The council insisted on freedom of speech, equality of voting power, and committee systems to arrive at common consent. Juan de Segovia emphasized that the church is held together not by handing over all authority to a single person, but in a network of mutual confidence created by leaders who are credible to their followers. "Authority arose in a web of trust created by open collegiality grounded in the one Holy Spirit."[31] Jean Gerson insisted on the corporate authority of all the bishops together, speaking of "the life-giving power by which the Mystical Body of the church can unify and vivify itself."[32] Gerson and others looked toward a council, which finally met in Constance. Its controversial decree, *Haec Sancta*, proclaimed: "This holy synod . . . holds its power immediately from Christ and anyone of whatsoever state or dignity — even the papal — is bound to obey it in matters relating to faith, the rooting out of schism and the general reform of the church in head and members."

The long scandal of papal schism in the fourteenth and fifteenth centuries compelled the best minds of the period to seek not only a solution to the immediate problem, but to probe deeply into the nature of the church. By trying to find the best understanding of the relationship of pope and council, they were impelled to examine the tradition of the early church. The result of this great rethinking convinced conciliarists of various stripes that the dominant papal monarchy of the high Middle Ages was an aberration or at least a historical accident that called for correction. It was Marsilius of Padua, writing before the schism, who captured the fundamentally corporate nature of the church as *universitas fidelium* in his influential *Defensor Pacis*. For Marsilius all believing Christians should participate in making church law. He invoked the ancient Roman dictum, *quod omnes tangit, ab omnibus judicetur* (that which affects all should be determined by everyone), which had become an important principle of patristic thought. Marsilius saw the monarchical constitution of the church as simply a matter of historical convenience.[33] In the fifteenth century, Nicholas of Cusa, a cardinal of the church engaged in the struggles of the Council of Basle, restated the ancient principles of consent and of authority deriving from the whole people, especially when these principles were endangered by the claims of centralizing monarchies.[34]

We should not see the conciliar movement as a perfect representation, even in theory, of an ideal democratic structure for the church today. It was a highly clericalist endeavor, which virtually excluded the laity from the councils. Again, this is understandable in the late medieval context of defending against the undo influence of secular princes. Moreover, few among the laity possessed the theological education requisite for resolving the complex problems of conciliarism. Moreover, conciliar thinkers were incapable of devising systems or constitutions for delegating authority in complex situations. Still influenced by the medieval mentality of paternalism, they were unable to work out needed forms of structured representation for a democratic church. But the conciliarists did tap into the basic scriptural insight that all ecclesiastical authority was conferred for the good of the church rather than for the personal glory of prelates, "that the clergy should be 'ministers' rather than masters."[35] This principle lends itself to fundamentally democratic potentials.

But we also know that the conciliar movement failed to reform the church in head and members. When it became tactically feasible after the Council of Basle, the popes returned to a policy of absolute monarchy. Yet the movement failed not because it was wrong, but because it was betrayed.[36] The collapse of these conciliar reforms proved disastrous for the church in the sixteenth century. Brian Tierney underscores the crucial importance of these disputes for the Catholic Church today:

> Now we live in the shadow of another great council. The doctrine of collegiality has been defined afresh. But the problem of constitutional structure remains quite open and unresolved. We have a second chance to solve it. And we have less excuse for failing than the men of the 15th century. We have not forgotten our history, and we are not condemned to repeat it.[37]

In an ecumenical age, the Catholic Church will also want to learn from experiments with democracy in the Protestant churches. During the Reformation of the sixteenth century and long after, most Protestant movements continued the patterns of geographical churches under aristocracies. This was generally true of Lutheran, Calvinist, and Anglican reforms. While these trajectories of the Reformation broke with Roman Catholic positions, they continued to live in state-church formats under royal leaders. One could look within each of these traditions for less autocratic lines of religious authority than the papal mode. But it was the radical, or left-wing, Protestant Reformation of Anabaptists, then Puritans and Pietists, that fostered within Christian churches more democratic forms.

Perhaps the greatest accomplishment of the radical wing of the Protestant Reformation was a freeing of Christianity from Christendom. The latter consisted of the forms of imperial or kingly monarchy that the church had incorporated since Constantine. The Anabaptists wanted not just a reform of that system, but a restoration of the pre-Constantinian church.[38] Today we may criticize the historical naiveté of the radical reformers in thinking that they could replicate first-century Christianity a millennium and a half later. But their key insight remains valid: the church must not be confined in its structure to any historical milieu. Their understanding of an adult covenant of believers who in faith create church follows from their desire to "de-territorialize" Christianity. The church was not to be wedded unconditionally to particular histories and cultures. Thus follows the radicals' intense call for separation of church and state. The lesson from this phase of history for Catholic reform today relates to freeing our ecclesial structures from their long bondage to patriarchal monarchy.

If we date the modern political era more or less from the Enlightenment and the French Revolution, we find the Catholic Church consistently opposed to liberal democracy through the nineteenth and early twentieth centuries. "Modern historians agree with . . . Lammenais and Acton that in general the Catholic Church set its face with equal firmness against political democracy, social equality, and religious liberty."[39]

A generation after the French Revolution the young priest Felicité de Lammenais launched a significant reform movement in French Catholicism. By the 1830s a minority of reformist Catholics, led by Lammenais, appreciated both the dangers and the promise of the postrevolutionary order. They criticized Napoleonic militarism as well as the alienation and poverty caused by *laissez faire* capitalism. But these reformers called for the church to adapt itself positively to the gains of the revolution. Lammenais's call for a free church in a free state echoed in some ways the stance of the radical reformers of the sixteenth century. He proposed a broad program for the reform of seminaries and clerical lifestyles. If the church was to offer positive inspiration to many disaffected Catholics in France, it would have to do more than condemn the excesses of the revolution and cling to restored monarchies.

Rome would have none of it. Lammenais's "pilgrims for God and liberty" were condemned by Pope Gregory XVI in *Mirari Vos*. "From the evil-smelling spring of indifferentism flows the erroneous and absurd opinion — or, rather, derangement — that freedom of conscience must be asserted and vindicated for everyone."[40] The pope derided "the vile attack on clerical celibacy" and "the deleterious liberty, which can never be execrated and detested sufficiently, of printing and publishing writings of every kind," as well as "the detestable insolence and impudence of those who, burning with an unbridled desire of baneful liberty, dedicate themselves entirely to the weakening and the destruction of all rights of government."[41] These orotund latinisms encapsulate the Vatican's pervasive attitude toward democracy in the nineteenth century. Beneath this negativity was the church's lack of confidence in human nature and in the ability of reasonably decent people to alter their political structures for the common benefit. Pope Gregory, like Pius IX and Leo XIII after him, urged obedience to rulers. Except for papal social encyclicals, this basic distrust in human freedom became a hallmark of most Catholic documents up to Vatican II. The church's antidemocratic bias played itself out in other major ecclesial events of the nineteenth century. The Syllabus of Errors in 1864 continued this tradition, as did Vatican I with its glorification of papal monarchical power.

In addition to Lammenais's efforts, other nineteenth-century movements showed the way toward a more democratic church. These minority groups and events were certainly not characteristic of the central church, but they offer important *loci* for current reflection. The controversy over lay trustees in the United States in the early nineteenth century is one such episode. Lay trustees in Charleston argued that they should be able to participate in the governance of the local Catholic church. In 1818 they argued that the old *jus patronatus*, enjoyed by European sovereigns in appointing clergy in particular locales, should be transferred to the whole body of the faithful in the American democratic environment.[42] In this new milieu, the American Constitution precluded any government exercise of the *jus patronatus*, the lay trustees contended, and, therefore, it was the Catholic community's right to appoint its leaders. This argument was based, as noted above, on a very old tradition in the church concerning the election of bishops by their people. But the embattled Vatican, tending its wounds after the French Revolution, would hear none of it. The ironically less traditional Ultramontanism of reactionary Catholicism prevailed, culminating in Vatican I, where monarchical power of the highest sort was dogmatically vested in the papacy.

In the conclusion of an exhaustive study of the lay trustee controversy, Patrick Carey reflects on its meaning for post–Vatican II Catholicism. Despite the theoretical gains toward democratic forms of the church in the Vatican II concept of collegiality, the practical structures or instruments for implementing a collegial theology are lacking.[43] In recent years the Vatican has shown intense reluctance to recognize the theological place and value of independent bishops' conferences on national and regional levels. This has been born out in the appointment of bishops of a conservative stamp in the Netherlands and Germany without local consultation and in spite of the opposition of local clergy and laity. Moreover, Cardinal Joseph Ratzinger, head of the Congregation for the Doctrine of the Faith, has maintained that local and regional conferences of bishops have only consultative, not deliberative, jurisdiction. In light of this current Vatican retrenchment on democratic structures, Carey's reflections on the meaning of the lay trustee controversy are particularly valuable:

> Even with the communal and collegial theology of the post–Vatican II era, the Catholic Church has failed to provide instruments that must take the lay voice seriously in parish and diocesan decision-making. The laity's voice is purely consultative and contributes effectively only when the clergy and bishops are open to such consultation.... The difficulties here appear to be inherent in a hierarchical church that is trying to incorporate congregational models of church government at the local level without fully incorporating either the theology behind congregationalism or a legal instrument that could provide for a constitutional balance of powers in the hierarchical church.[44]

The lay trustee dispute of the last century needs to be placed in a wider context of what came to be called the Americanist heresy. It is not important for purposes of this chapter to explore the intricacies that led to Leo XIII's condemnation of Americanism in 1899. But his letter *Testem Benevolentiae* demonstrated the Vatican's deep suspicion of "a certain liberty" connected with the church's experience in the American democratic milieu.[45] Pope Leo saw danger to Catholic doctrine and practice if that "certain liberty" were introduced into the church. Progressive American Catholic bishops of the nineteenth century, like Ireland, Keane, and Gibbons, came to experience the values of Lammenais's insight of a free church in a free state. These bishops and their priests were closer to the populist needs of their largely working-class, immigrant laity. Cardinal Gibbons, for example, supported the unionizing efforts of the Knights of Labor, led by the Catholic Terrence Powderly. Unlike the aristocratic hierarchies of Catholic Europe, these American churchmen kept close to the working classes. Not only did these populist experiences sensitize them to honor democracy's "certain liberty," but American separation of church and state proved to be beneficial to the expanding American church. Leo XIII rightly sensed the democratic thrust of Americanism and its potential for altering intrachurch structures. But his mentality reflected Vatican I's papal centralization and monarchism.

The Modernist crisis at the turn of the century brought these democratic tendencies to a sudden end. Catholic Modernism hit the Roman authorities like a theological thunderbolt. Official Catholic theology, especially after Leo XIII's letter reestablishing scholasticism in the seminaries, went forward in a traditionally conceptualist and ahistorical mode. Thinkers like Loisy and Tyrrell were basing their modernistic positions on very different presuppositions. For them, Catholic doctrines needed to be rethought as historically conditioned symbol systems ever open to new interpretation in the evolution of human consciousness. The Modernists were bringing to bear on Catholicism the fruits of Enlightenment reflection at a time when the church was ill-prepared to understand the flow of thought from Kant and Schleiermacher to Bergson and Schweitzer. Catholic ultramontanists interpreted these thinkers as enemies. The Modernists were also harkening forward to the hermeneutical conversations that dominate the contemporary theological world. Pius X's letters condemning Modernism in the first decade of this century demonstrated both unfair interpretations and authoritarian fear. As a result, these condemnations battened down the hatches on creative thought among Catholic theologians for nearly half a century. I am purposely not concentrating on the merits of Vatican or Modernist arguments. It is the procedure by which the controversy took place that underscores the pitfalls of an undemocratic church. There was no open discourse with dissident intellectuals within the church, as if the official church might learn something in such a dialogue. The problem was handled by divine-right-of-kings edict, followed by fear-inspiring purges of intellectuals in church institutions.

Beneath these heavy-handed procedures lurks a crucial issue still unresolved in Vatican dealings with the contemporary church: trust in the pluralistic experience of Catholic Christians. David O'Brien states it well: "What is at stake is the degree to which the church, having affirmed the rights of conscience and the dignity of the human person, is prepared to translate these values into pastoral policies based on trust and confidence in its own people."[46] Whether it is the condemnation of the Modernists or the firing of Charles Curran or the silencing of Matthew Fox and Leonardo Boff, controversial matters are not dealt with in ways that respect sincere and competent dialogue. Public discourse among theologians is curtailed by Vatican edicts poorly argued by "company" theologians. A most important lesson for the church to learn from the Modernist crisis is that suppression of dissent and of new ideas injures both the truth and the pastoral ministry. A democratic church does not mean that no official position can be reached or that no consequences can follow from such a decision. Rather a democratic church would cherish and protect by law the rights of its intellectuals to explore all avenues toward truth and to debate these issues among themselves in public. Even beyond trust in its own people, the church, through such procedures, would manifest confidence in the Spirit's ability to operate in an open exchange of ideas and experiences among the faithful.

Underlying the rationale for democratic structures in the Catholic Church are arguments both from the past and from the present. The argument from tradition can be succinctly stated in the scholastic dictum *ab esse ad posse valet illatio*, if it happened before, it can happen again. We have noted that the laity in the early church participated in the election of their leaders. They also had a right of recall. But even beyond these functions, the laity was actively engaged in conciliar events, that is, in vital decision making that affected the church on local, regional, and even international levels. This participation was not restricted to the emperors who convoked councils from the ancient church to the high Middle Ages. Laity also engaged actively in ecumenical councils from that of Carthage in the fourth century to Trent in the sixteenth century. Norbert Greinacher expresses well the fundamental task of democratization facing the Catholic Church:

> We must move toward a far-reaching *democratization of the structures of the Church*. Such a democratization corresponds on the one hand to an original and genuine stream of Christian tradition in the Church and on the other hand also to the mentality and structure of contemporary secular society.[47]

The argument from the present for a democratic Catholic Church should not be misconstrued as a capitulation to the contemporary secular mentality. There is, of course, much to criticize in modernity's individualism, consumerism, and lack of ecological awareness. This litany of negatives could be extended with its many forms of social violence. But the church that points out the evil ways of the world must be ever striving to live out within itself models for a better society. In important areas of respect for pluralism and dissent, the Catholic Church today trails behind many democratic secular institutions. The ecclesiastical structures of monarchy, and at times of totalitarian conduct, are not mandated by the gospel. They defy the freedom in God preached in the New Testament. To reestablish the structures that would honor the old *consensus fidelium*, that experience of the whole believing people, the church on the verge of a new millennium needs to take to heart its own admonition at Vatican II that it is both a teaching and learning church.

The church must extend the Vatican II doctrine of collegiality (and the principle of social encyclicals: subsidiarity) into its own internal, democratic reorganization. Reform in the Catholic Church toward a democratic polity is the basis for other desired changes. Whatever the specific issues, be they married clergy, women priests, or birth control and divorce, the underlying issue blocking creative rethinking is that of restrictive monarchical structures. Such a polity leads to rule by the judgment of a "king" who, in the end, does not have to listen to the experience and wisdom of the people. Channels of open communication, deliberation, and decision making still do not exist sufficiently in the Catholic Church.

Against the spirit of fearful retrenchment that has gripped the Vatican in recent years, a Catholic Church confident of its democratic possibilities needs to recapture the spirit of John XXIII, who, ten days before his death, urged the church to read the signs of the times with hope rather than despair:

> Today more than ever, certainly more than in previous centuries, we are called to serve man as such, and not merely Catholics; to defend above all and everywhere the rights of the human person, and not merely those of the Catholic Church. Present-day conditions, the demands of the last fifty years, doctrinal *approfondissement* have led us to new realities.... *It is not that the Gospel has changed; it is that we have begun to understand it better*. Anyone who has had a long life was faced with new tasks in the social order at the start of the century; anyone who was, as I was, twenty years in the East, eight years in France and been able to confront different cultures and traditions, knows the moment has come to discern the *signs of the times*, to seize the opportunity and to look far ahead.[48]

In this testament of John XXIII we see both respect for creative interpretation of tradition and a profound willingness to walk into a democratic future.

Notes

1. William J. Everett, *God's Federal Republic* (New York: Paulist Press, 1988), 20–21.

2. Ibid., 47ff.

3. J. Michael Miller, *The Divine Right of the Papacy in Recent Ecumenical Theology* (Rome: Università Gregoriana Editrice, 1980), 280ff.

4. Elisabeth Schüssler Fiorenza, *In Memory of Her* (New York: Crossroad, 1984), 104.

5. Roger Gryson, "The Authority of the Teacher in the Ancient and Medieval Church," in L. Swidler and P. F. Fransen, eds., *Authority in the Church and the Schillebeeckx Case* (New York: Crossroad, 1982), 176–77.

6. Fiorenza, *In Memory of Her*, 199.

7. Ibid.

8. Wayne D. Meeks, *The First Urban Christians* (New Haven: Yale University Press, 1983), 89.

9. Ibid., 191.

10. Halvor R. Moxnes, *The Economy of the Kingdom* (Philadelphia: Fortress, 1988).

11. Ibid., 96.

12. Ibid., 137.

13. Robert C. Gregg and Dennis E. Groh, *Early Arianism: A View of Salvation* (Philadelphia: Fortress, 1981), 47.

14. Ibid., 56.

15. Philip Rousseau, *Pachomius: The Making of a Community in Fourth-Century Egypt* (Berkeley: University of California Press, 1985), 73.

16. Ibid., 117.

17. *RB 1980: The Rule of St. Benedict* (Collegeville, Minn.: Liturgical Press, 1981), 347.

18. Ibid., 356.

19. Rousseau, *Pachomius*, 118.

20. Ralph W. Mathisen, *Ecclesiastical Factionalism and Religious Controversy in Fifth-Century Gaul* (Washington: Catholic University of America Press, 1989).

21. Ibid., 11.

22. Ibid., 68.

23. Lester K. Little, *Religious Poverty and the Profit Economy in Medieval Europe* (Ithaca, N.Y.: Cornell University Press, 1978), 124.

24. George Sabra, *Thomas Aquinas' Vision of the Church* (Mainz: Matthias-Grunewald Verlag, 1987), 120.

25. Ibid., 120–21.

26. Ibid., 181.

27. Ibid., 195.

28. William A. Hinnebusch, *The History of the Dominican Order* (New York: Alba House, 1966), 1:217.

29. Brian Tierney, "Pope and Bishops: A Historical Survey," *America* 158, no. 9 (March 5, 1988): 234.

30. Anthony Black, *Council and Commune: The Conciliar Movement and the Fifteenth Century Heritage* (London: Burns and Oates, 1979), 88.

31. Everett, *God's Federal Republic*, 73.

32. Tierney, "Pope and Bishops: A Historical Survey," 236.

33. Paul E. Sigmund, *Nicholas of Cusa and Medieval Political Thought* (Cambridge: Harvard University Press, 1963), 91.

34. Ibid., 310.

35. Brian Tierney, *Foundations of the Conciliar Theory* (Cambridge: Cambridge University Press, 1955), 242.

36. Tierney, "Pope and Bishops: A Historical Survey," 237.

37. Ibid.

38. Franklin H. Littell, "The Radical Reformation and the American Experience," in Thomas M. McFadden, ed., *America in Theological Perspective* (New York: Seabury Press, 1976), 72.

39. David J. O'Brien, "The Catholic Experience and Perspective," in Roger Van Allen, ed., *American Religious Values and the Future of America* (Philadelphia: Fortress Press, 1978), 72.

40. From *Mirari Vos*, as quoted in O'Brien, ibid., 74.

41. Ibid.

42. Dennis P. McCann, *New Experiment in Democracy: The Challenge for American Catholicism* (Kansas City, Mo.: Sheed and Ward, 1987), 162. See also Joseph Agonito, *The Building of an American Church: The Episcopacy of John Carroll* (New York: Garland Publishing, 1988), 212. Carroll tried to accommodate the new American Catholic Church to its republican environment by recognizing the role of the laity in parishes. He upheld the clergy's right to participate in the selection of bishops. But as Agonito also points out, Carroll faced the dilemma of relating these democratic ecclesial moves to the monarchical structure of the Roman Catholic Church. In the end, "he stifled the two movements — lay trusteeism and ecclesiastical democracy — which were valid expressions of republicanism" (ibid.).

43. Patrick W. Carey, *People, Priests and Prelates: Ecclesiastical Democracy and the Tensions of Trusteeism* (Notre Dame, Ind.: University of Notre Dame Press, 1987), 292.

44. Ibid.

45. McCann, *New Experiment in Democracy*, 11.

46. O'Brien, "The Catholic Experience and Perspective," 77.

47. Norbert Greinacher, "Der Vollzug der Kirche im Bistum," as cited in Swidler, *Authority in the Church and the Schillebeeckx Case*, 236.

48. Quoted from Swidler, *Authority in the Church and the Schillebeeckx Case*, 195, who in turn quotes from Angelina and Giuseppe Alberigo, *Giovanni XXIII* (Brescia: Queriniana, 1978), 494.

JOHN BEAL

-3-
Toward a Democratic Church:
The Canonical Heritage

Canon Law: An Unlikely Source
for a Democratic Church Polity

In light of its recent history, canon law seems an unlikely source to mine for elements that could contribute to a democratic church order. It is true, of course, that a revised Code of Canon Law has been promulgated in "a great effort to translate this same conciliar doctrine and ecclesiology into *canonical* language."[1] While this revised code is generally faithful to the letter of the council's teaching, it is often difficult to smell the fresh breeze of *aggiornamento* wafting through its 1752 canons. The church sketched in the revised code is not a democracy. Nevertheless, it would not be entirely accurate to say that the quest for the canonical contribution to a democratic church has reached a dead end with the 1983 code. To assert, as canonists of every ideological stripe are wont to do, that the Catholic Church is not a democracy is to mouth a tautology. Neither is the church a totalitarian dictatorship, an absolute monarchy, or a reincarnation of the Roman empire. The nature of the church is most adequately, but still imperfectly, defined not by political science but by theology, even though the social sciences can serve as a brake on the chronic temptation to ecclesiological mystification. Despite its somewhat suspect past, the canonical tradition does witness to institutes, principles, and practices that are consistent with the theological constitution of the church and that, if rescued from oblivion, could give the church a democratic face without transforming it into a "one-man-one-vote" democracy.

Brian Tierney has demonstrated that the glosses and treatises of medieval canon lawyers provided concepts and principles that, when taken over and assimilated by civil law, became the indispensable building blocks of constitutional theory in the West.[2] These concepts and principles and the texts that contain them are now interred beneath the debris of nearly half a millennium of history. Nevertheless, they still occasionally peek out from beneath the surface of the Latin text of the 1983 code. If these concepts and principles can be resurrected from their resting place, perhaps they can begin again to play the role in the development of the constitutional structure of the church that they once played in the development of constitutional democracy in the Western world.

The Harvest of Medieval Canonistry

In the midst of a complex and vibrant, but sometimes litigious, medieval society there appeared around 1140 Gratian's *Concordantia discordantium canonum* (*Concord of Discordant Canons*) or, more commonly, the *Decretum*. In this monumental tome, Gratian, a master at the University of Bologna, mustered, organized, synthesized, and, where possible, reconciled the whole discipline of the Christian church insofar as it was accessible to him. It was all here, a thousand years of church law — scriptural citations, patristic sayings, canons of great and not so great councils, papal decrees (including more than few fraudulent ones). Gratian organized this enormous mass of disparate material from all strata of the tradition topically, set off one authority against another, and attempted to resolve the inconsistencies and contradictions among the authorities. Although Gratian himself was more successful as a compiler and organizer than as a synthesizer, his work almost immediately became the standard starting point for canonical science. Soon Gratian's heirs, called decretists, or commentators on the *Decretum*, produced a vast literature of glosses and treatises on his gigantic, quasi-authoritative casebook.

While the works of Gratian and his successors are highly technical, "at the highest level of their thought, the decretists set themselves a great task — to provide an appropriate juridical formulation for the ancient theological doctrine of the church as a people of God, an ordered community of the faithful."[3] Two contributions to the medieval canonists are of particular relevance to the subject of this essay: their reflection on the relationship between the ruler and the community and their application of the principles of the law of corporations (*universitates*) to both the microscopic and macroscopic levels of the church.

The Shepherd and the Sheep

Since Gratian's *Decretum* contained numerous texts dealing with the papacy, his successors could hardly avoid discussion of the powers and prerogatives of the papal office. Medieval canonists were not at all shy about asserting and defending the "plenitude of power" the pope enjoyed by divine right, but they "were equally interested in the divine right of the community."[4] The decretists never forgot that popes — as indeed all prelates — did not stand outside and over against the church but within it.

The enormous powers they possessed within the church they enjoyed for the sake of the church and as its representatives. Unburdened by a defined dogma of papal infallibility, the decretists understood the scriptural texts about Peter to mean that it is the church, the whole body of the faithful, that is indefectible in the truth while individual popes could err in matters of faith.[5] The emergence of a clear notion of jurisdiction allowed the medieval canonists to distinguish clearly between the office of the pope and the individual human being who happened to hold the papal office at any given time.[6] The man who was pope worked out his salvation in fear and trembling like every other member of the faithful. The body of all the faithful was the heir of the Lord's promise that their "faith will never fail" (Luke 22:32), whatever the failings of its hierarchical leaders.

Given the vast powers that inhered in the papal office and the fallibility and peccability of individual office holders, canonists could not avoid ruminating on the possibility that a pope might fall into heresy or notorious sin or might otherwise abuse his trust. Short of direct divine intervention, what was to prevent a wayward or capricious pope from destroying the church? Gratian had included in the *Decretum* a text in which Gregory the Great held that the canons of the first general councils, because they had been instituted by universal consent (*universali consensu*), were unalterable.[7] In time, glosses on this text articulated the notion that there were matters of faith and "the general state of the church" that bound even the pope. Although the glossators never gave an exhaustive or even entirely consistent exposition of these matters touching "the general state of the church," the phrase does testify to the firm conviction of canonists that there existed "a framework of fundamental law which so defined the very nature and structure of the church that any licit ecclesiastical authority, even papal authority, had to be exercised within that framework."[8] The immutability of matters touching "the general state of the church" did not clash with the doctrine of the plenitude of papal power since the popes were an integral element of the general councils that had articulated this general state of the church by universal consent.[9] Thus, the inviolability of matters touching the general state of the church was essentially a self-limitation of papal authority or, perhaps more accurately, a humble acknowledgement of the limits of that authority.

Still the possibility remained that a pope might abuse his power and violate these fundamental canons of faith and discipline, a possibility that was not merely speculative as Gratian's inclusion of historical examples of such papal aberrations in his *Decretum* reminded canonists. Since it was an established principle of law that the pope had no superior on earth and, therefore, could be judged by no human, the decretists struggled to find a way for the church to protect itself from the excesses of a runaway papacy. Various theories were suggested. Some argued that a heretical pope excommunicated himself from the body of the faithful and, therefore, lost office by the law itself.[10] Others suggested that while the church could not initiate a judicial procedure against a pope, it could proceed deliberatively and declare the pope's default.[11] A more imaginative and satisfying solution to the problem required the evolution of canonical corporation law and its application to the church itself.

Corporation Law: The Juridic Articulation of Communio

THE LITTLE PICTURE.   In canon law, corporations, or *universitates* (moral or juridic persons in current law), are aggregates of persons or things that are treated at law as "fictitious persons" and as subjects of rights and obligations distinct from the persons or things that serve as their substratum. In both the religious and the secular spheres, new corporate groups of various kinds were springing up everywhere during the twelfth and thirteenth centuries. As *universitates* proliferated, intermural and intramural conflicts also multiplied. Since the pope was the judge of last resort in the church, many of these disputes were resolved by papal decretal. Eventually there emerged a body of law governing the structure and functioning of these corporate bodies. The canonists who glossed and commented on the collections of papal decretals came to be known as decretalists to distinguish them from their colleagues, the decretists, who continued to gloss Gratian's tome.

Canon law early on supplied for the deficiency of Roman law of agency by providing that a corporate group could be both represented and obligated by the action of its duly appointed representative.[12] Such representatives, essential for the smooth day-to-day functioning of *universitates,* were understood to represent the corporate body in its legal business and, within certain limits, to be empowered to bind the group even without the its prior consent. Within these defined limits, the representative possessed "full authority" (*plena potestas*). Canonists found in Justinian's *Digest* the principle of *private* law that "what touches all is to be approved by all" (*quod omnes tangit ab omnibus approbetur*).[13] Once this notion became established as a principle of corporate life, it took only a small step for the idea to gain currency that a majority of the corporate body (the *maior et sanior pars*) could bind the whole.[14] The marriage of the principle of representation *plena potestas* and the principle of binding majority consent soon gave birth to the idea that what "'touched' a whole community could be" — and indeed should be — "approved by a representative assembly acting on behalf of all."[15]

Many of the disputes that shaped this emerging body of law were conflicts between bishops and the canons of their cathedral chapters. It was the complex interrelationship of bishop and chapter that provided the fundamental model for the canonical *universitas*. The chapter of canons elected the bishop. However, the cathedral chapter did not disperse and disappear once the new bishop had taken possession of the see. Although the prerogatives of the episcopal office were defined by and derived from the divine law structure of the church, that authority came to the bishop not directly but through human mediation in the form of election by the majority of canons, a body that was understood to represent, however inadequate that representation may seem to us, the whole local church. Given the feudal provenance of the relationship between bishop and chapter, it was inevitable that the chapter of canons would retain its own properties, rights, and powers even after the elected bishop had taken possession of his office. Thus, in the best of times the bishop and chapter governed the local church collegially and a "major act involving the welfare of the whole church required the assent of both parties, the bishop and the majority of the canons."[16] In the worst of times, however, the bishop and the chapter found themselves in mortal combat over their respective prerogatives, combat that took the form of litigation in which canonists had an opportunity to hone the legal concepts and distinctions that would prove to be the cutting edge of constitutional thought.

The shared responsibility of bishop and chapter for the governance of the local church gave rise to two distinct but related forms of representation. On the one hand, following the patristic theology of the episcopacy that was generously represented in Gratian's *Decretum*, the bishop represented the church as its head or principal member.[17] On the other hand, following the sometimes messy realities of feudal life, the duly appointed representative of the chapter also represented the church with authority delegated to him as the agent of the chapter. "For the full representation of a cathedral church in a synod both types of representation were necessary — both the bishop and the proctor of the chapter were summoned."[18] The sometimes tension-filled collegial relationship of bishop and chapter would not let the thorny question of where authority in the local church ultimately inhered disappear. Some maintained that, on taking possession of the see, the bishop's jurisdiction extinguished whatever authority the chapter may have exercised during the vacancy.[19] The *maior et sanior pars* of canonists, however, held that the chapter did not wholly alienate its authority by electing a bishop but remained, to use a term that would not have occurred to the decretists, "coresponsible" for the state of the church.[20] Feudal realities and the fact that jurisdiction devolved to the chapter when the see was vacant or impeded or the bishop gravely derelict insured that the latter view would prevail. There was unanimity, however, that ultimately authority inhered in the church as an ordered community of the faithful and was exercised on the church's behalf by its duly chosen representatives.

THE BIG PICTURE. Although the tedious details of corporate law were worked out largely at the microscopic level of the particular church, abbey, or commune, canonists could not long ignore the consequences of this constitutional law for the macroscopic level, the church universal. Scriptural and patristic sources encouraged thinking of the communion of local churches scattered throughout the world but united in faith and discipline as the one body of Christ, an ordered community of communities of the faithful. For canonists, the principles of law forged for defining the structure of small-scale *universitates* were the most readily available vehicle for articulating the fundamental constitution of this corporate body ecclesiastic. The implications of this projection of these principles on to the larger screen of the church universal were enormous.

If the church could be analogized to a *universitas*, then authority resided ultimately in the church as the body of the faithful even as it was exercised by those office holders chosen according to the norms of divine and ecclesiastical law. If what touched all members of a corporate body had to be approved by all or at least by their legitimate representatives, then the membership of general councils in which the highest and most solemn form of the church's power of governance and teaching were exercised — and, *a fortiori*, in diocesan and provincial synods — should be representative of the church as a whole. Thus, when Innocent III convoked the Fourth Lateran Council in 1213, he summoned not only bishops and abbots but also representatives of chapters of cathedral and collegiate churches and religious orders as well as secular authorities.[21] This was to remain the norm for general councils until the First Vatican Council in 1870. The resignation of Celestine V in 1294 gave canonists ample reason to ponder the nature and source of papal power in the church. Celestine's resignation showed incontrovertibly that the authority of the church that inhered normally in the Petrine office was separable and distinguishable from the concrete individual who occupied that office at any given moment.[22]

With the emergence of the college of cardinals in something resembling its modern form, some canonists conceived the relationship between pope and cardinals by analogy to the collegial relationship between bishop and cathedral chapter. Hostiensis, one of the greatest commentators on the decretals and himself a cardinal, maintained that the Roman church had received from Christ the plenitude of power, which was exercised collegially by the pope and cardinals. Despite the enormous powers attributed to the pope, Hostiensis insisted the pope "ought not to settle difficult matters without the counsel of his brothers."[23] During the vacancy of the see of Rome, papal authority devolved to the college of cardinals or, should the college itself cease to exist during the vacancy, to the Roman church, which could reconstitute ecclesial government itself or through a general council.[24] Other canonists, less enthralled with the college of cardinals, conceded that college's right as representatives of the Roman church to elect the bishop of Rome but were more interested in plumbing the relationship between the Roman pontiff and the body of bishops both when gathered in general council and when scattered in their respective dioceses.

The pope was the superior and judge of every other person in the church and immune from judgment by any person, whether physical or juridic. As

Cardinal Zabarella noted at the time of the Great Western Schism: "The pope has plenitude of power not as an individual but as head of a corporation so that the power is in the corporate whole as its foundation and in the pope as the principal minister through whom it is exercised."[25] Logically, therefore, whatever power the pope might have over individuals, he could not judge the whole church, whose power he exercised as its principal minister.[26]

The development of constitutional thought by medieval canonists was not linear and uniform. Some ideas remained the scribbled musings of obscure lawyers; others were hotly disputed by rival camps; still others became the common intellectual heritage of the age. The democratic potential buried in these dusty volumes of quaint and forgotten lore surfaced during the Great Western Schism when the existence of two and eventually three rival claimants to the papacy threatened to destroy the church. This schism was the realization of the nightmare that had haunted canonists at least since the time of Gratian. The church's principal minister, whose function and duty was to preserve the unity of the church in faith and discipline and to maintain inviolate the state of the church, had become an agent of division and disintegration. In this desperate situation, canonists and theologians from extreme papalists to incipient Gallicans delved into the church's canonical heritage for a way to save the church. The solution they arrived at was the convocation of a general council representative of the whole corporate body of the church to restore unity and peace to the mystical body of Christ.

This council, assembled at Constance in 1415, evidenced no doubts about its identity and authority. In its initial decree, the council announced:

> This holy synod of Constance...declared that, legitimately assembled in the Holy Spirit, constituting a general council and representing the catholic church militant, it has power immediately from Christ; and that everyone of whatever state or dignity, even papal, is bound to obey it in those matters which pertain to the faith, the eradication of the said schism and the general reform of the said church of God in head and members.[27]

The council proceeded to depose the three rival popes, to arrange for the election of a new pope, Martin V, and to issue decrees aimed at the preservation of faith and the reform of the church. Noting that "the frequent holding of general councils is a pre-eminent means of cultivating the Lord's patrimony," Constance decreed "by perpetual edict" that general councils be held "every ten years for ever." Should a new schism break out, within one year "all prelates and others who are bound to attend a council shall assemble at the council without the need for any summons."[28] At Constance, the reflections on the constitution of the church by the generations of canonists since Gratian had provided the intellectual arsenal needed to protect the "state of the church" against a runaway papacy.

Although derived from sound and long established canonical principles, the conciliarism represented at Constance did not have a long life in the church once the crisis of the Western Schism was resolved. Those principles and the sort of constitutional thought they engendered did, however, flourish in secular political theory. Already in the Middle Ages, those who reflected on the political organization of cities and states were borrowing concepts forged in the canonical crucible. As Tierney explains: "The typical process that occurred was the assimilation of a text of Roman private law into church law, its adaptation and transmutation there to a principle of constitutional law, and then its reabsorption into the sphere of secular government in this new form."[29] The adaptation and development of principles of political theory of canonical provenance continued long after Constance. The exertions of the medieval canonists became part of a world of ideas that proved a critical element in the intellectual underpinnings for the emergence of constitutional democracy in the West. That the constitutional thought of the decretists and decretalists had no such impact in the Catholic Church goes without saying.

But why not? Why did principles and concepts originally devised to give juridic articulation to the constitution of the church support the development of democratic thought in the secular sphere but not in the church in which they originated? The easy — and endlessly repeated — answer to this question is that the church is not a democracy, that there is an inherent incompatibility between democracy and the divine law constitution of the church. This reflexive answer is too easy and the mindless incantation of this shibboleth begs the question. At its best, the constitutional thought of the medieval canonists tried to find and maintain a fragile balance between the divine law rights of the church's hierarchical leadership and the divine law rights of the ecclesial community itself.

During the nearly five hundred years after conciliarism self-destructed in the babble of Basle, the primary perceived threats to the church's integrity were those that challenged the legitimacy of its hierarchical leadership. The Reformation of the sixteenth century constituted, among other things, a theological assault on the legitimacy of the papacy and the received hierarchical order. Subsequently, Gallicanism, Febronianism, and Josephism and various other "isms" challenged the right of the church's hierarchy in the name of the secular state. In this atmosphere, the church saw itself as a besieged fortress and adopted a corresponding mentality. As a result, canonists and theologians inevitably focused their efforts on offering an intellectual and legal defense of the church's increasingly embattled hierarchical structure.

As ecclesiology became hierarchology, constitutional thought about the divine right of the ecclesial community atrophied. The dismantling of the fortress mentality that began with the Second Vatican Council has provided an opportunity to reflect again theologically and canonically on the long forgotten "divine right" of the people of God and to begin to recover the fragile balance between hierarchy and community that the medieval canonists had struggled to maintain.

Vatican II: The Unfinished Agenda

In its dogmatic constitution on the church, *Lumen Gentium*, the Second Vatican Council reversed the dominant tendency of half a millennium of canonico-theological reflection and teaching on the church by insisting on treating the church first as a mystery and then as the people of God embracing all of the baptized regardless of their state or condition before turning its attention to the church's hierarchical structure.[30] Beyond all distinctions between ordained and nonordained, prelate and parishioner, pope and pauper,

> those who are reborn in Christ, who are reborn not from a perishable but an imperishable seed through the Word of the living God, not from flesh but from water and the Holy Spirit, are finally established as "a chosen race, a royal priesthood, a holy nation, a purchased people." (*Lumen Gentium*, no. 9)

Each member of this people of God participates in his or her own way in the one priesthood of Christ and shares "a true equality with regard to the dignity and to the activity common to all the faithful for the building up of the body of Christ" (*Lumen Gentium*, no. 32). No longer can the nonordained be considered (or treated) as the mere passive subjects of clerical ministrations. The whole people of God succeeds to Christ's threefold office of priest, prophet, and king, and each member of this people participates in these three functions in his or her own way.

It has now been over a quarter of a century since the Second Vatican Council completed its work and adjourned. The texts of the council have been promulgated, studied, analyzed, and, in some respects, implemented. In accord with John XXIII's original intention, a revised Code of Canon Law has been promulgated to give juridic shape to the renewed ecclesiology articulated by the council. Despite some notable omissions, interpolations, and even not a few butcherings, the revised code is generally faithful to the letter of the council's documents. Nevertheless, the heavy baggage of the *societas perfecta* model of the church, a model that is endemic to the continental European form of codified law, does not allow the conciliar ecclesiology of the *communio* of the hierarchically ordered people of God to realize its full potential.[31] In many ways, the implementation of the code's translation of the conciliar image of the church into juridic form has been even more hesitant and half-hearted than the implementation of the conciliar documents themselves. The new habit of mind that Paul VI claimed was required to appreciate and incarnate the conciliar vision of the church[32] has often been less in evidence than a "business as usual" mentality reminiscent of triumphalism, clericalism, and juridicism.

Whatever the defects of the revised code and the mentality that has inspired its drafting and implementation, John Paul II has made clear that the council itself is the hermeneutical key for interpreting and implementing the code. In promulgating the code, the pope insisted: "If, however, it is impossible to translate perfectly into *canonical* language the conciliar image of the church, nevertheless the Code must always be referred to this image as the primary pattern whose outline the code ought to express insofar as it can by its very nature."[33] When the provisions of the revised code are resituated in the context of the conciliar texts that gave them birth and interpreted in the light of the constitutional principles and concepts developed by medieval canonists, new avenues toward a more "democratic" approach to church governance emerge.

The Macroscopic Level

The great achievement of Vatican II was to place once again in the forefront of ecclesial consciousness that the church is the *communio* of the people of God. What had been the point of departure for the glosses, commentaries, and sometimes diatribes of the medieval canonists has been set forth by the council as the touchstone for the reform and renewal of the mystical but historically visible Body of Christ. Although the hierarchical element of the church's constitutional structure was present at the creation, all ranks of the hierarchy stand not outside but within the ordered people of God. This is a hierarchy in service to the edification and sanctification of the communion of the faithful. Of course, this is a truth that never completely disappeared from ecclesial consciousness even when it was given little more than lip service. Thus, the dogma of papal infallibility defined by Vatican I and reaffirmed by Vatican II accords to the Roman pontiff (and to the college of bishops unified with him) the exercise of only that "infallibility with which the divine Redeemer willed His Church to be endowed" (*Lumen Gentium,* no. 25).

It is, after all, the faith of the church that pope and bishops are charged to protect and nurture. The hierarchy is also bound to preserve inviolate the fundamental constitutional structures of the church (what the medieval canonists called the *status ecclesiae*). Since popes and bishops are part of a sinful, pilgrim people, their actions or inactions may jeopardize the integrity of the faith or of the church's fundamental constitution and, thus, severely disrupt ecclesial communion. Even the pope is not immune from the consequences of damage he inflicts on ecclesial communion.

Despite the explicit ban in current law on individuals' appealing to a council or the college of bishops against an act of the Roman pontiff (can. 1372), the pope cannot judge the whole church without putting himself outside its communion. As it did through its representatives at Constance in 1415, the church has the right to defend its existence and integrity against a papacy run amok.

Not much progress has been made since the council in resolving two critical theological dilemmas that conciliar ecclesiology bequeathed to the church. Failure to reach a theological consensus has in turn impeded giving practical form to the conciliar theology of *communio*.

ROMAN PONTIFF AND COLLEGE OF BISHOPS. The first dilemma is this: how does one reconcile the supreme and full power of the Roman pontiff over the universal church with the supreme and full power of the college of bishops? Resolution of this problem has been impeded by the inability of theologians (and, therefore, canonists) to agree whether there are one or two subjects of supreme power in the church. If the bishop of Rome *with* the college of bishops is the sole subject of supreme power, then it would be possible to conceive the communion of pope and college of bishops, as some medieval canonists already had, by analogy to a *universitas*, with the pope as head and the bishops as members. Participation is of the essence of communion at all levels and in all degrees of its expression.[34] The communion of pope and college of bishops achieves its fullest, albeit only occasional and temporary, expression in their mutual participation in an ecumenical council. Nevertheless, collegiality should permeate — and should be in evidence in — every aspect of the relationship of pope and college whether gathered in council or scattered throughout the world. If this were taken seriously both in theory and in practice, the limits imposed on papal authority by collegiality would not materially reduce the leadership role of the pope, but they would radically alter the mode in which it is exercised.[35]

Representing their own particular churches the members of the college would have a genuinely participatory role in all the major deliberations and decision making in the universal church. The hallowed principle that "what touches all as individuals must be approved by all" (can. 119, 3°) remains a norm governing the decision-making processes of collegial bodies, one of which is clearly and preeminently the college of bishops. Although "it is for the Roman Pontiff, in keeping with the needs of the Church, to select and promote the ways by which the college of bishops is to exercise its collegial function regarding the universal Church" (can. 337, §3), it is hard to imagine anything that touches all in the church as individuals more directly and intimately than weighty matters of faith and universal discipline. It is of the nature of collegial bodies that their "members determine its action through participation in making its decisions, whether by equal right or not" (can. 115, §2).

While neither the individual members of the college of bishops nor the body of bishops as a whole has equal right with the head of the college in its deliberations, both the demands of collegiality and the common law itself seem to accord bishops a right to some meaningful participation with the bishop of Rome in decisions affecting the whole church. If so, then the church's law can and must provide vehicles for the college of bishops to exercise their "solicitude for all the churches" (*Lumen Gentium,* no. 23), not to mention to represent their own particular church, in matters touching all the churches in communion with the church of Rome. Perhaps Hostiensis's ideal that the pope "ought not to settle difficult matters without the counsel of his brothers," not just in the college of cardinals, as Hostiensis envisaged, but in the college of bishops, could be realized.

POPE AND DIOCESAN BISHOP. A second dilemma inherited by the post-conciliar church was how to reconcile the primacy of ordinary power enjoyed by the pope over all particular churches with the proper, ordinary, and immediate power of diocesan bishops in the dioceses entrusted to their care. The idea of two individuals with proper, ordinary, and immediate power over the same particular church seems hopelessly contradictory even if both the council and the code offer the reassurance that the pope's concurrent jurisdiction over a particular church is a way by which the diocesan bishop's authority "is both strengthened and safeguarded" (*Lumen Gentium,* no. 27). Resolving this apparent contradiction has been hampered by the insistence of official authorities on clinging to

> the governmental model of the Roman Empire with its passion for uniformity and impatience with diversity, its monarchical centralization of authority, its subordination of imperially appointed provincial governors to centralized bureaucracy, and its subordination of concern for the individual person to the perpetuation of the divinized institutions of the Empire.[36]

It is hard to avoid noticing the striking similarities between this capsule summary of the dominant tendencies of the ancient Roman empire and penchants of the Apostolic See in our day. Tensions between the papacy and the episcopacy are not, of course, modern inventions. From Paul's confrontation with Peter in Antioch "because he was clearly wrong" (Gal. 2:11), to Cyprian's wrangling with Pope Stephen, to the feuding between secular masters and mendicants at the University of Paris in the thirteenth century, to the internecine battle of Gallicans and Ultramontanes in nineteenth century France, to the postconciliar upheaval of our own day, tension between papacy and the episcopacy has been a constant theme in church history. What has been lacking has been a viable model for containing the tension and the will to implement that model.

Vatican II made a noteworthy departure from the received Roman empire model when it asserted that the Petrine ministry in the church not only sees to the preservation of unity in the church's faith and discipline but also "protects legitimate differences, while at the same time it sees that such differences do not hinder unity but rather contribute toward it" (*Lu-*

men Gentium, no. 13). (This statement, it might be noted, is conspicuously absent from the revised code.) To exercise his ministry of protecting legitimate diversity within the communion of churches, the pope, it would seem, would have to refrain voluntarily from exercising his discretionary authority to micro-manage the affairs of the particular churches in the *communio ecclesiarum,* except when urgent concern about the unity of faith and discipline dictated such an intervention.

The council and the revised code took an essential first step in this direction by asserting unequivocally that the diocesan bishop "possesses all the proper, ordinary and immediate power which is required for the exercise of his pastoral office" (*Lumen Gentium,* no. 27; see also can. 381, §1). The upshot of this assertion has been a significant shift away from a system in which bishops governed their particular churches largely in virtue of faculties conceded from above to a system in which the diocesan bishop is presumed to have all the authority needed to exercise his pastoral office *unless* a particular cause had been reserved to a higher authority.[37] While this shift has resulted in a considerable enhancement of prerogatives of diocesan bishops, the list of reserved causes remains long, hard to justify on the basis of the requirements of communion or the irreducible divine law role of the successor of Peter, and obstructive to the flowering of legitimate diversity in the particular churches.

As Karl Rahner noted, there is no dogmatic principle that prevents the pope from waiving prerogatives that have accrued to the Apostolic See in the course of history or voluntarily limiting his own authority to areas essential to the exercise of the Petrine ministry when the good of the communion of churches so counsels.[38] Indeed, for a variety of reasons, popes have legitimately done so in the past and continue to do so today. For years, no cavil was raised when popes have restricted their rights to name bishops freely or to control other aspects of ecclesiastical life through concordats with secular authorities when the common good of the church seemed to dictate such self-limitation.[39] Nor has anyone recently argued that the relative autonomy that has allowed the Eastern Catholic churches to develop their own discipline, liturgical practice, and theological and spiritual heritage within the parameters of communion results from the free concession of the Roman pontiff that he can revoke.[40] If such diversity in the framework of unity is not simply a fossilized relic that must be tolerated but a value to be fostered in the present, it can be argued that the pope is obligated, at least morally, to restrict his own authority to what is necessary for the preservation of unity in the communion of churches and thereby to allow all the particular churches the relative autonomy needed for the flowering of that legitimate diversity that makes the church catholic, not only in geographical expanse but in inclusivity.

The voluntary self-limitation of primatial power by the bishop of Rome need not lead inevitably to cacophony and chaos. Once it has been accepted that the model of the Roman empire is not part of the divine law structure of the church, another model, more attractive and more appropriate to a communion of churches, is available. Robert Kennedy has argued that the federalism embodied in the Constitution of the United States, if applied analogously to the structuring of the church, has the potential both to maintain unity in essentials and to foster legitimate diversity.[41] Such a federalism would retain the immediate authority of the Roman pontiff over every member of the faithful in matters essential to the unity of faith and discipline while legitimating "in the conceptual order increased initiative, creativity, and experimentation in structural and procedural matters at the diocesan level."[42] The voluntary self-restraint of the bishop of Rome in a federal model of the communion of churches might give some intellectual and practical credibility to the claim that papal authority does not destroy but affirms, strengthens, and vindicates episcopal authority.

The Microscopic Level

In the present climate of the church, it is unlikely that any of these changes of attitude and structure are likely to become the prevailing practice of the church universal in the near future. Nevertheless, there is some hope that courageous and imaginative leadership at the local level could carry through the renewed conciliar vision of the church in the particular churches. During the Middle Ages, it was in large measure from theological and canonical reflection on and attempts to resolve concrete conflicts between bishops and chapters that there evolved principles and concepts governing collegial structures that could be applied to the analogous tensions in the universal church. Perhaps it is not too much to hope that systematic reflection on the constitutional structure of the particular church can show the way to a satisfactory resolution of the as yet unresolved and unresolvable theoretical and practical tensions between the papacy and the episcopacy and between the one bishop of Rome and many diocesan bishops. Indeed, if the particular church is fashioned after the model of the universal church, and if the universal church comes into being in and from such individual churches, it would be expected that developments at the microscopic level would have their reverberations at the macroscopic level of the church. To give an ecclesiological spin to Justice Brandeis's famous observation, perhaps the particular churches can be laboratories of democracy in the church.

SELECTION OF BISHOPS. In the ecclesiology of the council, the diocesan bishop functions as "the visible principle and foundation of unity in his particular church" and "represents his own church" (*Lumen Gentium,* no. 23). There is an inextricable link between these two roles, a link expressed in Cyprian's celebrated *dictum* that the bishop is in the church and the church in the bishop. The bishop represents his church because he is the principle and foundation of its unity, but the bishop can be a source of unity in that church only because he genuinely and legitimately represents it. Even though Vatican II cites only patristic sources for its teaching, the link between the legitimacy of the bishop's authority in the local church and his representative function is redolent of medieval canon law of corporate bodies.

In the patristic and medieval (and, indeed, early modern) church, the link between these two episcopal roles in the particular church was unproblematic since the bishop was chosen by the particular church (or at least by its recognized representatives). Until rather recent times, Leo I's principle, by then traditional, that the bishop who is to preside over all should be elected by all remained the norm rather than the exception.[43] For the medieval canonists, election according to the norm of then prevailing law was the assurance of the legitimacy of the exercise of episcopal authority and the mode through which the authority of the episcopal office was mediated to the bishop. Duly elected by the particular church, the bishop could fully and authentically represent that church.

Gradually, the right of the particular church to choose its bishop was eroded both by secular government and the centralized papacy until canon 329, §2, of the 1917 code asserted baldly that bishops are freely nominated by the Roman pontiff, a norm repeated in canon 377, §1, of the revised code. Although traditional methods of selecting bishops have been retained in the Eastern churches, the appointment of diocesan bishops in the Latin church is now the exclusive prerogative of the pope. According to current norms, the pope exercises his power of appointment primarily in consultation with papal diplomatic representatives except in the rare cases where concordatory law or approved customs still prevail.[44] Recently, rancor has erupted when papal efforts have been made (as in Cologne and Chur) to encroach on even these remnants of local participation in the selection of bishops. By this development a long canonical tradition has been "entirely turned upside down."[45]

Unfettered papal discretion in the selection of bishops was less incongruous in an age in which the prevailing ecclesiology treated diocesan bishops in practice if not in theory as little more than delegates of the pope for a particular territory. However, the rehabilitation of the theology of the particular church as a portion of the people of God and of the diocesan bishop as representative of that church renders the current law for the selection of bishops increasingly untenable from an ecclesiological and, therefore, canonical perspective. It is rather difficult to see how a bishop imposed from above, without any meaningful consultation with the local church as a community of faith (and not merely facultative consultation with just random individuals under seal of the papal secret as in the current norms),[46] can be considered a legitimate representative of that church. Although the present code, like its predecessor, precludes such meaningful consultation with the particular church about the selection of its bishop, no great theological or canonical principles bar a change in the current norms toward a more "democratic" process for the selection of bishops.[47] In fact, if anything, conciliar theology and canonical tradition dictate such a change not for the sake of democracy *per se* but for the sake of an authentic realization of *communio*.

THE DIOCESAN SYNOD. Just as an ecumenical council is the most solemn and complete expression of the communion of the Roman pontiff and the college of bishops, so the diocesan synod is the most solemn manifestation of the communion of the diocesan bishop and the faithful of the particular church. From the fourth century, the diocesan synod was the preeminent vehicle for legislating and making pastoral policy for the local church. So important was the diocesan synod seen for the ongoing reform and renewal of the local church that the Fourth Lateran Council (1215) decreed that such synods should be convoked annually in every diocese,[48] a norm reiterated by the Council of Trent in the sixteenth century.[49] The 1917 code prescribed that a diocesan synod should be held every ten years;[50] the revised code specifies only that a synod is to be celebrated "when circumstances warrant it in the judgment of the diocesan bishop, after he has consulted the presbyteral council" (can. 461, §1). The desuetude into which the diocesan synod has fallen has been caused in part by the tedious and time-consuming planning and preparation required for the synod to be conducted efficiently and effectively. Unfortunately, the vacuum left by the decline in frequency of the celebration of synods has been filled by legislation and policy making by decree with or, more commonly, without consultation with the local church.

Despite the enormous practical and logistical problems associated with the celebration of a synod, synodal governance does involve the whole local church directly through discussions in the preparatory phase and indirectly through representatives present at the synod itself in setting the direction and agenda of the diocese. The 1983 code went a long way toward eliminating the clericalism that had characterized synods under the previous law. Current law requires that the membership of the synod be truly reflective and representative of the composition of the local church and gives the bishop discretion to appoint additional members if the mandatory members do not accurately represent the church (can. 463). The agenda of the synod is wide-ranging. It is the primary vehicle for the whole church to assist the bishop in fulfilling his ministry

> by adapting the laws and norms of the universal church to local conditions, by pointing out the policy and program of apostolic work in the diocese, by resolving problems encountered in the apostolate and administration, by giving impetus to projects and undertakings, and by correcting errors in doctrine and morals if any have crept in.[51]

During the sessions of the synod, "all the proposed questions are to be subject to the free discussion of the members" (can. 465). The synod may even be an appropriate occasion for the election of members of various consultative bodies in the diocese and of the commissions and offices of the diocesan curia.[52] The concrete realization of the communion of the local church in the synod and the "ownership" the participants take of the results of the synod because of their involvement in its deliberations may well be worth the time, energy, and expense expended in preparing and celebrating a synod.

Although the diocesan synod is to be composed of members who represent and are representative of the particular church, it is not a democratic legislative body. The members of the synod have only a consultative vote and "the diocesan bishop is the sole legislator at a diocesan synod" (can. 466). More importance should not be attributed to the apparent disparity of power between the bishop and the synodal membership than it actually deserves. As Robert Kennedy has pointed out, the reservation of the sole deliberative vote to the bishop in synod (and in the discussions of other consultative bodies) is akin to the veto power exercised by the president and governors of states over the enactments of legislatures.[53] Moreover, choice making is only one, and not necessarily the most important, component of the decision-making process. In addition to choice making, the decision-making process also involves at least collection of factual data, generation of creative ideas, implementation of choices and evaluation, "all of which entail the exercise of influence and power."[54]

While current law reserves choice making in synods to the diocesan bishop, the members of synods have the right to participate fully in the other moments of the decision-making process, a participation that may well be more determinative of the outcome than the deliberative vote of the bishop. Even the consultative vote of the members of the synod is not without its weight. Although the diocesan bishop is not required to accept the recommendation of a synod even if it is unanimous, the code cautions that the bishop "should not act contrary to it, especially when there is a consensus, unless there is a reason which, in [his] judgment, is overriding" (can. 127, §2, 2°). A synod whose recommendation has been rejected by the bishop would surely have a legitimate expectation of a reasonable explanation of the overriding reason that motivated his decision.

Despite the council's fervent desire that "the venerable institution of synods and councils flourish with new vigor" (*Christus Dominus,* no. 37), synodal activity in the postconciliar church has been less than flourishing. Nevertheless, both the amount of material devoted to the diocesan synod in the revised code and the tenor of the code's language about synods make clear that the expectation of the law is that synods will be restored to their preeminent place in the policy-making processes of the particular church and be a visible manifestation and realization of the *communio* of the local church. Although the enormous organizational burdens of planning and executing a synod cannot be gainsaid, one suspects that a deeper reason for the desuetude of the diocesan synod is an old habit of mind that pays lip service to *communio* without an appreciation of its meaning and implications, that values speed and efficiency over participation, and that cultivates rugged individualism in both leaders and the led.

THE PRESBYTERAL COUNCIL. Although the collegiality of the bishop of Rome with the college of bishops and with individual bishops has received the lion's share of attention in the years since the council, it should not be forgotten that the council conceived the relationship between the diocesan bishop and the presbyterate on the analogy of the relationship between the pope and college of bishops. Just as the successor of Peter and the successors of the apostles constitute one college, so the diocesan bishop and his presbyters form one *presbyterium* (*Lumen Gentium,* no. 28).[55] Just as collegiality suffuses the relationship of pope and bishops both when they are gathered in council and when they are scattered throughout the world, so an analogous synodality permeates the relationship of bishop and presbyters both in synod and outside it. If collegiality does not materially limit the pope's *plena potestas*, but does limit the mode in which it is exercised, so synodality does not materially detract from the authority of the diocesan bishop in the particular church but it does qualify the modality of its exercise. Quietly omitting the conciliar qualification "necessary" of the sort of cooperation presbyters offer to the bishop, the revised code asserts the obligation of diocesan bishops to "attend to presbyters with special concern and listen to them as his assistants and advisers" (can. 384).

To structure this ongoing dialogue between the diocesan bishop and his presbyters, the code, following the directive of the council, mandates the existence in each diocese of a presbyteral council to represent the presbyterate and to serve as a sort of senate to the bishop (can. 495, §1). The role of this council is to "aid the bishop in the governance of the diocese according to the norm of law, in order that the pastoral welfare of the portion of the people of God entrusted to him may be promoted as effectively as possible" (can. 495, §1). Although the presbyteral council is sometimes seen as the successor of the old cathedral chapter, it is something more. The presbyteral council is part of an attempt to retrieve the ancient notion of the presbyterium as a constituent element of a particular church, a notion of which the cathedral chapter was but a fossilized relic.[56]

The presbyteral council should be representative of the presbyterate in all its diversity. Thus, "the council will have a representative character if, in as far as possible, the various ministries, regions and pastoral areas of the diocese are represented, as well as the various age-groups of the priests."[57] Toward that end, the law specifies that about half the members are to be freely elected by the presbyterate (can. 497, 1°). While some members may serve *ex officio* and the bishop is free to appoint other members, it would be a serious abuse for the bishop to use his appointive power to dilute the representative character of the body.

Unlike the diocesan synod, the presbyteral council has a continuous existence even though it ceases to exist when the see is vacant and can be disbanded for up to a year by the diocesan bishop if it is negligent or abuses its function (can. 501, §§2–3). As the preeminent consultative body in the diocese, it "deals with more important questions . . . whether they concern the holiness of life, sacred science, and other needs of the priests, or the sanctification and religious instruction of the faithful, or the government of the diocese in general."[58] The presbyteral council is an effort in law to give structural expression to the right of presbyters, as the bishop's "necessary cooperators," to be heard by the bishop in what pertains to the good of the church. As Corecco notes:

> The hearing the bishop is to give to the presbyters does not reflect sim-
> ply a moral, legal, or vaguely communional obligation, but flows from the
> ontological structure of communio itself, which implies an immanence of
> the component parts. . . . It follows, that the obligation to have a presbyteral
> council is not justified by corporative principles, but has its raison d'etre in
> the fact that the ministry of the diocesan bishop is not purely personal but
> essentially synodal.[59]

Although the code specifies only a relatively few instances when the diocesan bishop must consult the presbyteral council, the bishop's habitual failure to consult with the presbyteral council about decisions, plans, and policies of major moment — or to take its counsel seriously — would constitute a grave violation of *communio*. The council, after all, represents the presbyterate, which is coresponsible with the bishop for the good of the particular church.

Despite the consultative character of the presbyteral council, implementation of the current law governing this council has the potential to give the governance of the particular church a more participatory, if not democratic, style. Unfortunately, experience with presbyteral councils since Vatican II has been mixed at best.[60] The relationship of members of the councils to the diocesan bishop have ranged the full spectrum from adversarial to supine. Some councils have become so wrapped up in issues regarding the life and welfare of the clergy that they have completely neglected the larger issues affecting the pastoral welfare of the portion of the people of God entrusted to the care of the bishop and his presbyters. Bishops have, sometimes with good reason, withheld important issues in diocesan governance from the agenda of the presbyteral council.

At times, personality conflicts and internecine feuds have made presbyteral councils more manifestations of the divisions within the presbyterate than signs of its unity. No doubt, the performance of presbyteral councils can be improved by learning from the mistakes of the past, tinkering with structures and processes, and even revising the law to clarify the role of these councils and enhance their roles. Perhaps, however, technical improvements will not allow the potential of presbyteral councils to be realized until both presbyters and bishops actually understand themselves and act as one *presbyterium* and not as ecclesiastical "Lone Rangers" in rivalry with one another. Until a new way of thinking prevails, efforts to ameliorate the functioning of presbyteral councils may be putting new wine in old wineskins.

PASTORAL COUNCILS. By defining particular churches (and, by implication, the smaller communities of faith within them) as "portions of the people of God," the council took a giant step beyond the residue of feudalism in the church. The 1917 code merely continued centuries of canonical tradition when it treated dioceses and parishes structurally as benefices. A benefice was "a juridic entity constituted or erected in perpetuity by competent ecclesiastical authority, consisting in a sacred office and the right of receiving revenue from the dowry attached to the office."[61] Thus a benefice was a noncollegial juridic or moral person, i.e, one whose substratum lay not in persons but in things. The legal affairs of the benefice were conducted by its legitimate rector or administrator, who was directly accountable to hierarchical superiors for his stewardship but not to the people of the diocese or parish. If in times past bishops and pastors administered their benefices like feudal lords, there was a basis in law for their style of leadership.

Following the lead of the council, the revised code recognizes dioceses and parishes no longer as aggregates of things but as communities of persons. Although still considered noncollegial juridic persons, dioceses and parishes are firmly rooted in the communion of the faithful. This change in the legal constitution of these communities of the faithful, and the corresponding change in mentality it necessitates, cannot be overlooked when making provision for the administration and governance of these communities. The communion of the faithful in parishes and dioceses derives not merely from affective or juridic bonds but from participation.

As Castillo Lara has noted,

> At the very heart of the concept of communion is found the concept of participation. Communion is not only a relational bond but also participation in common goods: in the mystery of the trinitarian communion, in the gifts of the Holy Spirit, in salvation, in charisms in the faith, in hope and charity, in the mission of the Church, etc.[62]

In virtue of their baptisms, all the members of the faithful participate in the threefold ministry of Christ and the church "in accord with the condition proper to each one" (can. 204, §1). Although the revised code does make progress toward empowering the nonordained to exercise the church's teaching and sanctifying mission, it does "not attend in a sufficiently rigorous way to the fact that the participation of the faithful in the governance is no less necessary theologically than their participation in the other functions."[63]

The code does recognize the right and at times the duty of all members of the faithful as individuals "to manifest to their sacred pastors their opinion on matters which pertain to the good of the church and... to make their opinion known to the other Christian faithful" (can. 212, §3). What is lacking, however, are structures and institutions to translate that right and duty from rhetoric into reality. The pastoral councils whose establishment is recommended in every diocese (albeit with notably less enthusiasm than in *Christus Dominus*, (can. 511), and permitted at the discretion of the bishop in every parish (can. 536, §1), might help to fill this void. The function of the diocesan pastoral council is "to investigate under the authority of the bishop all those things which pertain to pastoral works, to ponder them and to propose practical conclusions about them" (can. 511). Its members are clerics, religious and "especially lay persons" (can. 512, §1). Like the presbyteral council, the diocesan pastoral council is to represent the full diversity of the particular church. Thus,

> The Christian faithful who are appointed to the pastoral council are to be so selected that the entire portion of the people of God which constitutes the diocese is reflected, with due regard for the diverse regions, social conditions and professions of the diocese as well as the role they have in the apostolate, either as individuals or in conjunction with others. (can. 512, §2)

The code leaves the structuring of parish pastoral councils to particular law. However, the nature of the council and the dynamic of *communio* suggest that these councils too should reflect the diversity of the parish community and be truly representative bodies. Moreover, nothing prevents diocesan law from stipulating that they should be such.

The code states simply that the members of diocesan pastoral councils "are designated in a manner determined by the diocesan bishop" (can. 512, §1). The common law does not preclude election of some or all of the members by the faithful. Indeed, there is some faint suggestion that election would be appropriate. *The Directory on the Pastoral Ministry of Bishops* observes:

> To make the [diocesan pastoral] council's work more effective, the bishop can order, if the good of the faithful requires it, that in every parish... parish pastoral councils be set up and that these be aligned with the diocesan council. These councils, grouped together according to areas, could choose their representatives to serve on the diocesan council, so that the whole diocesan community may feel that it is offering its cooperation to its bishop through the diocesan council.[64]

If implemented this suggestion might help to dispel the parochialism that too often characterizes parish pastoral councils. This suggestion might also give members of the diocesan pastoral council a stronger sense of the constituency they represent.[65] Although the diocesan pastoral council's voice is only consultative, "nevertheless the bishop has great respect for its recommendations, for they offer his apostolic office the serious and settled cooperation of the ecclesiastical community."[66] A similar obligation to consider seriously the voice of the parish pastoral council is, of course, incumbent on pastors.

The performance of pastoral councils both at the diocesan level and at the parish level since Vatican II has been as spotty as that of presbyteral councils. However, what empirical evidence exists suggests that pastoral councils can function effectively if they are empowered to do so from above.[67] Expending the time and energy necessary to enhance the performance of pastoral councils at both the diocesan and at the parish level would be a genuine service to the realization of the communion of the local church and to enabling the Christian faithful, possessing the Spirit of Christ, to exercise their right and duty to make known their opinions on what is for the good of the church. However, old attitudes and styles of leadership and of being led, the residue of the feudal past, die hard.

THE RIGHTS OF THE FAITHFUL.   One of the far-reaching accomplishments of the Second Vatican Council was its enunciation of the rights and duties of all of the faithful not only in the world but also in the church. Reflecting the conciliar concern for rights, the principles that were to guide the revision of the code, drafted by the revision committee and unanimously approved by the 1967 synod of bishops, assert:

> The rights of each and every faithful must be acknowledged and safeguarded, both the rights which they have by natural law and the rights contained in divine positive law, as also the rights which are duly derived from these laws because of the social condition the faithful acquire or possess in the Church.[68]

Noting the widely acknowledged inadequacy of existing procedures to protect these rights, the principle called for an overhaul of the system and the establishment of administrative tribunals to redress violations of the rights of the faithful "so that every suspicion of arbitrariness in church administration may completely disappear."[69]

It cannot be denied that the revised code does indeed articulate many of the rights of the faithful. In promulgating the revised code, John Paul II noted that such a code was "extremely necessary . . . in order that the mutual relations of the faithful may be regulated according to justice based upon charity, with the right of individuals guaranteed and well defined."[70] Nevertheless, the rights recognized in the revised code are hedged with conditions and qualifications. Moreover, the administrative tribunals for which "the need is everywhere strongly felt"[71] were completely eliminated from the final version of the code. The only method of remedying violations of rights is the old system of administrative recourse, a system that has long been considered inadequate for the protection of rights.

Despite the glaring inadequacies of the code's articulation of the rights of the faithful and of its procedures for vindicating rights, what is significant for the future is the fact that the rights of the faithful are mentioned in the code at all. After having long preached and championed human rights against totalitarian regimes of every ideological hue, the church has recognized that it must practice what it preaches. As the 1967 synod of bishops observed:

> While the Church is bound to give witness to justice, she recognizes that everyone who ventures to speak to people about justice must first be just in their eyes. Hence we must undertake an examination of the modes of acting and of the possessions and life style found within the Church herself.[72]

That examination and consequent "purification . . . in internal practices and procedures"[73] is still going on.

As Andrei Sakharov was aware, it was the idea of human rights rooted in the inalienable dignity of the human person that exposed the moral bankruptcy of the Soviet empire and made its collapse inevitable. As Michael Scammell recently noted in a review of Sakharov's *Memoirs*, after the Soviet Union agreed to the Helsinki accords,

> the words "human rights" began to appear with increasing frequency on the front pages of *Pravda* and other Soviet newspapers, and no matter how they were twisted and turned inside out to mean their opposite, or unfavorably contrasted with the "economic rights" supposedly guaranteed by the Soviet regime, there they were for all Soviet citizens to read and digest. . . . The very readiness of the Soviet press to argue the merits of human rights was a battle lost, even if the larger war was to continue for another ten years.[74]

We now gaze in amazement over the smoldering ruins of the Soviet empire. Perhaps we can hope that the timid articulation of the rights of the faithful in the revised code guarantees the totalitarian temptation will at last be banished from the church.

Conclusion

Rummaging in the attic often turns up long forgotten family heirlooms that had been squirreled away rather than tossed out because someone was sure these treasures, although no longer needed or fashionable, would prove useful on another day. In a similar way, rummaging in the canonical attic unearths the long neglected heritage of medieval glossators and commentators, a heritage of ideas and principles that once proved useful for laying the intellectual foundations of constitutional democracy in secular society but fell out of fashion in the church once they had served to rescue the church from the disaster of the Great Western Schism. Consultation and consent, representation and participation, colleges and councils, episcopacy and primacy, the divine law right of the hierarchy and the divine law right of the ecclesial community — these were the ideas used by the decretists and decretalists to give juridic articulation to the communion of the ordered people of God.

The democratic potential of these ideas was not realized in the church as the Middle Ages gave way to the Modern Age, but the ideas themselves were stored away — and, with them, their democratic potential for today. Other ideas and principles of the medieval canonists were reupholstered and rearranged to fit with what eventually became the "perfect society" ecclesiological model that was fashionable in the age of absolutism, restoration, and later in what Karl Rahner has called the "Pian epoch."[75] However, the Second Vatican Council went rummaging in the church's theological and canonical attic for ideas and models more serviceable for a church facing a brave new world.

Although Vatican II and those who are faithful not only to its letter but also to its spirit are often labeled "liberals," the truth is that the council, despite notable innovations, was essentially "conservative" in the most noble sense of the term. It recovered and conserved a part of the rich tradition of the church that had been buried under the debris of centuries. Vatican II reminded us that the church's tradition did not begin (or end) at Vatican I or even at the Council of Trent. It recovered the strata of the church's tradition that stretched back to the Middle Ages, to the patristic era, and to the Scriptures themselves. Nevertheless, those to whom the task has fallen to reconfigure the church in the postconciliar era, as the church approaches the end of its second millennium, cannot simply wipe away the developments of centuries as if they had never occurred and begin anew. The architects of the church of the future cannot escape the burden of the church's past — all of it.

The torch of reform once carried by the decretists and decretalists has now been passed to a new generation, a generation that has been made aware of the breadth and depth, the problems and contradictions of the Catholic tradition by Vatican II, much as an earlier generation of canonists were made aware of the consistencies and inconsistencies, the scope and limitations of the church's tradition by Gratian's *Decretum*.

The Second Vatican Council has set this new generation of theologians, canonists and church people of all sorts squarely at the point where the medieval canonists (and every generation in the church before them) began — face to face with the communion of the people of God, hierarchically ordered but endowed with a fundamental equality. That the exertions of the medieval canonists did not yield a church with a democratic face does not necessarily mean that the quest for a more democratic church is doomed to get bogged down in the quagmire of canon law. Rather, as Brian Tierney observed, "A recurring paradox of Western thought is that ideas originally

presented to justify an established order of things often prove to have revolutionary implications, when they are taken over by critics of the existing
order."76

The recovery of the ancient theology of the church as the communion
of the people of God and the remembrance of the juridic structuring of that
people through a delicate balance between the divine right of the hierarchy
and the divine right of the community of faith have revolutionary implications today, as they did centuries ago. The medieval canonists began their
reflection with a vivid awareness of themselves and the rest of the faithful as intimately and inextricably bound up in a network of communities.
Ironically, whether the democratic potential for the church in the present
moment is realized or not may depend less on the erudition of scholars than
on the ability of the church community to rise above the rampant individualism of our age and to understand ourselves, both in rhetoric and reality,
as a community of faith. Perhaps it is only as faith-filled men and women,
conscious of our individuality but painfully aware of the communal bonds
that shape and sustain that individuality, that we can reflect consciously and
fruitfully on the rules by which we form ourselves as the ordered people
of God.77 That, at least, is the lesson to be learned from rummaging in the
canonical attic.

Notes

1. John Paul II, apostolic constitution *Sacrae Disciplinae Leges*, January 25,
1983, *Acta Apostolicae Sedis (AAS)* 75 (1983): xi.

2. Brian Tierney, *Religion, Law and the Growth of Constitutional Thought, 1150–
1650* (Cambridge: Cambridge University Press, 1982). Here and throughout the
discussion of the contribution and continued relevance of the medieval canonists I
rely on and summarize, I hope faithfully, Tierney's work.

3. Ibid., 13.

4. Ibid., 14.

5. Ibid., 15.

6. Ibid., 33.

7. Ibid., 16.

8. Ibid. For a fuller discussion of the notion of the "state of the church," see
Gaines Post, "The Theory of Public Law and the State in the Thirteenth Century,"
The Jurist Seminar 6 (1948): 42–59; John H. Hackett, "State of the Church: A
Concept of the Medieval Canonists," *The Jurist* 23 (1963): 259–90; Yves Con-
gar, "Status Ecclesiae, " in *Droit ancien et structures ecclesiales* (London: Variorum
Reprints, 1982), 3–31.

9. Tierney, *Religion, Law and the Growth of Constitutional Thought*, 17.

10. Ibid.

11. Ibid., 18.

12. Ibid., 23.

13. Ibid., 20–21. See also Yves Congar, "Quod omnes tangit, ab omnibus tractari
et approbari debet," in *Droit ancien*, 210–59.

14. Ibid., 23.
15. Ibid., 25.
16. Ibid., 27.
17. Ibid.
18. Ibid.
19. Ibid.
20. Ibid.
21. Ibid., 25.
22. Ibid., 33.
23. *Com. ad X.* 5.38.14, 1.6.6. Cited in Tierney, *Religion, Law and the Growth of Constitutional Thought*, 6.
24. Ibid.
25. Zabarella, *Tractatus de schismate*, in Schardius, *De iurisdictione . . . imperialis ac potestate ecclesiastica* (Basle, 1566), 688–711. Cited in Tierney, 59.
26. Tierney, *Religion, Law and the Growth of Constitutional Thought*, 59.
27. Council of Constance, decree, *Haec sancta*, April 6, 1415 in *Decrees of the Ecumenical Councils*, ed. Norbert Tanner, vol. 1 (Washington: Georgetown University Press, 1990), 409.
28. Council of Constance, decree, *Frequens*, October 9, 1417 in ibid., 1:438–39.
29. Tierney, *Religion, Law and the Growth of Constitutional Thought*, 25.
30. Aloys Grillmeier, "The People of God" in Herbert Vorgrimler, ed., *Commentary on the Documents of Vatican II* (New York: Crossroad, 1989), 1:153–54.
31. Eugenio Corecco, "Aspects of the Reception of Vatican II in the Code of Canon Law," in *The Reception of Vatican II*, ed. Giuseppi Alberigo et al. (Washington, D.C.: Catholic University of America Press, 1987), 251.
32. Paul VI, "Allocutio ad Tribunalis Sacrae Romanae Rotae Decanum, Praelatos Auditores, Officiales et Advocatos, novo Litibus Iudicandis ineunte anno, de protectione iustitiae reddenda," *AAS* 69 (1977): 153.
33. John Paul II, "Sacrae Disciplinae Leges."
34. Rosario Castillo Lara, "La communion ecclesiale dans le nouveau Code de droit canonique," *Studia Canonica* 17 (1983): 335.
35. Corecco, "Aspects of the Reception of Vatican II," 286.
36. Robert T. Kennedy, "The Early Republic's Challenge to Catholic Church Governance: Bicentennial Reflections of an American Canonist," *CLSA Proceedings* 38 (1976): 9.
37. Thomas J. Green, "The Pastoral Governance Role of the Diocesan Bishop: Foundations, Scope and Limitations," *The Jurist* 49 (1989): 480.
38. Karl Rahner, "Structural Change in the Church of the Future," in *Theological Investigations*, vol. 20 (New York: Crossroad, 1981), 118–22.
39. Ibid., 121.
40. Ibid., 122.
41. Kennedy, "The Early Republic's Challenge," 10.
42. Ibid.
43. See John E. Lynch, "Co-Responsibility in the First Five Centuries: Presbyteral Colleges and the Election of Bishops," in *Who Decides for the Church?*, ed. James Coriden (Washington: Canon Law Society of America, 1971), 48.

44. Council for the Public Affairs of the Church, "Normae de promovendis ad episcopale ministerium in Ecclesia Latina," March 25, 1972, *AAS* 64 (1972): 386–91, especially 391.

45. Knut Walf, "Dead End or New Beginnings? On the Future of Church Law," in *Ius Sequitur Vitam: Studies in Canon Law*, ed. James Provost and Knut Walf (Leuven: Leuven University Press, 1991), 232.

46. Council for the Public Affairs of the Church, "Normae," 391.

47. See, for example, Canon Law Society of America, "Procedure for the Selection of Bishops in the United States: A Suggested Implementation of Present Papal Norms" (Washington: CLSA, 1973).

48. Fourth Lateran Council, decree §6, De conciliis provincialibus, in Tanner, *Decrees of the Ecumenical Councils*, 1:236–37.

49. Council of Trent, Sess. XXIV, *de ref.*, can. 2, in ibid., 2:761.

50. 1917 Code, can. 356, §1.

51. Congregation for Bishops, *Directory on the Pastoral Ministry of Bishops* (Ottawa: Publication Service of the Canadian Catholic Conference, 1974), §163.

52. Ibid., §165.

53. Kennedy, "The New Republic's Challenge," 12.

54. Robert T. Kennedy, "Shared Responsibility in Ecclesial Decision-Making," *Studia Canonica* 14 (1980): 9.

55. See also Aloys Grillmeier, "The Hierarchical Structure of the Church with Special Reference to the Episcopate, Article 28," in Herbert Vorgrimler, ed., *Commentary on the Documents of Vatican II*, 1:221–25.

56. Tomas Garcia Barbarena, "Collegiality at the Diocesan Level: The Western Presbyterate," in *Pastoral Reform in Church Government*, Concilium 8 (New York: Paulist Press, 1965), 25.

57. Congregation for Bishops, *Directory*, §203, d.

58. Ibid., §203, b.

59. Corecco, "Aspects of the Reception of Vatican II," 252.

60. James H. Provost, "The Working Together of Consultative Bodies — Great Expectations?," *The Jurist* 40 (1980): 257–81.

61. 1917 Code, can. 1409.

62. Castillo Lara, "La communion ecclesiale dans le nouveau Code de droit canonique," 347.

63. Corecco, "Aspects of the Reception of Vatican II," 252.

64. Congregation for Bishops, *Directory*, §204.

65. Provost, "Working Together of Consultative Bodies," 275.

66. Congregation for Bishops, *Directory*, §204.

67. Provost, "Working Together of Consultative Bodies," 281.

68. Pontificia Commissio Codicis Iuris Canonici Recognoscendo, "Principia quae Codicis Iuris Canonici recognitionem dirigant," *Communicationes* 1 (1969): 82–83.

69. Ibid.

70. John Paul II, "Sacrae Disciplinae Leges," xiii.

71. Pontificia Commissio Codicis Iuris Canonici Recognoscendo, "Principia," 83.

72. Documenta Synodi Episcoporum, "De iustitia in mundo," *AAS* 63 (1971): 933.

73. Paul VI and the Synod of Bishops, "Diritti dell'uomo e reconciliazione," *L'Osservatore Romano*, October 26, 1974, 5; Pontifical Commission *Iustitia et Pax*, *The Church and Human Rights* (Vatican City: Pontifical Commission *Iustitia et Pax*, 1975), 41–42.

74. Michael Scammell, "The Prophet and the Wilderness: How the Idea of Human Rights Crippled Communism," *New Republic* 204 (February 25, 1991): 34–35.

75. Karl Rahner, "Structural Changes in the Church of the Future," 116–18.

76. Tierney, *Religion, Law, and the Growth of Constitutional Thought*, 49.

77. Ibid., 37.

HANS KÜNG

–4–

Participation of the Laity in Church Leadership and in Church Elections

A Blind Spot in the Decree on the Laity

The theme to be treated here is, surprisingly, not to be found in the Vatican II Decree on the Apostolate of the Laity. That fact makes the matter difficult. Participation, cooperation, collaboration of the laity in the decisions of the church? People like to talk of the participation of the laity in the *life* (not the decisions) of the church. They also like to speak of the participation of the laity in the decisions of the *world* (but not of the church). They do not at all like to speak, at least in official binding documents, of the participation of the laity in the *decisions* of the *church*. Nevertheless it is precisely here that the question of the status of the laity in the church arises in the most practical way. For, as long as I can contribute advice and work but am excluded from decision making, I remain, no matter how many fine things are said about my status, a second-class member of this community: I am more an object that is utilized than a subject who is actively responsible. Persons who can advise and collaborate but not participate in decision making in a manner befitting their status *are* not really the church but only *belong to* the church.

Unfortunately the Decree on the Apostolate of the Laity of Vatican II, that carries on in a very long-winded and paternal fashion on various subjects which are quite obvious, remains on this point, which is so decisive in practical life, far behind what Yves Congar had already pioneered with concrete possibilities in the difficult preconciliar days by his courageous and epoch-making *Jalons pour une théologie du laïcat*.[1] Did this happen solely

This article originally appeared in *Journal of Ecumenical Studies* 6, no. 4 (Fall 1969) and subsequently in Hans Küng, *Reforming the Church Today* (New York: Crossroad, 1992), 75–94, under the title "On the Way to a New Church Order: A Theological Case for Shared Decision-Making by the Laity." It appears here in a revised form.

because this decree on the Apostolate of the Laity came about without the active participation of the laity itself in the decision making and thus is essentially a product of clerics? Well, even Yves Congar is not a layman but a cleric. That the decree has here a blind spot should not so much be ascribed to the clergy as clergy as to the clericalism of the clergy, a trait that can also be found among the laity.

The basis for joint decision in the church was itself laid out thoroughly in the decree, inasmuch as in the first section of the first preparatory chapter it was said that the laity "share in the priestly, prophetic, and royal office of Christ" and that from thence they "have their own role to play in the mission of the whole People of God in the Church and in the world" (no. 2). And at the same time the decree alludes to the pertinent section of the Dogmatic Constitution on the Church.

If the community of all those in the church goes so deep in spite of all differences of gifts and services that it is not possible to go deeper, then why, considering the communality of the one Lord, of the one Spirit and the one Body, of one faith and one baptism, of one grace and vocation, of one hope and love, and finally of one responsibility and task — why then, despite all the diversity of functions, is there not also in the church a communality of *decision?* On this one point the Dogmatic Constitution on the Church as well as the Decree on the Apostolate of the Laity remains timid.

Fundamental Principles

But are there perhaps serious theological objections, and not merely a centuries-long tradition of clericalism in the Catholic Church, that do indeed favor the participation of the laity in advising and working but not in decision making in the church? Is this not perhaps a misunderstanding of the real essence of the church, which is grounded not on a free accord of a believing individual but on the call by God in Christ? Has not an essential differentness — a differentness that does not admit a translation of the modern democratic model to the church — been overlooked? Has not the hierarchical character of the church, which is built upon the apostles and the apostolic succession of the office-bearers and thus excludes any democratization, been forgotten? These and similar serious considerations should be answered, and of course not simply from the conciliar decrees, which in their treatment of this question have remained superficial, but from the original Christian message, as it expressed itself and operated in the church or the churches of the original New Testament age. What was originally correct cannot later on be rejected as false in principle by those who call themselves followers.

1. If we may, to begin with, argue from a more sociological point of view: Some of those who today reject joint decision making with the laity in the church earlier rejected on the same basis any serious participation

of the laity through collaboration and advising in the church. And some of those who protest today against a democratization of the church and against any translation of secular sociological models to the church not too long ago accepted without reflection the secular sociological model of the monarchy for the church, and even in practice did nothing against the monarchization of the church.

Basically it is better even in the church to speak of a democracy (the entire holy people of God) than of the "hierocracy" (a holy caste). For while in the New Testament all worldly honorary titles are strictly shunned in connection with bearers of office, they are in fact given to the entire believing people, which is designated "a chosen race, a royal priesthood, a consecrated nation" (1 Pet. 2:9) and made "a line of kings and priests, to serve our God and to rule the world" (Rev. 5:10).

But that already demonstrates that in decisive matters we are careful to argue not in sociological but in theological categories. Only in this way can we show that joint decision making and regulation on the part of the laity is not only a timely concession to modern democratic developments but is a move thoroughly rooted in the church's own origins.

2. Out of a correct — that is to say, biblical and historical — perspective of "apostolic succession" there arises the question of the joint role of the laity in the decision making in the church.[2] Here this can be indicated only briefly.[3] The special and unquestionable apostolic succession of the multiple pastoral service (the bishops with the pope, but in their way also the pastors with their co-workers) must not be isolated but must be seen in its functionality:

a. The church *as a whole* (Credo Ecclesisam apostolicam!), and thus each individual church member, also stands in succession to the apostles. In what sense? The church, as well as all individuals, remains bound to the basic witness and service of the original witnesses without which there would be no church. The church is founded on the apostles (and the prophets). All the faithful thus are supposed to succeed the apostles in apostolic faith and confessing, life and service. This service takes the most diverse forms of proclamation, baptism, the community of prayer and the Supper, the building up of the congregation, and service to the world.

b. The special apostolic succession of the diverse *pastoral service*, important as it is, is not thereby an end in itself. The pastoral service continues the special task of the apostles, in which they differentiate from other important and likewise permanent services in the church, such as that of the prophets or the teachers: namely, to establish and guide the churches. From this service of guiding the church, these office-bearers (bishops, pastors, further co-workers) also have a special authority; only in service can their authority have any foundation at all. The shepherds in the church are thus in no way a management class with a unilateral imperial power, toward which the single possible attitude is unilateral obedience. They are no *dominium* but a *ministerium*. They form no power structure but a special service structure. "You know that among the pagans their so-called rulers lord it over them, and their great men make their authority felt. This is not to happen among you. No; anyone who wants to become great among you must be your servant, and anyone who wants to be first among you must be slave to all. For the Son of Man himself did not come to be served but to serve, and to give his life as a ransom for many" (Mark 10:42–45).

So the purpose of shepherds in the church is special service to the apostolic church, which is made up of all the believers. For this reason the term "hierarchy" or "holy rule" (customary only since the time of Dionysius the Pseudo-Areopagite, five hundred years after Christ) is misleading. To be relevant biblically, it is better to speak of "diakonia" or "church service."

> For the nurturing and constant growth of the People of God, Christ the Lord instituted in His Church a variety of ministries, which work for the good of the whole body. For those ministers who are endowed with sacred power are servants of their brethren, so that all who are of the People of God, and therefore enjoy a true Christian dignity, can work toward a common goal freely and in an orderly way, and arrive at salvation. (Dogmatic Constitution on the Church, no. 18)

Thus if from a biblical perspective the shepherds are not the masters but the servants of the church or the congregation (=the "laity"), why then should it in practice be possible to exclude the church or the congregation (=the "laity") from joint decision making? This can happen only if the shepherds are seen not as the servants of the church, but as its exclusive owners or fathers or teachers.

But the shepherds are *not* the *owners* of the church, toward whom laity are only dependents who have nothing to say in the management. The church is not a huge industry: All members of the church *are* church; the church belongs to all of them. And the shepherds are also *not* the *fathers* of the church, in contrast to whom the laity are only minors who still cannot have any responsibility of their own for the church. The church cannot be considered simply as a family (except as under God, the one Father): All grown-up members of the church are adult members who have an established inalienable responsibility for the whole. And, finally, the shepherds are also *not* the *teachers* of the church, in contrast to whom the laity are only learning pupils who have only to listen and obey. The church is not a school: All church members have "learned from God" (1 Thess. 4:9) and "do not need anyone to teach" them (1 John 2:27).

In brief: In the church, despite all the variations of office, which we must return to, all are ultimately equal insofar as they all are believers and, as such, adult brothers and sisters under the one Father and the one Lord Jesus. Teaching and advising, like listening and obeying, are, because all members are filled by the Spirit, *reciprocal*. To this extent the church, despite all differences of services, is no two-class society of possessor and nonpossessor, empowered and powerless, adults and minors, knowledge-able and ignorant, but a community of love filled and authorized by the Spirit, in which only greater service bestows greater authority.

3. If then within this community of basic equality the variety of services and the special fullness of power of the pastoral office are nevertheless to be taken seriously, the question of relation of the church (the local church or parish, the diocesan church, the universal church) to the relevant pastoral office (pastor and his co-workers, bishop, pope) must be defined anew: Does the universal fullness of power of the church confirm the particular fullness of power of the pastoral office, or is it the other way around — does the particular fullness of power of the pastoral office confirm the universal fullness of power of the church? This must be examined carefully.

a. The joint decision making of the laity in the church can obviously *not be founded* on the fact that the fullness of power of the shepherds is derived simply from the fullness of power of the church or congregation, from the fullness of power of the universal priesthood. Then the special pastoral office would simply be leveled within the church and within the universal priesthood: an unbiblical democratization!

b. But on the other hand the participation of the laity in the decision making of the church can also *not be excluded* on the basis that the fullness of power of the church or congregation is simply derived from the fullness of power of the shepherd, as though the shepherds alone stood in succession to the apostles and were not the servants of the church but its masters or mediators. Thus the pastoral service would be isolated from the church or congregation, from the universal priesthood, and its apostolic succession would be absolutized: an unbiblical hierarchicalization or clericalization of the church!

c. If, however, as we saw, the church and its shepherds stand all together under the one Father and Lord, who makes them all sisters and brothers; if they all stand under the one message of Christ and all are called into the same discipleship and the same obedience to God and God's Word; if they then ultimately all are the hearing church and precisely as hearers are all filled with the Spirit, then it follows that the fullness of power of the church or congregation is not derived from the fullness of power of the shepherds, and the fullness of power of the shepherds is not derived from the fullness of power of church or congregation, but the fullness of power of *both* is directly derived from the fullness of power of the Lord of the church in his Spirit. This common origin of their fullness of power establishes the universal authorization of the congregation as well as the special fullness of power of the service of the shepherds. It is the support of the authority of the shepherds as well as of the participation of the "laity" in decision making.

4. The joint decision making of the "laity" in the church will, then, be seen correctly only if church or congregation and the shepherds are seen as

intimately related as well as different. It is this perspective that eliminates all absolutistic decision making by either the shepherds *or* the congregation alone, which excludes both ecclesiastical oligarchy (monarchy) *and* ochlocracy. If, as we have emphasized, the universal priesthood, if the various charismatic gifts and offices, and if especially the charismata of the prophets and teachers are taken seriously in the church, then the *special office of the shepherds* (presiding officers) in the church must and will also be taken very seriously: It is the special vocation of individual believing persons (in principle — for there is no biblical or dogmatic objection to it — both men and women) to the permanent and regular (not only occasional), public (not only private) service to the congregation as such (and not only to individual members) through the laying on of hands or ordination (and not only through the equally possible charism of the Spirit breaking through where the Spirit wills).

From the *special* service the shepherds have also *special* authority that can never be simply eliminated or passed over in the church or congregation. From this special *service*, however, they have their authority only within, for, and in collaboration with the church or congregation. So the *shepherds from the very outset are oriented to the joint collaboration, decision making, and regulating of the congregation*. This orientation does not mean a constraint and restriction but a protection against all stifling isolation, a help in all their need, a liberation into true togetherness. The shepherds must see their special fullness of power embedded and protected in the universal authorization of the church and of each individual church member. Solitary responsibility stifles; common responsibility sustains.

The word, baptism, the Eucharist, forgiveness, the office of love are given to the entire church. But a few must discharge the service of the word, the sacrament, and the church permanently, regularly, and publicly in the church, strengthened and legitimized for this through prayer and the power of ordination, which itself should occur in cooperation with the entire church. Concretely: *All* Christians are empowered to preach the word and to witness to the faith in the church and in the world; but only to the shepherds of the congregation who are called, or to those delegated by them, is the special fullness of power to preach in the congregational assembly given. *All* Christians are empowered to exhort others to forgive their brother or sister in a crisis of conscience; but only to the called shepherds is given the special fullness of power of the words of reconciliation and absolution, which is exercised in the congregational assembly upon the congregation and thus upon the individuals. For the coexecution of baptism and the Eucharist *all* Christians are authorized; but only to the called shepherds is given the special fullness of power to perform baptisms in public in the congregation and to conduct responsibly the congregational Eucharist.

5. Thus of their innermost essence the church or congregation and the

shepherds are oriented toward one another in decision making. On the basis of his special mission with which he steps before the congregation, the ordained shepherd has a pregiven authority in the church or the congregation. On the basis of his ordination the shepherd need not demonstrate his vocation, like every other charismatic, by the exhibition of his charism (in proof of the Spirit and the power). Rather he is appointed from the very beginning: legitimized as the one who is fully authorized for this office in a special way for the public activity of the congregation in the Spirit. But this must not be misunderstood, as though the shepherd ultimately were raised over the congregation to become the lord of the congregation, where he no longer remained dependent on the congregation.

So the shepherd and the congregation have their mutual obligations: The shepherd has the duty and the task to proclaim the Christian message to the congregation again and again, even when it is uncomfortable for the congregation. The congregation, on the other hand, has the duty and the task of retesting again and again whether the shepherd is remaining true to his commission, whether he is acting according to the gospel. For there are not only false prophets but also faithless shepherds.

Thus everyone is helped by this mutual respectful examination, this reciprocal criticism without disputation, this universal *correctio fraterna* in modesty. And all this is a presupposition for common action, for which all that we have said is basically true: No individual decisions, either of the church or congregation or of the shepherd! No going-it-alone, either of the "laity" without the shepherd or of the shepherd without the "laity." No sole control, either dictatorship of the one or dictatorship of the many! Instead of seclusion and isolation, openness and solidarity. Instead of paternalism, brotherliness. Instead of autocracy and despotism, service and love. Instead of servitude, freedom; instead of egotistic power, existence for others.[4]

6. If common responsibility, if joint decision making of the congregation with the shepherd is seen in this way, then one need have no anxiety for the order of the congregation, even if it is threatened again and again from all sides. Then a first principle will be true for the shepherd as well as for the members of the congregation: *To each their own!* Then the shepherd will not assume a superiority over the congregation nor the congregation over the shepherd. Then neither shepherd nor laity will wish to commandeer and subordinate everything for themselves but they will each give and relinquish what belongs to the other. And then a second principle is valid: *With one another for one another!* Then neither the shepherd nor the laity will use their fullness of power as a weapon against the other in order to grasp a position for themselves and seize the power in the church, but they will use this fullness of power in the only way it makes sense, to serve one another and the whole. And finally there is one supreme criterion: *Obedience to the Lord!* Then neither the shepherd nor the laity will play the role of lord of the church, but they will find true freedom, imperturbable peace,

and a permanent joy even amid difficulties and affliction in subordination to the one Lord and his word in love.

Embodiment

The embodiment of an ecclesiastical order that is justified by the original Christian message and church must be different for different times and different places. In every case a transposition is necessary. Thus it is far from our intention to deliver a hard unhistorical judgment on times in which this ecclesiastical order was realized only very imperfectly.[5] And likewise it is not our intention to give a simple prescription or a universal remedy for a better realization of such a truly Christian order to all the varied areas of the church. Nevertheless attention ought to be called to a few points of a general nature.

The Collegial Church Leadership on the Various Levels

The "collegiality" emphasized by the council, that is the brother-communal character of church leadership, must not arbitrarily remain limited to the uppermost level of the universal church (pope-bishops). It must also be realized on the level of the national church, the diocesan church, and above all the local church (and correspondingly also in the religious orders with their lay brothers). That means very clearly a dissolution of that authoritarian one-man rule — whether on the level of the parish, bishopric, nation, or the universal church — which, as we have seen, is consonant neither with the original New Testament organization nor with contemporary democratic thought.

According to what we have already said about the shepherds, it is quite clear that the decisive authority of the pastor, the bishop, and the pope should remain explicitly preserved; only in this way can the mutual paralysis of the various powers normally be avoided. Nevertheless at the same time not only collaboration and counseling but also participation in decision making by representative councils of the churches in question should be guaranteed. In order that these councils be truly representative it is necessary that the greater part of the members be elected in free and secret elections; a minority can be members ex officio because of certain important service functions or through their nomination by responsible shepherds (pastor, bishop, bishops' conference, or pope).

The constitutional foundations for these pressing and incisive reforms are laid down, at least for the diocese, by the council itself: It was resolved by Vatican II that in every diocese a diocesan pastoral council should be established, to be composed of priests, religious, and laity. This pastoral council is already a reality in some dioceses, wherein the priests' council, also decreed by Vatican II, is partly integrated into this pastoral council, and the laity often have a two-thirds majority.

Analogous to the diocesan level, collegial leadership of the church must also be realized on the other levels:

a. For the universal church it would mean a lay council parallel to the bishops' council that is already constituted, though still not permanent, still not assembling regularly, and still possessing no authority. This could come about as a result of the international lay congress, which in the postconciliar period showed more vitality, courage, and resolution than the synod of bishops. This lay council, together with the bishops' council under the decisive leadership of the pope (the veto power), could not only give advice but also decide on the important concerns of the universal church.

b. For each nation there should be constituted, again paralleling the diocesan pastoral council, a national pastoral council, consisting of bishops, priests, and laity, for counseling and communal decision making in all important concerns of the national church.

c. For every parish there should be constituted, where this has not already happened, a parish council of men and women, paralleling the diocesan pastoral council, for the purposes of counseling and participation in decision making with the pastor (who would have veto power) in all important parish concerns.

For the concrete statute the following should be observed:

a. In all the decision making councils we have described, from the parish council to the lay senate and the bishops' council of the entire church, it should be self-explanatory that a sufficient number of qualified *women* are also to be admitted as members. Such representation is a part of the full participation of women in the life of the church on the basis of equality. On the various levels care must be taken eventually for the education and inclusion of women in active coresponsibility.

b. On every level theological and other *professional people* are to be drawn in, corresponding to the scholarly areas under discussion.

c. For practical functioning the American principle of "checks and balances," which precludes a monopolization of power in certain hands, is helpful. In the United States the president as well as Congress have strong posts.

Free Election of Presiding Officers through a Representation of the Pertinent Churches:

This should hold true for pastors, bishops, and pope. Such an election can be arranged with the cooperation of the representative councils discussed above, to which, circumstances permitting, other members can be enlisted for the electoral college: For the election of the pope in the universal church the bishops' council and lay council would be duly qualified, for the election of the bishop in the diocese the diocesan pastoral council, for the election of the pastor in the local church the parish council (or, as in some Swiss cantons, the assembled congregation).

In the election of the pastor and bishops a control function would belong to the superior pastoral offices: The election of pastors would have to be approved by the bishops, the election of bishops by the episcopal conference in its majority or by the pope. In this way the old axioms of canon law would once again hold good and could be applied by analogy to all ecclesiastical offices: "No bishop should be installed against the will of the people" (Pope Celestine I) and "He who presides over all should be elected by all" (Pope Leo the Great).

As to concrete regulations, several points would be important:

a. Election not only of the superiors of religious orders, or, as in certain church areas, the pastor, but also of the bishops and all office holders for a substantial but stipulated time (e.g., six or eight years with the possibility of reelection) is a justified as well as a pressing desideratum in today's situation.

b. Directives for obligatory (e.g., at seventy years) or optional (e.g., at sixty-five years) resignation from ecclesiastical offices are necessary. On the other side, demands of a congregation for the retirement of a shepherd should never be legally binding without the agreement of the superior office holder (bishop for the pastor, pope or episcopal conference for the bishop); in this way illegitimate attempts at pressure can be averted.

c. A special committee should advise the bishop in all personnel concerns; such a group can consider each case carefully — the special peculiarities and requisites of the position concerned as well as the wishes of the congregation and of the person in question. Special attention must be given to the pastor-assistant relationship, which is full of vexation.

Only one example, though one that has central significance, shall be investigated here more closely: election of bishops.[6] The election of the bishop of Rome, the pope, will not be treated specially here; nevertheless it must be clear even without a long explanation how pressing the transferral of the election from the college of cardinals, which is in no way representative and in any case is anachronistic, to the episcopal and lay councils is: Today more than ever the pope needs the broadest consensus in the church!

The election of the bishop by a representative council of the pertinent church satisfies the following:

1. the theological as well as practical high esteem for the particular and local church, for the diocese and the congregation (see especially the Dogmatic Constitution on the Church, no. 26, and the Decree on the Bishops' Pastoral Office in the Church, e.g., no. 27);

2. the demand for decentralization, which stipulates a dismantling of the power of the Roman curia in favor of the churches in the individual nations (establishment of national bishops conferences, etc.; see the Decree on the Bishops' Pastoral Office in the Church, e.g., nos. 36–38);

3. the demand for a curial reform (which, unfortunately, has still not been radically accomplished), which will provide not a broadening of the

area of curial competence over against the episcopates of individual countries, but on the contrary the insertion of representatives of the most varied countries into the ecclesiastical central administration (see the Decree on the Bishops' Pastoral Office in the Church, nos. 9–10);

4. the strict definition (which here would mean limitation) of the authority of the nuncio, as desired by the council: "The Fathers also eagerly desire that, in view of the pastoral role proper to bishops, the office of legates of the Roman Pontiff be more precisely determined" (Decree on the Bishops' Pastoral Office in the Church, no. 9; cf. no. 10).

For a historical understanding of these conclusions of Vatican II it must be remembered that these conclusions doubtless stand in a clear front line against Roman centralism, dirigism, and absolutism, as it has prevailed in the West since the Gregorian reform and the High Middle Ages and reached its unsurpassable high point in the period after Vatican I with the codification of the Code of Canon Law. But on the basis of what has been stated here from the New Testament, it must be clear that these conclusions are not concerned with attempted "innovations," but with a return to tradition,[7] the truly good old tradition.

The election of bishops is itself an excellent model for this, as it was earlier. In the election of bishops it was from the beginning kept in mind that not only a clerical hierarchy of functionaries but rather the entire community of believers, the entire people of God, is the church. In ancient Christian times the bishop was *elected by clergy and people*, even if he then was ordained generally by the neighboring bishops. Some of the greatest bishops of all times, like Ambrose of Milan and Augustine of Hippo, were elected decisively by the people. "Nos eligimus eum," "We elect him" — ran the formula of acclamation of the people in the Latin congregations. Not the Roman bishop but the neighboring bishops authoritatively cooperated in the election. The right of corroboration and consecration also belong later, according to the stipulations of the First Ecumenical Council of Nicaea, not to the Roman See but to the metropolitan of the ecclesiastical province involved.

How the nomination to the episcopal sees passed in later times in part to the princes and how the biblically based right of the people of the church was more and more limited cannot be treated here in detail. In any case the reform movement of the Middle Ages still demanded the free election of bishops by clergy and people (so decreed Leo IX at the Synod of Rheims in 1049). The free episcopal election as over against nomination by the princes succeeded in principle in the battle over investiture. Indeed because of the growing predominance of the cathedral chapter, the lower clergy and the laity were more and more excluded from the election. At first the cathedral chapter had only to assent to an election; then more and more it could determine the election. The election right of the cathedral chapter became common toward the end of the twelfth century and was established as obligatory by Innocent III for the entire church.

Through this development, favored by the popes, the right of corroboration and ordination increasingly fell to the Roman see, although in the early centuries the influence of the Roman bishop in reference to episcopal elections did not extend essentially beyond his metropolitan (or patriarchal) right, and only after the ninth century in case of complications (removal, promotion, election controversies) did he regularly interfere in the filling of a vacancy. After the High Middle Ages the right of corroboration was often used for the purpose of exerting influence on the election itself. This resulted in the reservations by which the popes withheld to themselves the filling of episcopal seats: first of all for isolated cases, then for certain seats, finally after the fourteenth century (under the Avignon pope Urban V, in 1361) in general. Thus the suffrage of the chapter was undermined and in time even legally suppressed.

Only after the Western Schism and in the struggle over the Council of Basel was an at least circumscribed episcopal suffrage of the cathedral chapter again recognized through the Viennese Concordat of 1448. Indeed it came about in the aftermath of the development of a royal or noble right of nomination that took many forms. With the abolition of the Catholic ruling houses these rights declined vastly. In this manner the way was first cleared for a general papal naming of bishops, which had already long been in the making and now was established in proper form in the new Codex Juris Canonici, which was proclaimed by Rome in 1918 without any essential participation of the episcopacy and amid the complete exclusion of the universal church. The chiefly unrestricted right to elect bishops in the Swiss bishoprics of Basel, Chur, and St. Gall as well as Olmütz remain now the great exceptions. Only in the Eastern churches united to Rome has the right of nomination formed in the ancient church era to an extent remained preserved, and the new law of the Eastern churches recently accepted the rule that the bishop be elected by the synod of bishops and patriarchs. Yet this freedom of election is diluted insofar as the list of candidates must be approved by Rome in advance! The spirit of the resolutions of Vatican II means a reinclusion of clergy and laity in the election of bishops after the model of the ancient church.[8]

In conclusion let us say only this: Obviously there is no perfect system of organization; in concrete life each has its specific defects and dangers. But a system better than that canonized by the present Code of Canon Law is not difficult to think of![9] The one suggested here in some of its basic features corresponds better both to the original organization of the apostolic church and to our contemporary democratic times.

Postscript

The reader will certainly be surprised to learn that this article, written after the Second Vatican Council, in which I participated, first appeared in German and French in 1969. Of course, I am glad that this article is still of relevance in 1992. At the same time, it is a sad sign of how little the Catholic Church has really changed during the past three pontificates. I hope that it will not be necessary to reprint this article again in another twenty-three years and that by then the problem of the laity in the Catholic Church will have been resolved in a positive way.

Notes

1. Yves Congar, *Jalons pour une théologie du laïcat* (Paris, 1953); *Lay People in the Church* (Westminster, Md., 1957).

2. On apostolic succession see besides the usual works on the church in the New Testament (by O. Linton and F. M. Braun, and the monographs by F. J. Leenhardt, N. A. Dahl, O. Michel, G. Johnston, W. Robinson, A. Oepke, G. Aulén, L. G. Champion, A. Nygren, P. Minear, K. H. Schelkle, R. Schnackenburg, L. Cervaux) the more specialized researches by P. H. Menoud, *L'Eglise et le ministère selon le Nouveau Testament* (Neuchâtel, 1949); G. W. H. Lampe, *Some Aspects of the New Testament Ministry* (London, 1949); H. von Campenhausen, *Kirchliches Amt und geistliche Vollmacht in den ersten drei Jahrhunderten* (Tübingen, 1953); H. Schlier, *Die Zeit der Kirche* (Freiburg im Breisgau, 1955), 129–47; G. Dix, *Le Ministère dans l'église ancienne* (Neuchâtel/Paris, 1955); E. Schweizer, *Gemeinde und Gemeindeordnung im Neuen Testament* (Zurich, 1959); E. Käsemann, *Exegetische Versuchs und Besinnungen* (Göttingen, 1960), 1:109–34; H. U. von Balthasar, *Sponsa Verbi* (Einsiedeln, 1960), 80–147; E. Schlink, *Der kommende Christus und die kirchlichen Traditionen* (Göttingen, 1961), 160–95; for literature from the fields of history and systematic theology on the subject of ecclesiastical office, see H. Küng, *Structures of the Church* (New York, 1964), chapter 4 (includes a response to the positions of Käsemann and Schlink), and the pertinent lexicon articles.

3. For the basic foundation of all that follows see H. Küng, *The Church* (New York, 1968), chapter E.

4. See N. Greinacher, "Der Vollzug der Kirche im Bistum," in *Handbuch der Pastoraltheologie* (Freiburg, 1968), 3:106–7: "If we are in earnest when we speak of Christian brotherliness and the equality of the members of the diocese, we must move toward a far-reaching *democratization of the structures of the church.* Such a democratization corresponds on the one hand to an original and genuine stream of Christian tradition in the church and on the other hand also to the mentality and the structures of contemporary secular society, which, as we have shown, cannot conceal its own Christian origins. One thing must be clear: one cannot speak of the coresponsibility of the laity if participation in *decision making* is not granted. The summons of the laity to coresponsibility and care for the diocese has meaning really only if this laity is also guaranteed a genuine role in diocesan decision making. If this is not the case, then one not unjustly runs the danger that this summons to joint care will be regarded as a farce. If the complaint is heard so often the laity show so

slight an interest in the call to participation in the apostolate, then it should be asked whether the necessary place has also been made for their role in decision making. Only under this condition of genuine participation in decision making will it be possible in the long run to integrate the laity into the church in any authentic way."

5. Peter Stockmeier, "Gemeinde und Bischofsamt in der alten Kirche," *Theologische Quartalschrift* (Tübingen) 149, no. 2 (1969): 133–46, shows of course that the constitution of the ancient church was very much closer, and not only just in time, to the original Christian message and church than is the constitution of the post-Tridentine church.

6. On the election of bishops see besides the manuals on the history of canon law (especially E. Feine, W. Plöchl), the short summary by K. Mörsdorf in the article "Bischof III. Kirchenrechtlich," in *Lexikon für Theologie und Kirche* (Freiburg im Breisgau, 1958), 2:497–505; Günter Biemer, "Die Bischofswahl als neues Desiderat kirchlicher Praxis," *Theologische Quartalschrift* 149, no. 2 (1969): 171–84; Johannes Neumann, "Wahl und Amtszeitbegrenzung nach kanonischem Recht," ibid., 117–32; Stockmeier, "Gemeinde und Bischofsamt in der alten Kirche."

7. See especially Stockmeier, "Gemeinde und Bischofsamt in der alten Kirche."

8. Greinacher, 107: "If it is correct that every believing Christian is a brother or sister of Jesus and that the Spirit of Christ operates in each, that the Spirit blows where it will, and that there is also charisma outside office, then the idea cannot be excluded that these Christians should also exert an influence on the fulfillment of the church in the diocese and on the *filling of posts of service*. In the election of the apostle Matthias (Acts 1:15–26) as well as in the election of deacons (Acts 6:1–6), the collaboration of the entire community was considered self-explanatory (see also Acts 15:22f.). It is well-known that the leaders of the congregations in the first centuries up to the time of Ambrose and Augustine were determined with the collaboration of the congregation. Until recently the church tolerated a situation in which the nobility exerted an influence on the filling of certain parish positions. Even up to the year 1903 the church countenanced the fact that in practice the kaiser influenced the papal elections. Up until our own time — and not only in Eastern countries — the governments in some countries exerted a massive influence on the episcopal elections. Would it not be more appropriate to give some influence in the filling of offices to everyone who is immediately concerned and who is coresponsible for the bishopric — namely, the members of the local church? Is it not time to give the old democratic tendencies in the church another chance and endow them with a new meaning and a new expression that would be suitable for our time, which is characterized by the process of 'fundamental democratization'?"

9. See especially Biemer, "Die Bischofswahl als neues Desiderat kirchlicher Praxis," and Neumann, "Wahl und Amtszeitbegrenzung nach kanonischem Recht."

Translated by Arlene Swidler

CHARLES E. CURRAN

– 5 –
What Catholic Ecclesiology Can Learn from Official Catholic Social Teaching

Ecclesiology deals with the mystery of the church together with its structures and organization. Official Catholic social teaching refers to what the hierarchical teaching office in the Catholic Church has proposed; modern official Catholic social teaching generally refers to the teaching on the social order, especially the economic order, begun by Pope Leo XIII's encyclical *Rerum Novarum* in 1891. Catholic social ethics is broader than official Catholic social teaching since it involves the disciplined and systematic study of Catholic social morality. The thesis of this essay is that Catholic ecclesiology can learn much from official Catholic social teaching.

Preliminary Considerations

Some preliminary considerations are in order. It is necessary to show that Catholic ecclesiology can learn from Catholic social teaching before explaining what, if anything, Catholic social teaching has said that is pertinent. Some might object that Catholic ecclesiology can and should learn nothing from Catholic social teaching. The two — ecclesiology and social teaching — deal with two very different realities — the church and the human social order. The church as a unique community founded on the grace and the call of God has a very distinctive structure, which by definition is different from human structures and especially from human political society. Since we are dealing with apples and oranges, there is no real relationship between them.

Traditional Catholic self-understanding does not see such a dichotomy or difference between the two. Catholic faith has always seen the divine as working in and through the human. The human as such never stands in opposition to the divine. This characteristic understanding of Roman Catholicism has been seen as distinctive and is referred to by different names — the analogical imagination, the principle of mediation, the sacramental principle, or an incarnational approach.[1] Since the divine uses the human and is mediated in and through the human, the church can and should learn from human understandings. The church and the human political order are not the same, but there can be and are important similarities.

The fact of God's working in and through the human is very evident in Catholic ecclesiology.[2] Catholicism insists in contradistinction to some Reformation perspectives that the church is a visible human society with a visible human structure. The church is not an invisible relationship of the individual believer with God but is rather a visible, human community animated by the Holy Spirit. As the incarnational principle brought the divine and human together in Jesus, so too in the church there is both the divine and the human aspect but not merely existing in juxtaposition.

History reminds us of how the early church took its structural components from the contemporary human scene. As the church grew in Roman soil, the Roman empire furnished many of the structures and institutions that were taken over by the church. The understanding of leadership in the church borrowed much from the secular models of the day. To this day the church recognizes the need for a legal and structural model to be employed in a way that best serves the needs of the people of God. One criticism of the new Code of Canon Law that went into effect in 1983 is its reliance more on Roman law than on the common law tradition.[3] Notice that the problem is not that of a divine versus a human model but which human model best serves the people of God in its present circumstances.

Yes, the church is different from a secular political community, but there are many similarities and agreements. Both theology and history show how the Catholic Church has borrowed much from human models in the very structure of the church itself.

Has official Catholic social teaching ever acknowledged that the church can and should learn from the models and structures of secular government and the political order? The modern period of official Catholic social teaching began with the papal encyclicals of Pope Leo XIII over a hundred years ago. The first explicit mention of the relationship between life in the church and life in human political society is found in the 1971 document of the world synod of bishops, *Justitia in Mundo:* "While the church is bound to give witness to justice, she recognizes that anyone who ventures to speak to people about justice must first be just in their eyes. Hence, we must undertake an examination of the modes of acting and of the possessions and life style found within the church herself."

The first area mentioned in this document is human rights, including the right of workers in the church to a suitable livelihood and social security, the right to a suitable freedom of expression and thought, and the right to procedural justice, including the accuser's right to know the accused. *Justitia in Mundo* also insists on the right of all members of the church to "have some share in the drawing up of decisions" and urges that women should have their own share of responsibility and participation in the life of society and in the community life of the church.[4]

The U.S. Catholic bishops in their pastoral letter on the economy cite *Justitia in Mundo* and assert, "All the moral principles that govern the just operation of any economic endeavor apply to the church and its agencies and institutions; indeed the church should be exemplary."[5] The bishops then reflect in a special way on five areas — wages and salaries, rights of employees, investments and property, works of charity, and working for economic justice. Even though this particular letter deals with economic activity, the bishops in their closing paragraph of this section recognize that the principle involves more than just the economic order and includes the cultural order. "As we have proposed a new experiment in collaboration and participation in decision making by all those affected at all levels of United States society, so we also commit the church to become a model of collaboration and participation."[6] Thus the American bishops firmly insist that the principles of justice, collaboration, and participation that must exist in the political order should also be present in the church. In fact, the church should be exemplary in this matter.

The comparatively late linking of the internal life of the church with the life of human political society raises some significant questions. Why was the linkage never mentioned earlier? What explains why the connection was made in 1971?

This development coheres with the great changes that occurred in Roman Catholicism at the time of the Second Vatican Council. A pre–Vatican II understanding of the church and the relationship between the church and the human political order saw no basic bond or connection between the two. From a purely ecclesiological perspective pre–Vatican II Catholicism tended to see the church as the kingdom of God and thus basically holy, without spot, and in no need of reform or change. A later theology characterized such an approach as triumphalistic.

In the relationship between the church and the state both societies were said to be perfect societies insofar as they contain within themselves all they needed to achieve their purposes. These two societies are distinguished from the family, which is not a perfect society because it does not have within it everything that is needed for its members to achieve their end. The family depends upon both the church and the state.[7] Since the church and state are two perfect societies, there is little or no room for linkage between them. Note that perfect in this sense means complete and does not mean morally perfect or holy. However, especially in the light of the triumphalistic ecclesiology, such a connotation of perfection was also present.

The peculiar circumstances of the Catholic Church in the United States, and the theory that went along with such an understanding, also discouraged any recognition of a direct link between the church and the political society. In the United States Roman Catholicism for the first time faced in a conscious way the relationship of the church to a democratic form of government and especially to a religiously pluralistic society. Before that time it was generally accepted by both Catholics and Magisterial Protestants immediately after the Reformation that civic unity required religious unity. The state thus supported and defended the church in the system known as the union of church and state.

The U.S. experiment involved civic unity without religious unity. Could Catholics fully support this American system and work together in the political and social order with those belonging to other religions and no religion? In practice American Catholics wholeheartedly accepted the American separation of church and state and religious pluralism, but the theory justifying such an approach matured only in the 1950s; it was finally accepted by the hierarchical church at the Second Vatican Council in 1965.

John Courtney Murray, a U.S. Jesuit, was the principal architect of the theory accepting religious freedom and the so-called separation of church and state.[8] (Note that the acceptance of the separation of church and state did not involve the separation of the church and society.) In the 1940s Murray had advocated intercreedal cooperation, or the working together of Catholics with all others, to bring about a greater peace and justice in the temporal society. To justify such cooperation Murray clearly distinguished between the supernatural order and the natural order, between the role of the church and the role of the state. In the supernatural order the Catholic Church rightly claims to be the one true church of Jesus Christ and does not permit any common worship, or *communicatio in sacris*. However, in the natural order the Catholic approach of natural law has recognized that all people share the same basic human nature and are therefore called to the same morality and should work together for the common good.[9] The defense of the separation of church and state likewise began with recognizing the distinction between the supernatural and the natural orders, the spiritual and the temporal.[10]

In Murray's earlier approach to justify intercreedal cooperation in the temporal and social realms and in his later defense of religious liberty, it was important to emphasize the differences between the supernatural and the natural orders and between the church and the state. In such a perspective any direct linkage between the supernatural order and the natural order was downplayed. Murray thus stressed Catholic distinctiveness and differences in the supernatural order but common ground and the cooperation of Catholics with all others in the temporal realm. In common with general Catholic social teaching, Murray himself before Vatican II saw no direct link between anthropology in general, with the important role of freedom called for in the temporal political order, and the anthropology and freedom required in the life of the church. Only in 1966 did Murray directly link through analogy the freedom in the political order with freedom in the realm of the church.[11] Why did both Murray and official Catholic social teaching see a direct link between the temporal order and the spiritual order in terms of their common understanding of the human only at the time of Vatican II?

One extremely significant change involved the overcoming of the supernatural-natural dichotomy, which had become almost a dualism in Catholic thought and practice. The Pastoral Constitution on the Church in the Modern World of Vatican II insisted that the gospel, grace, and the supernatural have to affect all reality.[12] Redemption is not limited only to the sphere of the supernatural and the church. The distinction between the two orders and the two realms of the supernatural and the natural had been used to prevent any direct linkage between ecclesiology and Catholic social teaching. The Pastoral Constitution insisted on the need to overcome the split between faith and daily life and to apply the gospel and God's grace to our life in the world (no. 43).

The most significant changes occurred in ecclesiology itself.[13] Vatican Council II accepted the notion of the church as always in need of reform. The principle of *aggiornamento*, or updating, included considering both the signs of the times and the historical sources. The structures of the present had developed and grown over time. The return to the sources and the needs of the present provided criteria for judging and reforming the existing structures and laws of the church.[14] The theological basis for reform came from eschatology. The church lives in the tension between the now and the future of the fullness of grace. The church is a pilgrim church. In the light of its eschatological fullness the church is never perfect and always in need of change and reform.

Vatican II recognized that the church is the people of God and not primarily the hierarchical structure, thus opening the door for rethinking the role of authority in the church. The church is the community of the baptized, the people of God animated by the Holy Spirit and served by the office holders in the church. Catholic ecclesiology before Vatican II had almost identified the church with the kingdom of God. Now the kingdom of God was seen as much broader than the church. The church is a sign of the kingdom, which in its eschatological fullness and even its contemporary reality is more than the church. The church is now seen in terms of its service to the kingdom and to the world. The church is not the be all and end all in itself, identified with the kingdom of God and served by all others.

In addition, Vatican II accepted a sacramental ecclesiology — the church is a sign of the kingdom. The sign must point out to others the presence of the kingdom. The church must show to others the meaning, dignity, and respect of the human person. The church as a sign helped pave the way for a reforming effort to make sure that the church was such a sign and beacon in our world.

All these changes brought about a more direct link between Catholic ecclesiology and Catholic social teaching. This connection was made very clear in the Pastoral Constitution on the Church in the Modern World: "Everything we have said about the dignity of the human person and about the human community and the profound meaning of human activity, lays the foundation for the relationship between the church and the world, and promotes the basis for the dialogue between them.... Thus the church, at once a visible assembly and a spiritual community, goes forward together with humanity and experiences the same earthly lot which the world does. She serves as a leaven and as a kind of soul for human society as it is to be renewed in Christ and transformed into God's family" (no. 40).

Since the church and the world are mutually related, there is a reciprocal relationship between them. One would expect the Pastoral Constitution on the Church in the Modern World to point out the help that the church tries to bring to human persons, society, and human activity. However, one paragraph (no. 44) also recognizes the help that the church receives from the modern world: "The church knows how richly she has profited by the history and development of humanity.... Thanks to the experience of past ages, the progress of the sciences, and the treasures hidden in the various forms of human culture, the nature of man himself [sic] is more clearly revealed and new roads to truth are opened.... Since the church has a visible and social structure as a sign of her unity in Christ, she can and ought to be enriched by the development of human social life" (no. 44). The dialogue and reciprocal relationship between church and world link the two and recognize that the church can and should learn from the world in its understanding, proclamation, and living as a human community.

Subsequent documents in official Catholic social teaching take up the same theme. In his *Sollicitudo Rei Socialis*, Pope John Paul II commemorated the twentieth anniversary of Pope Paul's encyclical, *Populorum Progressio* (1967) and quoted the phrase that the church is an "expert in humanity."[15] In a special way John Paul II has called attention to anthropology in both social teaching and ecclesiology. In *Redemptor Hominis*, his first encyclical, John Paul II emphasized that "man [sic] is the primary route that the church must travel in fulfilling her mission — he [sic] is the primary and fundamental way for the church...."[16] Catholic social teaching itself now recognizes a mutual relationship between ecclesiology and Catholic social teaching.

Specific Points That Can Be Learned

In the light of that direct link and relationship between ecclesiology and Catholic teaching this essay will now discuss the more important values and aspects that Catholic ecclesiology can learn from Catholic social teaching. One of the most distinctive characteristics of official Catholic social teaching in the last few decades has been the development that has taken place. Within Catholic social teaching one can readily see areas of continuity and of change. At the same time the methodology of Catholic social teaching has itself changed, even somewhat dramatically, in the one hundred years of modern official teaching. This section of the essay will consider aspects from three different areas where Catholic social teaching can provide helpful guidance to Catholic ecclesiology: continuing emphases in Catholic social teaching, newer developments, and a historically conscious methodology.

Continuing Emphases in Catholic Social Teaching

Two important continuing emphases in Catholic social teaching that are helpful and applicable to Catholic ecclesiology are the principles of subsidiarity and the subordination of authority to justice and truth.

Modern official Catholic social teaching has strongly insisted on the principle of subsidiarity. The principle was enunciated by Pope Pius XI in *Quadragesimo Anno* in 1931 and described as "a fundamental principle of social philosophy, fixed and unchangeable." The principle primarily delineates the proper role and function of government. One should not withdraw from individuals and give over to the community what individuals can accomplish by their own enterprise and activity. It is an injustice and a disturbance of right order to transfer to the larger and higher collectivity functions that can be performed by lesser and subordinate bodies. The government is a help (*subsidium*) that should enable individuals, voluntary groups, and smaller and more local governmental bodies to do what they can; and the larger unit of government should intervene only when the individuals, voluntary groups, and local governments are not able to deal with the issue.[17]

The principle of subsidiarity coheres with Catholic social teaching's attempt to avoid the two extremes of individualism and collectivism in its approach to political society. Individualism wants to restrict the role of government as much as possible and supports the axiom that the least government is the best government. Collectivism so extols the role of the collectivity that it subordinates all to the whole and takes over the rightful role of individuals, of voluntary associations, and of more local governments.

The very phrasing of the principle lent credence to some in the United States and elsewhere in the 1950s who were employing this principle to deny a larger role to government.[18] In 1961 Pope John XXIII in *Mater et Magistra* recognized the growing complexity and socialization (multiplication of social relationships) of modern life and the need for the federal government to intervene more than in the past to reduce imbalances in economic life and to bring about justice. The common good in these circumstances requires greater government involvement because only the federal government is big enough to deal with the complexity and the many aspects of the issues. However, John XXIII still strongly upholds the principle of subsidiarity itself.[19]

Can and should the principle of subsidiarity be applied in the church? The answer to both the can and the should questions is yes. The ecclesiology of Vatican II recognizes that too much emphasis has been given to the universal church and to the hierarchical leadership in the church. The church is primarily the people of God and not just the universal governing function in the church. Vatican II emphasizes the importance of the local church. The church is above all the church as the community of God gathered around the eucharistic banquet table. The universal church is a community of local churches. More importance is also given to the local or diocesan church and to the local bishop and the college of bishops.[20]

Especially in the light of the growing centralization in Roman Catholicism in the pre–Vatican II period, there is a great need for the principle of subsidiarity today. More emphasis must be given to local, national, and regional churches with the church universal truly exercising only a subsidiary function. The 1971 synod of bishops approved ten principles for the revision of the canon law of the church. The fifth principle stated that the principle of subsidiarity should be more broadly and completely applied to church legislation.[21] In the judgment of many the subsequent 1983 Code of Canon Law fails to put into practice the principle of subsidiarity. The new code is basically the same as the old with only a few comparatively peripheral changes. The consistent application of the principle of subsidiarity would call for a much more radical change.[22] The church will always experience the tension between the local and the universal; there are no easy or pat answers that will do away with these tensions. However, the recognition of growing diversities within the Catholic Church today and the ecumenical requirements of the time call for a much more thorough and complete application of the principle of subsidiarity to the life of the church.

Catholic social ethics and teaching have traditionally emphasized the primacy of justice and have seen the role of authority as discerning and ordering in accord with justice. Without doubt Catholic social teaching recognized an important role for authority. For many in the tradition monarchy was the accepted and best form of government. Recall that Catholic social ethics came into existence when monarchies of some type were the accepted form of government. One of the fascinating developments in the tradition has been the move toward the recognition of democracy as the best form of government. It was only beginning with the speeches of Pope Pius XII in the early 1940s in the midst of World War II that Catholic social teaching moved to support democratic forms of government as the best. An earlier approach had maintained that the forms of government could be diverse provided that they brought about justice for society.[23]

A later section will discuss this and other related developments in greater detail. For our present purposes I want to raise the question of how it was possible for Catholic social ethics in general and its official teaching to make this very significant change when in its history it had been strongly supportive of monarchies and in the nineteenth and early twentieth centuries had condemned liberal democracy. One of the significant factors making such a development possible was the approach taken to authority. Authority was never absolutized and was always subordinated to justice, human reason, and natural law.

In the Thomistic and Catholic traditions a just and well ordered society is governed by law. The eternal law is the plan of God for the world, whereas the natural law is the participation of the eternal law in the rational creature. Human reason reflecting on human nature can arrive at ethical wisdom and knowledge. Human law is an ordering of reason for the common good made by the one who has charge of the community. This human law either reiterates the principles of natural law or applies the natural law in changing circumstances. The natural law as based on human nature is universal and binding on all. In the changing historical and cultural circumstances of time and place, human law specifies the demands of the natural law. Thus, for example, the natural law argues that there should be progressive taxation but human law works out the precise details of this. The natural law would demand that people drive cars carefully and safely, but human or positive law fleshes out what is careful and safe in the different conditions. The purely human or positive law thus specifies the demands of the natural law.[24]

At first glance it would seem that a model based on law would give great emphasis and power to those in authority as the ones who make the law. The legislator or authority determines what is right or is to be done by all others. However, there are two characteristics of Catholic natural law theory that stand in the way of such an understanding. The first is the rational or intrinsic understanding of law in the Catholic tradition, and the second is the important role of mediation in Catholic theology and ethics. The intrinsic or rational aspect of law is prominent in the Thomistic tradition.[25] Human law is an ordering of reason for the common good made by the one who has charge of the community. Law is not primarily an act of the will but an act of reason. The legislator or authority must conform oneself to reason, justice, and the demands of the common good. The will of the legislator does not make something right or wrong. The most important virtue for the ruler is not power but wisdom — to know what is right, just, and helpful for the common good and to direct all people toward it.

Voluntaristic and extrinsic approaches to law have a very different perspective. If law is primarily an act of the will of the legislator, then the source of its obligation comes from the will of the ruler. Something is good because it is commanded. Note that the Catholic tradition is the opposite — something is commanded because it is good. A rational and intrinsic notion of law emphasizes that legislators or rulers must conform themselves to what is reasonable and just. The legislator is neither ultimate nor the last word.

The intrinsic and rational understandings of human law have other important ramifications. The Catholic tradition in theory has had no problem with the legitimacy of civil disobedience. Some have maintained that the Thomistic tradition too readily and easily accepts civil disobedience by simply maintaining that an unjust law is no law and does not oblige in conscience. Not only does Thomistic theory justify possible civil disobedience but it also sees the going against the letter of the law as a matter of virtue — the virtue of *epikeia*. By its very nature purely human law admits of exceptions because it is not based, as is natural law, on immutable and universal human nature (a very disputed point) but on changing historical and cultural circumstances. The legislator determines what is for the common good in the usual circumstances, but other circumstances can enter in and change the reality. In other words, the letter of the law can get in the way of its spirit. To go against the word of the law is not always wrong. In fact, *epikeia* is the crown of the virtue of legal justice, which at times calls for an individual to go against the letter of the law in order to achieve true justice and right ordering.[26]

The Catholic insistence on mediation sees human law as a mediation of natural law and natural law as a mediation of the eternal law. Thus the human lawgiver is not free to decide what the law should be. The human law is determined not primarily by the will of authority but by the plan of God, the natural law, and the concrete determination of what is best for the common good.

In Catholic political ethics the will of the ruler does not make something right or wrong. Yes, for a long time Catholic social ethics favored monarchies, but the monarch was never an absolute ruler. The monarch had to correspond to the demands of reason, justice, and the common good, which were the true basis of a just law. It is true that the older Catholic political theory stressed justice and right ordering at the expense of the freedom of the individual, but for the same basic reason it also severely limited the freedom of the ruler. Catholic social teaching has always insisted that rulers or lawgivers are not supreme but must conform themselves to the just, the reasonable, and the demands of the common good.

The same fundamental principles can and should hold for the church. Church authority does not make something true or right. Church authority must conform itself to the true and the right and the just. Church authority should be seen as a mediator and servant of God's grace and must conform itself to God's grace. Authoritarianism can never be accepted in the church. The Holy Spirit assists authority to discern more readily and surely what is the call of God and the needs of the church community. Vatican Council II proposed such an understanding of the hierarchical teaching office in the church. "This teaching office is not above the word of God but serves it, teaching only what has been handed on, listening to it devoutly, guarding it scrupulously, and explaining it faithfully by divine commission and with the help of the Holy Spirit; it draws from this one deposit of faith everything which it presents for belief as divinely revealed."[27] Authority in the church thus must always be exercised in this manner, recognizing that it is not the ultimate or the last word but itself is striving to discern and correspond to the word of God, the grace of the Holy Spirit, and the needs of the faith community here and now in these circumstances.[28]

Dramatic New Emphases in Official Catholic Social Teaching

Modern official Catholic social teaching as found in official church documents tends to emphasize continuity with the past. The rule was to cite only official church documents, Scripture, and earlier writings from the tradition, such as the fathers of the church or Thomas Aquinas. Only one of the 167 footnotes of the Pastoral Constitution on the Church in the Modern World refers to a contemporary book — a 1964 book on Galileo published by the Vatican Press.[29] Populorum Progressio in 1967 makes a decided shift since nine of the sixty-nine footnotes refer to contemporary publications. Seldom if ever have the documents explicitly recognized a change in the teaching or contrasted the newer teaching with the older teaching. However, in reality, very significant and deep changes have occurred in Catholic social teaching in the last century. For our purposes, here, the significant changes involve anthropology, the central criteria for judging a just social order, and the best form of government.

In Octogesima Adveniens in 1971, Pope Paul VI maintained: "Two aspirations persistently make themselves felt in these new contexts, and they grow stronger to the extent that human beings become better informed and better educated: the aspiration to equality and the aspiration to participation, two forms of human dignity and freedom."[30] The anthropology stressing freedom, equality, and participation becomes normative for the entire letter. Subsequent documents such as Pope John Paul II's Laborem Exercens and Sollicitudo Rei Socialis continue these emphases. Karol Wojtyla's earlier major philosophical treatise, The Acting Person, published originally in Polish in 1969 and in English in 1979, devotes the fourth and final part of the book to participation.[31]

The condemnations of freedom in nineteenth-century official Catholic social teaching are well known. This very negative attitude to freedom is found especially in the teachings of Pope Pius IX, but it is still present in the corpus of Pope Leo XIII, who began the tradition of modern official Catholic social teaching with Rerum Novarum in 1891. Many commemorations of Rerum Novarum occurred in 1991, and rightly so because this encyclical dealing with the rights of workers continues to ring true today. However, the contemporary church no longer celebrates or often cites the encyclicals of Leo XIII dealing primarily with the political order and the legal order. There were no celebrations in 1988 of the one hundredth anniversary of Leo's encyclical *Libertas Praestantissimum*, which dealt with freedom. This document was a strong denunciation of liberalism.

Pope Leo XIII in *Libertas Praestantissimum*, condemned "the modern liberties." The liberty of worship goes against the "chiefest and holiest" duty, which commands human beings to worship the one true God in the one true church. The theory calling for the separation of church and state is an "absurdity." Liberty of speech and of the press are condemned because the authority of the law must protect "the untutored multitude" from error and falsehood just as it protects the weak from violence inflicted by the powerful. Since the truth alone should imbue the human mind, the liberty of teaching is greatly opposed to reason and tends absolutely to pervert human minds inasmuch as it claims for itself the right of teaching whatever it pleases — a liberty that the state cannot grant without failing in its duty. The only way in which the liberty of conscience can be understood is the freedom to follow God's commands and to do one's duty.[32] Recall that it was only at Vatican Council II in 1965 that Roman Catholicism finally accepted religious freedom. Pope Leo XIII was no supporter of civil liberties and human freedom.

Leo's position on equality is very clear. His general discussions usually begin by recognizing that although there is a true equality insofar as all are children of God and called to eternal happiness, there is no equality in civil society and culture. "The inequality of rights and of power proceeds from the very Author of nature, 'from whom all paternity in heaven and earth is named.'"[33] The metaphor of the human body with its various organs and parts is used to justify the inequality that must exist in society: "But, as the abilities of all are not equal, as one differs from another in the powers of mind or body, and as there are many dissimilarities of manner, disposition, and character, it is most repugnant to reason to endeavor to confine all within the same measure and to extend complete equality to the institutions of civil life."[34]

There was no place for participation of the people in civil society and in the political order in Leo's understanding. The people were the "untutored multitude."[35] Authorities in society were called the rulers (*principes*). Leo's understanding of the political order was authoritarian or at best paternalistic. Religion "is wonderfully helpful to the state. For, since it derives the prime origin of all power directly from God himself, with grave authority it charges rulers to be mindful of their duty, to govern without injustice or severity, to rule their people kindly and with almost paternal charity; it admonishes subjects to be obedient to lawful authority, as to the ministers of God; and it binds them to their rulers, not merely by obedience, but by reverence and affection, forbidding all seditions and venturesome enterprises calculated to disturb public order and tranquility."[36]

Thus there has been a most significant change in the anthropology found in official Catholic social teaching since the time of Pope Leo XIII in the latter part of the nineteenth century until today. Above all these changes have seen a strong contemporary emphasis on freedom, equality, and participation as essential characteristics of the human person today. In contemporary Catholic social teaching David Hollenbach refers to "an astounding development" whereby human rights has become "a prime focus" of official Catholic social teaching."[37] J. Bryan Hehir maintains that the "principal way in which John Paul II addresses the social questions is through human rights categories."[38]

In the eighteenth and nineteenth centuries official Catholic teaching strongly opposed "The Rights of Man" as associated especially with the French Revolution. Human rights by definition are intimately connected with human freedom. Recall the general opposition of Catholicism to these freedoms in the nineteenth century. It was only at the Second Vatican Council in 1965 that Catholics finally accepted the right to religious freedom. In the nineteenth century Catholic emphasis fell on law and duties but not on rights.[39] *Pacem in Terris* in 1963 gives the first full-blown discussion of human rights in official Catholic social teaching.[40] Since then human rights have become a central criterion in judging the justice of existing social systems.

The Pastoral Constitution on the Church in the Modern World of Vatican II recognized the "profound changes" that have occurred in the political order. The document then goes on to affirm the role of democratic structures:

It is in full accord with human nature that juridical-political structures should, with ever better success and without any discrimination, afford all their citizens the chance to participate freely and actively in establishing the constitutional bases of a political community, governing the state, determining the scope and purpose of various institutions, and choosing leaders.... Let the rights of all persons, families, and associations along with the exercise of those rights be recognized, honored, and fostered. The same holds for those duties which bind all citizens.[41]

Today there seems to be nothing startling about such a statement, but in the eighteenth and nineteenth centuries Catholicism strongly opposed the emergence of democracies. As late as the twentieth century the Vatican entered into concordats or treaties with the governments of both Mussolini and Hitler. Catholic teaching often insisted that it was indifferent to the forms of government. The first official praise of democracy as the best form of government came with the Christmas addresses of Pope Pius XII in the 1940s.[42]

What explains these changes that have occurred in a comparatively short period of time in these three aspects of official Catholic social teaching? One very significant and overarching factor for acceptance of these particular changes was the church's response to the challenge of liberalism. Over the course of time it came to accept many aspects of liberalism, but not all. Liberalism is too closely connected with a one-sided individualism. Thus, for example, in finally accepting human rights Catholic teaching insists on both political and economic rights. Liberalism was strong on political and civil rights but weak on economic and social rights. Catholic social teaching today has accepted, obviously with some modifications, what it had strongly opposed a century or more ago. Yes, the church should not uncritically accept any movement, but all must admit that the church has learned from liberalism, even while criticizing some aspects of it.[43]

Catholic ecclesiology can and must learn from these dramatic changes in official Catholic social teaching. I admit that the church and the political order are not exactly the same, but there are definite similarities and congruencies, especially in the light of the fact that the church is a sign of the presence of the reign of God and looks forward to the future fulfillment of that reign. I have purposely not spoken only of democracy in this section but have stressed the developments in anthropology, the criteria of a just society, and the best form of the political order. These three are intimately connected, with anthropology being the most general and democracy the most specific of the concepts. Since the church now understands itself as an expert in humanity, this anthropology must be proclaimed and lived by the church itself. Freedom, equality, and participation must become more evident and be promoted and protected in the life of the church, if it is truly to carry out its function as an expert in humanity. Today, Catholic ecclesiology must incorporate and promote the contemporary Catholic approaches to anthropology found in official Catholic social teaching.

Human rights as a central criterion of justice can and should be present in the church itself. Yes, these rights will not be exactly the same as rights in the political order, but they must enshrine and defend the same basic values. Canonists in the last few decades have called for a bill of rights that would be part of the constitution of the church. The official documents guiding the work of the revision of canon law made the safeguarding of rights one of its ten guiding principles. Pope Paul VI had originally called for a first section or "fundamental law of the church," which would be a constitutional statement including the rights of the people of God. However, the fundamental law was ultimately scuttled and never saw the light of day.[44] The 1983 Code of Canon Law has a section on the rights of the faithful (canons 208–23), but in my judgment the rights presented in this section are very inadequate.[45]

The Catholic Church can and should learn from democratic forms of government. These forms incorporate the anthropological concerns and the human rights emphasis mentioned above. Since the church is primarily the people of God, it is open to learning from truly democratic societies. It is beyond the scope of this paper to point out exactly what democracy in the Catholic Church should look like. Many other authors such as Dennis McCann in the United States, Edward Schillebeeckx in Europe, and Leonardo Boff in South America have addressed these issues.[46]

Some have objected that this emphasis on freedom, equality, participation, human rights, and democracy is an attempt to Americanize the church. This is not true. Recall that these emphases are found in the official documents of the universal teaching authority of the church and do not come just from American documents. Many theologians and canonists from outside the United States have also been advocating a more free, equal, participative, and just church. Rosemary Ruether, an American who has called for a greater democratization of the church, has also been very critical of many social, cultural, economic, and political institutions in the United States.[47] To be true to its own mission, function, and purpose, the Catholic Church must be more open to incorporate into its structures the anthropology, criteria of justice, and form of government mentioned here.

A Historically Conscious Methodology

As the last section has pointed out, very significant substantive changes have occurred in official Catholic social teaching. Substance, however, is intimately connected with method. These substantive changes point to an underlying methodological change in official Catholic social teaching, which developed in the last few decades.

In my judgment the more recent official documents of Catholic social teaching have adopted a more historically conscious methodology, as distinguished from the classicism of the earlier documents in this tradition. Classicism tends to think in terms of the eternal, the immutable, and the unchanging, whereas historical consciousness recognizes continuity and discontinuity but gives importance to the particular, the individual, the contingent, and the changing. While classicism employs a deductive approach, historical consciousness sees a greater but not absolute role for inductive reasoning.[48]

These contrasting methodologies can be readily illustrated from the documents themselves. Pope Pius XI's 1931 encyclical, *Quadragesimo Anno*, called in English "On Reconstructing the Social Order," proposes a general plan or blueprint that he thought had universal validity and was to be applied to the whole world. The methodology of *Quadragesimo Anno* is decidedly deductive.[49] Forty years later in 1971 Pope Paul VI in *Octogesima Adveniens* recognizes the diversity of situations in the contemporary world: "In the face of such widely varying situations it is difficult for us to utter a unified message and to put forward a solution which has universal validity. Such is not our ambition, nor is it our mission. It is up to the Christian communities to analyze with objectivity the situation which is proper to their own country, to shed on it the light of the gospel's unalterable words, and to draw principles of reflection, norms of judgment, and directives for action from the social teaching of the church."[50] Notice how such an approach recognizes both continuities and discontinuities.

The dramatic substantive changes outlined in the previous section could have occurred only because official Catholic teaching adopted a more historically conscious methodology. In the process Catholic social teaching was able to change its approach to freedom, equality, participation, human rights, and democratic forms of government. A truly historically conscious approach will not merely accept or canonize what is happening here and now but will critically evaluate the present in the light of the past and of the future. The Christian perspective thus gives great significance to the scriptural witness, the tradition, and the future eschatological fullness as God's gracious gift as well as to the signs of the times. The pilgrim church in its ongoing life learns from what is happening in the world, but at the same time it is always ready to oppose and criticize what stands in the way of the gospel and the reign of God.

Catholic ecclesiology can and should learn from official Catholic social teaching and from other sources to employ on a regular basis a more historically conscious methodology. In reality the reforms of Vatican II came about because of a more historically conscious methodology at work. The existing church structures were criticized and reformed in the light of Scripture, tradition, the signs of the times, and the coming of the reign of God.[51] Once again such a historically conscious methodology will not uncritically canonize all that is occurring today. However, such an approach can and should learn from the contemporary historical realities that Vatican II referred to as the signs of the times. A more rigorously consistent historically conscious methodology in ecclesiology will share with official Catholic social teaching the importance of freedom, equality, participation, basic human rights, and democratic forms of government.

In conclusion Catholic ecclesiology can and should learn from official Catholic social teaching. This essay has pointed out some very important substantive and methodological approaches that will enable ecclesiology to make the church more truly a sign and servant both of humanity and of the reign of God.

Notes

1. Andrew M. Greeley, *The Catholic Myth: The Behavior and Beliefs of American Catholics* (New York: Scribner, 1990); David Tracy, *The Analogical Imagination: Christian Theology and the Culture of Pluralism* (New York: Crossroad, 1981).

2. For a very helpful contemporary summary and overview of Catholic ecclesiology, see Richard P. McBrien, *Catholicism*, study ed. (Minneapolis: Winston, 1981), 567–729.

3. Ladislas Orsy, "Title I: Ecclesiastical Laws (cc. 7–22)," in James A. Coriden,

Thomas J. Green, and Donald E. Heintschel, eds., *The Code of Canon Law: A Text and Commentary* (New York: Paulist, 1985), 34ff.

4. *Justitia in Mundo*, in David M. Byers, ed., *Justice in the Marketplace: Collected Statements of the Vatican and United States Catholic Bishops on Economic Policy, 1891–1984* (Washington, D.C.: United States Catholic Conference, 1985), 257–58.

5. National Conference of Catholic Bishops, *Economic Justice for All: Pastoral Letter on Catholic Social Teaching and the United States Economy* (Washington, D.C.: United States Catholic Conference, 1986), 174, no. 347.

6. Ibid., 179, no. 358.

7. Marcellinus Zalba, *Theologiae Moralis Summa II: Theologia Moralis Specialis, Tractatus de Mandatis Dei et Ecclesiae* (Madrid: Biblioteca de Autores Cristianos, 1953), 199ff.

8. Important studies of John Courtney Murray include the following: Donald E. Pelotte, *John Courtney Murray: Theologian in Conflict* (New York: Paulist, 1976); J. Leon Hooper, *The Ethics of Discourse: The Social Philosophy of John Courtney Murray* (Washington, D.C.: Georgetown University, 1986); Robert W. McElroy, *The Search for an American Public Theology: The Contribution of John Courtney Murray* (New York: Paulist, 1989).

9. John Courtney Murray, "Current Theology: Christian Co-operation," *Theological Studies* 3 (1942): 413–31; "Current Theology: Co-operation, Some Further Views," *Theological Studies* 4 (1943): 110–11; "Current Theology: Intercredal Co-operation: Its Theory and Its Organization," *Theological Studies* 4 (1943): 267–86; "On the Problem of Co-operation: Some Clarifications, Reply to Father P. H. Furfey," *American Ecclesiastical Review* 112 (1945): 194–214.

10. John Courtney Murray, *The Problem of Religious Freedom* (Westminster, Md.: Newman, 1965), 28.

11. John Courtney Murray, "Freedom, Authority, Community," *America* 115 (1966): 592–93; see Hooper, *The Ethics of Discourse*, 184ff.

12. The Pastoral Constitution on the Church in the Modern World, Part I, nos. 11–45, in Walter M. Abbott, ed., *The Documents of Vatican II* (New York: Guild, 1966), 209–48. For a discussion of this development in official Catholic social teaching, see my *Directions in Catholic Social Ethics* (Notre Dame, Ind.: University of Notre Dame, 1985), 43–69.

13. For a succinct and very helpful delineation of the new vision of the church in society proposed by Vatican II, see Richard P. McBrien, "The Future Role of the Church in American Society," in Leslie Griffin, ed., *Religion and Politics* (Notre Dame, Ind.: Review of Politics, n.d.), 87–101. The following paragraphs summarize some of McBrien's six theses elaborated in this article.

14. John W. O'Malley, *Tradition and Transition: Historical Perspectives on Vatican II* (Wilmington, Del.: Michael Glazier, 1989).

15. Pope John Paul II, *Redemptor Hominis*, no. 14, in Byers, *Justice in the Marketplace*, 281.

16. See J. Bryan Hehir, "John Paul II: Continuity and Change in Social Teaching," in Charles E. Curran and Richard A. McCormick, eds., *Readings in Moral Theology No. 5: Official Catholic Social Teaching* (New York: Paulist, 1986), 253–55.

17. Pope Pius XI, *Quadragesimo Anno*, nos. 17, 18, in Terence P. McLaughlin,

ed., *The Church and the Reconstruction of the Modern World: The Social Encyclicals of Pius XI* (Garden City, N.Y.: Doubleday Image, 1957), 246–47.

18. See Benjamin L. Masse, *Justice for All: An Introduction to the Social Teaching of the Catholic Church* (Milwaukee: Bruce, 1964), 77.

19. Pope John XXIII, *Mater et Magistra*, nos. 54–58, in Byers, *Justice in the Marketplace*, 115.

20. Patrick Granfield, *The Limits of the Papacy: Authority and Autonomy in the Church* (New York: Crossroad, 1987), 107–33.

21. John A. Alesandro, "General Introduction," in Coriden, Green, Heintschel, *The Code of Canon Law*, 6.

22. Knut Walf, "The New Canon Law — the Same Old System," in Hans Küng and Leonard Swidler, eds., *The Church in Anguish: Has the Vatican Betrayed Vatican II?* (San Francisco: Harper & Row, 1987), 91–105.

23. Paul Sigmund, "The Catholic Tradition and Modern Democracy," in Griffin, *Religion and Politics*, 3–21.

24. Thomas Aquinas, *Summa Theologiae,* Ia–IIae (Rome: Marietti, 1952), qq. 90–97, 410–23.

25. For a more complete discussion of the meaning and ramifications of an intrinsic or rational approach to law, see John Mahoney, *The Making of Moral Theology: A Study of the Roman Catholic Tradition* (Oxford: Clarendon, 1987), 224–58.

26. Édouard Hamel, "La vertù d' épikie," *Sciénces Ecclesiastiques* 13 (1961): 35–56.

27. Dogmatic Constitution on Divine Revelation, no. 10, in Abbott, *Documents of Vatican II*, 118.

28. The literature on authority in the church is immense. For a very competent overview, see Thomas P. Rausch, *Authority and Leadership in the Church: Past Directions and Future Possibilities* (Wilmington, Del.: Glazier, 1989).

29. Pastoral Constitution on the Church in the Modern World, no. 36, fn. 100, in Abbott, *Documents of Vatican II*, 234. Note that the Abbott edition adds unofficial footnotes to the document. The official footnote number is 62.

30. Pope Paul VI, *Octogesima Adveniens*, no. 22, in Byers, *Justice in the Marketplace*, 234–35.

31. Cardinal Karol Wojtyla, *The Acting Person* (Boston: D. Reidel, 1979), 261–300.

32. Pope Leo XIII, "On Human Liberty" (*Libertas Praestantissimum*), nos. 18–30, in Etienne Gilson, ed., *The Church Speaks to the Modern World: The Social Teachings of Leo XIII* (Garden City, N.Y.: Doubleday Image, 1954), 69–76.

33. Pope Leo XIII, "On Socialism" (*Quod Apostolici Muneris*), in Gilson, *The Church Speaks to the Modern World*, 193.

34. Pope Leo XIII, "On Freemasonry" (*Humanum Genus*), no. 26, in Gilson, *The Church Speaks to the Modern World*, 130.

35. Pope Leo XIII, "On Human Liberty" (*Libertas Praestantissimum*), no. 23, in Gilson, *The Church Speaks to the Modern World*, 72.

36. Pope Leo XIII, "On Human Liberty" (*Libertas Praestantissimum*), no. 22, in Gilson, *The Pope Speaks to the Modern World*, 22–23.

37. David Hollenbach, *Justice, Peace, and Human Rights: American Catholic Social Ethics in a Pluralistic World* (New York: Crossroad, 1988), 87.

38. Hehir, "John Paul II: Continuity and Change," in *Readings in Moral Theology No. 5*, 260. See Otfried Höffe et al., *Jean Paul II et les droits de l'homme* (Fribourg: Editions Universitaires, 1980).

39. Fr. Refoulé, "L'Église et les libertés de Léon XIII à Jean XXIII," *Le Supplément* 125 (1978): 243–59.

40. Pope John XXIII, *Pacem in Terris*, nos. 11–45, in Byers, *Justice in the Marketplace*, 152–59.

41. Pastoral Constitution on the Church in the Modern World, no. 75, in Abbott, *Documents of Vatican II*, 285, 286.

42. Sigmund, in Griffin, *Religion and Politics*, 3–21.

43. Rosemary Radford Ruether, *Contemporary Roman Catholicism: Crises and Challenges* (Kansas City, Mo.: Sheed and Ward, 1987), 1–23.

44. James A. Coriden, "A Challenge: Making the Rights Real," in Leonard Swidler and Herbert O'Brien, eds., *A Catholic Bill of Rights* (Kansas City, Mo.: Sheed and Ward, 1988), 7–32. This book serves as a commentary on the "Charter of the Rights of Catholics in the Church" proposed in 1983 by the Association for the Rights of Catholics in the Church (ARCC).

45. See my *Toward an American Catholic Moral Theology* (Notre Dame, Ind.: University of Notre Dame Press, 1987), 161–69.

46. Dennis P. McCann, *New Experiment in Democracy: The Challenge for American Catholicism* (Kansas City, Mo.: Sheed and Ward, 1987); Edward Schillebeeckx, *The Church: The Human Story of God* (New York: Crossroad, 1991); Leonardo Boff, *Church, Charism, and Power: Liberation Theology and the Institutional Church* (New York: Crossroad, 1985).

47. Ruether, *Contemporary Roman Catholicism*, 24–75.

48. Richard M. Gula, *Reason Informed by Faith: Foundations of Catholic Morality* (New York: Paulist, 1989), 30–39.

49. Pope Pius XI, *Quadragesimo Anno*, in McLaughlin, *The Church and the Reconstruction of the Modern World*, 219–78.

50. Pope Paul VI, *Octogesima Adveniens*, no. 4, in Byers, *Justice in the Marketplace*, 225.

51. O'Malley, *Tradition and Transition*, 44–125.

JAY P. DOLAN

–6–

The Desire for Democracy
in the American Catholic Church

The history of American Catholicism clearly indicates that the desire for democracy in the church is not a recent phenomenon. It first surfaced in the aftermath of the American Revolution, an era that historians have labelled the age of democracy, and it remained popular through much of the nineteenth century. Throughout these decades many Catholics desired that the spirit of democracy shape the government of the local church so that leadership in the church would be more democratic or populist and less clerical or aristocratic. Historically this is what comprised the desire for democracy in American Catholicism until very recently. It was a quest for a democratic form of government at the level of the local church. Even though this democratic thrust was primarily political in nature, namely the government of the local church, it clearly had theological implications. In becoming involved in local church politics and advocating a more democratic form of government, people were endorsing a distinct model of church for the local community.

What was only implied in the pre–Vatican II era became very explicit after the council when a new theology of church emerged that was much more democratic and populist than the model of church endorsed at the First Vatican Council. A new theological agenda replaced the older political agenda as the desire for democracy went far beyond the issue of local church government.

Although the search for democracy began in the republican era, 1780–1820, important precedents were established in the colonial period. The Jesuits were an integral part of the Maryland settlement from its founding in 1634, and a major concern of theirs was to gain a privileged position in the colony. They wanted to reproduce the type of church-state relationship that prevailed in the Old World, a situation in which religion legally enjoyed a special place in society and the church and its clergy were invested with a privileged status. Cecil Calvert, the founder of the colony, strongly opposed this, and after a decade of bitter wrangling the Jesuits gave in and accepted the authority of Calvert and the New World arrangement between church and state. This meant that the clergy would enjoy no special privileges from the government, and they would have to support themselves financially.

With the Glorious Revolution of William and Mary in 1688–89 the rule of the Catholic Calvert family was overthrown and the Church of England became the established religion in Maryland. This further diminished the prestige of the clergy and the church, since being a Catholic in Maryland now became a liability rather than an asset. Until the Revolution of 1776 Maryland Catholicism remained a small religious sect, politically disenfranchised and religiously suspect. The clergy did not know the meaning of privilege and power, and the idea of having a bishop in the colony was out of the question. With the Revolution of 1776 and the writing of the Constitution Americans officially severed the relationship between church and state. Henceforth, no denomination would enjoy special privileges. All churches were on their own.

The significance of this colonial tradition is twofold. First, it underscores a major theme in American religious history, adaptation. When various religious traditions came to the New World as part of the cultural baggage of the immigrants, they underwent significant adaptations. The people who first settled this land as well as those who came after them would have to adapt the patterns of the past to the challenges presented by the American geographical, social, and political environment. This was as true for Protestants and Jews as it was for Catholics. Secondly, when Catholics began to organize themselves after the Revolution they did not have to contend with a time-honored tradition of a privileged clergy and church as was true in the Old World. The idea of the church as a clerical preserve was not part of the colonial heritage, and the absence of a bishop undercut the tradition of monarchical rule in the church. For this reason it would be much easier for Catholics to graft the spirit of democracy onto the church during the period of organization that took place after the Revolution.

The American Revolution marked the beginning of a new era in world history. Historians have labelled it the age of democracy, and its effects are still being felt in the closing decade of the twentieth century. On one side of 1776 was an age of privilege and deference. The aristocratic values of English society with its kings and lords were visible throughout all the colonies, but most especially in the South. In Virginia the greater ruled over the lesser. The well-to-do planter lived in a home distinguished not only by its size, but also by its elaborate ornaments and orderly design. The tailored dress of the privileged set them apart, and English soldiers paraded about in colorful uniforms. Even the churches reflected the values of old England. Built of brick they were imposing structures, fitting for the established Church of England, which enjoyed the support and protection of the local government. The design of the church mirrored this ordered society. People sat according to their rank in society, and the pulpit, the clergyman's perch, towered above all. A formal liturgy "read in the midst of a community ranged in order of precedence, continuously evoked postures of deference and submission. Liturgy and church plan thus readily combined to offer a powerful representation of a structured, hierarchical community."[1]

Then came the Revolution. It was a revolution of mind as well as a war for independence. The world was turned upside down, and a new nation appeared. Privilege and deference were cast aside. Freedom, independence, and equality became cherished values of the new republic. Shunning the type of dress worn by English soldiers, patriots donned hunting shirts and took up arms to fight against the king. Deference vanished and the prerogatives of privilege no longer counted for much. The will of the people became supreme, and the people's choice occupied the seats of power.

Rank in society counted for little in the new evangelical churches that appeared during this period, and plain tables set in the midst of the congregation replaced ornamented and elevated pulpits. People sensed that a "new order of the ages" had arrived, and this Latin phrase (*novus ordo saeclorum*) became part of the nation's seal. By the turn of the century a new type of person had stepped onto the world stage, a republican, one who had inherited "a revolutionary legacy in a world ruled by aristocrats and kings."[2]

This transitional age transformed American Christianity in the same manner that it changed American political life. In religion as in politics the people's choice became determinative. People sought to gain control over their own destiny, spiritual as well as political. Thus, they cast aside any monopoly that sought to control their eternal life; in Virginia this meant an end to the established church and the beginning of religious freedom for all people. Heaven was democratized and salvation now became a possibility for all of God's children, not just the Calvinist elect.

In this new atmosphere people "wanted their leaders unpretentious, their doctrines self-evident and down-to-earth, their music lively and singable, their churches in local hands. It was this upsurge of democratic hope," wrote historian Nathan Hatch, "that characterised so many religious cultures in the early republic and brought Baptists, Methodists, Disciples and a host of other insurgent groups to the fore. The rise of evangelical Christianity in the early republic is, in some measure, a story of the success of common people in shaping the culture after their own priorities rather than those outlined by gentlemen such as the Founding Fathers."[3] This democratic contagion infected people everywhere, and it changed the landscape of American religion. It created a spirit of populism that left an indelible imprint on religion in America, as evangelical fervor and ritual informality replaced decorum and formality. The people's choice, not the preacher's prerogative, became determinative.

This new populist spirit in religion affected all denominations. It was the driving force behind the growth and expansion of Methodism; it gave birth to the Disciples of Christ and was a major reason for the popularity of Joseph Smith and the founding of the Mormon church. It shaped the organization of Jewish synagogues as Jews sought to declare their rights and privileges. This passion for democracy also permeated the Catholic community. Where this was most visible was in the government of the local parish.

The vital element in the development of American Catholicism was the parish. Between 1780 and 1820 many parish communities were organized across Catholic America. Perhaps as many as 124 Catholic churches dotted the landscape in 1820, and each one represented a community of Catholics. In the vast majority of these communities laymen were very involved in the government of the parish as members of a board of trustees. The principal reason for such a trustee system was the new spirit of democracy that was rising across the land.

At that moment in history the traditional understanding of authority was being questioned in a variety of places. In France, Ireland, and the United States people were redefining the meaning of authority and coming up with a much more democratic understanding of how authority should be exercised in society. Such questioning ushered in the democratic age. Much like the civil rights movement of the 1950s and 1960s this democratic awakening touched people everywhere, in Paris, France, as well as Bardstown, Kentucky. It changed the lives of kings as well as farmers. In Catholic communities it meant that laypeople wanted to have more control over their parish churches.

In emphasizing the influence of the democratic spirit on the Catholic parish it is well to remember that tradition played a very important role in this development. When they fashioned a democratic design for parish government, American Catholics were attempting to blend the old with the new, the past with the present. The establishment of a trustee system was not a break with the past, as they understood it, but a continuation of past practices adapted to a new environment. Nor were they wrong in their arguments. Lay participation in church government was an accepted practice in France and Germany; English and Irish lay Catholics were also becoming more involved in parish government. Thus, when they were forced to defend their actions against opponents of the lay trustee system, the trustees appealed to the Catholic tradition and longstanding precedents for such involvement. This blending of the old with the new captured the meaning of the Catholic heritage and enabled the people to adapt an ancient tradition to the circumstances of an emerging new society.

The first step in establishing a lay trustee type of parish government was to select the trustees. This took place in a very American manner, by election. Elections would take place each year to select the board of trustees. Only those people who rented pews in the church were eligible to vote; this meant that white males over the age of twenty-one and of some financial means were the only people that voted. Though the trustee system could vary from parish to parish, two types were popular prior to 1820. In one type laymen were in control, and the clergy were looked upon as hired servants of the parish. The clergy worked for the board and were subject to the trustees' wishes. The trustees hired them and the trustees could also fire them. This system in which lay trustees had exclusive control over parish affairs was in operation in such cities as New Orleans, Philadelphia, Buffalo, New York, and Norfolk, Virginia. The other model explicitly provided for the participation of the clergy on the board of trustees and made them *ex officio* members of the board. This type of arrangement was found in parishes in Philadelphia, Baltimore, Boston, and Detroit.

An important aspect of lay trusteeism was the separation between the temporal and the spiritual realms. The American tradition of the separation of church and state that developed in this democratic age affected the nature of local church government. Lay trustees were responsible for what they described as "temporal concerns." In other words, they were the parish business managers and their major concern was financial: collection of pew rents, purchasing an organ, selling gravesites in the parish cemetery, determining the salary of the priest, and paying off debts. They also supervised the work of those who worked for the parish such as the organist and the priest. The priest was responsible for the church's spiritual affairs. When the priest and the trustees did not agree on some issue, be it salary or the quality of preaching, then conflict did occur and it could be very bitter and prolonged. But as Patrick Carey, the recognized authority on this issue noted, such conflict took place in relatively few Catholic parishes.[4]

In the vast majority of the one hundred or more parishes in the country at this time the trustee system worked well, and it remained the people's choice for local church government. While it is true that there were European precedents for lay involvement in parish government, the primary influence in the adoption of the trustee system was the democratic spirit that was surging through the nation at this time.

Roman Catholicism was a religion of the Old World. Many Catholic immigrants, as well as those born and raised in the land that was to become the United States, recognized the contrast between the European tradition of Catholicism and the American style of independence and freedom. They realized that there was a need for the Roman Catholic church to adapt itself to the American situation. They were not talking about Catholic dogma or religious beliefs, but the way that the church operated through its bishops and clergy. Mathew Carey, an Irish immigrant and a prominent Philadelphia Catholic at this time, believed that the Irish clergy in particular had to adapt to American culture. In Ireland, he wrote, "too frequently the relations between the pastor and his flock partake of the nature of extravagantly high toned authority on the one side and servile submission on the other."

In the United States people would not accept this. As Carey put it, "This people never will submit to the regime in civil or ecclesiastical affairs that prevails in Europe." As regards the hierarchy, he observed that "an overweening idea of the extent of episcopal authority is not suited to this meridian." [5] In the United States the European monarchical tradition was no longer acceptable; as Carey put it, "a different order of things prevails in this country."[6] Catholics in New Orleans made the same point when they petitioned the state legislature to enact a law that would force the bishop "to govern the Catholic church here in accordance with the spirit of our national customs and political institutions."[7] This need for adaptation was paramount in the minds of Catholics across the country.

In desiring to have the church adapt to American culture Catholics wanted Roman Catholicism to be more in step with the times and incorporate some of the democratic spirit that was blowing across the landscape. In doing so they believed that they would be establishing "a National American Church with liberties consonant to the spirit of government under which they live." The way that this could happen would be to adopt what they called "republican" principles in the government of the local church.[8] In doing this they endorsed four major principles of the American democratic experience — the sovereignty of the people, popular elections, religious freedom, and a written constitution.

In the old country the will of the monarch was sovereign; in the New World the will of the people was supreme. One of the more popular slogans of the day was "the voice of the people is the voice of God." Catholic trustees appropriated this maxim and applied it to the church. "Is it wise," asked a Philadelphia Catholic, "is it prudent, that those whose voice is law in everything else, should be made to feel, that in that very thing, in which they are most deeply interested they have no voice at all?"[9] The way that the voice of the people would be heard would be through elections. They were considered a natural right and a natural consequence of popular sovereignty. In advocating elections in the church, trustees included not just election of trustees, but also the election of pastors and bishops.

Freedom or what was often described as "the spirit of independence" was another principle advocated by Catholics. As Mathew Carey noted, the freedom exercised in the civil realm "has produced a corresponding independent spirit respecting our church affairs."[10] This meant that the European style of absolutism and the arbitrary exercise of authority were not suited to the American scene. Independent as Americans they also wanted to be independent as Catholics. This did not mean casting off "the spiritual supremacy of the Apostolic See," as a Philadelphia trustee put it, but keeping it "as the bond of a federal union, not as the yoke of a servile dependency."[11]

The final republican principle was the need for a written constitution. Constitution writing had a long heritage in the Anglo-Saxon tradition and was very much in vogue in the republican era. From the federal level to the local level people engaged in the process of writing a constitution. In Scott County, Kentucky, a group of Catholics organized themselves into a religious society in 1806, and one of the first steps they took was to draw up a constitution. Described as a "Republican Constitution," it had a preamble and set of articles that sought to regulate and define the government of the local church in Scott County.[12] Such a constitution was to serve as a protection against the arbitrary use of authority by incorporating certain checks and balances into the government of the local church. By establishing a balance of power the likelihood of conflict would be diminished. Moreover, a constitution spelled out the areas of responsibility for both clergy and laity, giving to one the responsibility for the spiritual and to the other the responsibility for the temporal. Such constitutions were commonplace in Catholic America in the early years of settlement.

These four principles — the sovereignty of the people, popular elections, religious freedom, and a written constitution — provided the rationale for the trustee system in the American Catholic community. Very American and clearly republican, they showed how much democratic thought had permeated the Catholic community.

The widespread acceptance of the trustee form of parish government during the republican era was not without its problems. The most troublesome issue centered about the right to appoint and dismiss the parish priest. Some trustees and clergy asserted that this right rested with the laypeople. John Carroll, the first bishop of Baltimore (1790–1815), adamantly opposed this point of view, stating that the bishop alone possessed the final authority in such decisions. These disputes became very bitter at times and lasted for years, not months. The Germans in Baltimore carried on a bitter battle against Carroll for more than a decade, and in Charleston the Irish locked horns with him over this issue of authority.

As adamant as Carroll was in defending this aspect of ecclesiastical authority, he was equally consistent in supporting the concept of the trustee system. For him it was not a question of tolerating a bad idea, but of actively supporting a concept of the church that endorsed democracy in the government of the local church. In doing so he recognized the need of the church to adapt to the American situation. His episcopal contemporaries, Benedict Flaget of Bardstown, Kentucky, and Jean Cheverus of Boston, concurred in this position and supported the people in their efforts to organize parishes governed by lay trustees.

There were others, however, who thought otherwise; the best known opponents of the trustee system were Carroll's auxiliary bishop, Leonard Neale, and the pioneer priest of Kentucky, Stephen Badin. These men, along with other clergy and laity, viewed the church in a more monarchical manner, as a church that, in Neale's words, "places the clergyman over the vestrymen whom he appoints and dismisses at will."[13] Despite such a hard-line attitude among some clerics, the idea of the trustee system was not to be denied, and it remained the most popular form of local church government during the first quarter of the nineteenth century.

The most ambitious and comprehensive example of lay trusteeism was in the southern regions of Virginia and the Carolinas in the 1820s and 1830s. Led by their Irish-born bishop, John England, Catholics in this region fashioned an elaborate system of church government. The centerpiece of this was a written diocesan constitution. It provided for periodic conventions of Catholics where clergy and people discussed the needs of Catholic life in the region, and it spelled out the nature of the trustee system that each parish adopted. For John England, whom his contemporaries described as a "republican" Catholic, this system of church government sought to achieve a situation in which, as he put it, "the laity are empowered to cooperate but not to dominate."[14]

Like John Carroll, England had an understanding of the church that incorporated democratic ideas. But by the 1830s he was very much alone in this regard. The enthusiasm for democracy that characterized the early years of the American republic had waned by this time. In Rome the papacy was regaining strength and prestige after the humiliation endured during the Napoleonic era. The popes of this era were opposed to such modern political ideas as democracy and clearly endorsed the traditional, monarchical model of the church. England's colleagues in the American hierarchy were as traditional as the pope when it came to democracy in the church. When they gathered together in 1829 at their first national meeting, they passed legislation aimed at weakening the lay trustee system and strengthening the authority of the bishop. This marked the first concerted effort of the American hierarchy to establish clerical control over the government of the local church. Throughout the rest of the nineteenth century they continually sought to strengthen their position in this regard.

The republican period, 1780 to 1820, encouraged the development of a new model of the church in which democracy was acceptable. It challenged the traditional monarchical model of the church and gained wide support. Given the scarcity of clergy at this time and the underdeveloped nature of the church's bureaucracy, such a model of church that encouraged lay involvement in the government of the local parish made sense. As Catholics moved into a new era of their history, the immigrant period, the democratic model of church did not vanish. Each wave of new immigrants sought to organize parishes around a democratic model of church that would allow for lay involvement in the government of the parish in much the same manner that was operative in the republican period. This view of the church continually challenged the dominance of the traditional, monarchical model. A major issue in the history of the immigrant church was the struggle that went on in local communities between supporters of these opposing views of the church.

Religion was central to the organization of the immigrant community, and the most common way this took place was through the organization of a local church community. Each group of immigrants wanted to have their own church where they could worship and pray in their own language and according to the traditions and customs of the Old World. The solution to this was the national parish, a parish organized along the lines of language and culture rather than territory. An important feature of the national parish was the central role that the laity had in its organization. Wherever the immigrants settled, a familiar pattern emerged. Lay leaders in the community would emerge and organize the people around the goal of founding a parish; they would purchase some land, canvass the city for funds, and then proceed to build a church. Then they would ask the bishop to send them a priest who could minister to them in their own language. The founding of the German parish of St. John the Baptist in Cincinnati illustrates the extent to which laypeople became involved in the organization of a parish.

The new church was to be situated in the Over the Rhine area, Cincinnati's Little Germany. The first organizational meeting took place during the last week of October 1844 in a German church in Over the Rhine. A building committee of ten laymen was chosen, and they then proceeded to draft a constitution outlining the procedures for building the church. At another public meeting, German Catholics ratified the constitution, and the establishment of St. John the Baptist parish was underway. The people purchased land for the church in the name of the bishop, John Purcell, and voted to name the church after his patron saint. Between October and March they held eight public meetings and voted upon such issues as the maximum price to be paid for the property, the number of doors in the church, the thickness of its walls, and the size of its windows. As was true elsewhere, a collection committee, organized at a public meeting, solicited funds throughout the city for the church's construction.

On March 25, 1845, the laying of the cornerstone took place, highlighted by an elaborate procession through Over the Rhine. The people had planned the ceremony, procession, and accompanying festivities. In November the dedication of the church took place. While all this was going on, the people also decided to build a school, and like the planning of the church, this "was agreed to and carried out with the accustomed meetings."[15]

Lay involvement in the parish did not end with the opening of the new church. In Cincinnati and in other places as well, German congregations established the lay trustee system of parish government. In Cincinnati the lay trustee system had a unique twist to it: even though the bishop owned all church property, the Germans still supported the idea of lay government in the parish. Every parish in the city had lay trustees, and this style of local church government persisted throughout the nineteenth century. All evidence suggests that in Cincinnati both prelates and people were satisfied with it. Moreover, Cincinnati was not unique in this regard. A study of nineteenth century German parishes indicates that three out of five of the parishes (62 percent) had lay trustees.[16]

A key question is why were the Germans so inclined to such lay initiative in the organization and government of the parish? One reason can be traced back to the cultural and religious experience of the old country. Among German Catholics there was a strong tradition of lay involvement in parish affairs, and this was maintained in the United States. In addition, the ideal of the German hometown, a distinctive autonomous form of local government that developed in the seventeenth and eighteenth centuries, was a strong tradition that formed the political and social experience of many immigrants. Independence, self-government, and a community closely bound together by consensus were trademarks of the German hometown, and it would not be surprising to find such ideals surfacing in the United States. Once these ideals crossed the ocean they adapted to the American legal and religious environment and became actualized through the lay trustee system of church government.

The German immigrant experience clearly suggests that elements of democracy were present in the church. There were also elements of monarchical rule. No one model of church was totally dominant at this time; rather there was a mixture of both. The bishop's authority was supreme in certain areas such as the ownership of property, but the people did have a voice in the organization and government of the local parish. A similar pattern was evident in the Polish community.

In the old country the parish was the center of village life for Polish Catholics. "The most important events of individual, familial, and communal life" took place there, and it bound people together, giving them a sense of identity as both Polish and Catholic. When they emigrated to the New World, the parish became the primary form of association among Polish Catholics. It was "simply the old primary community, reorganized and concentrated" in the United States.[17]

The organization of the parish in the Polish community followed a pattern similar to that of other immigrant groups. When people first arrived, they generally attended services in a local Catholic church. For many Poles, this often meant a German church, since those from Prussia and Austria could understand German. But this was not a satisfactory arrangement. Like all immigrants, they wanted to pray in their native language and sing Polish hymns, not German ones. To remedy this, Polish immigrants organized themselves into a mutual benefit society, whose express purpose was to found a Polish parish church.

The mutual benefit society was a commonplace organization in immigrant communities. Most often transplanted from the Old World, such societies provided insurance benefits for their members in times of sickness and death and gave the newcomers a sense of identity and belonging in the New World. More than an insurance institution, the mutual benefit society became a source of initiative in the broader community, and among the Polish "the great work of the society . . . is the formation of a parish."[18]

Wherever the Polish settled, a mutual benefit society was quickly organized, and it became the catalyst in the organization of a parish church. The pattern was a familiar one. Feeling a deep need for their own national parish, where they could hear sermons in Polish and practice their own religious customs, the society would collect money to purchase land for a church; then they would petition the local bishop to send them a Polish-speaking priest. Once a priest arrived, the church was built and the parish began to take shape. Even though every parish community was not organized in the same way, a definite pattern of lay initiative existed in each instance. Sometimes people acted on their own, sometimes they acted with the aid of a priest, but with few exceptions the source of the initiative for the organization of the parish was the people's mutual benefit society.

A key issue in the establishment of Polish parishes was the ownership of property. Most often, the parish was incorporated in the name of the mutual benefit society and its officers became the trustees of the parish. This arrangement conflicted with the prevailing custom in the late nineteenth century of bishop and clergy owning all church property. Thus, the stage was set for conflict, and conflict there was. In virtually every city where they settled, Polish Catholics went to battle over the issue of the ownership of church property. From their point of view, the tradition of the old country allowed for lay involvement in parish affairs, and they sought to continue this in the United States. As one Polish editor put it, "In the old country the founders and benefactors [of a parish] had a voice not only in the running of church affairs, but in the selection of the pastor. Here in America, the founders and benefactors of the Polish churches, that is the Polish people should certainly have the same rights and privileges."[19]

The editor had made an important point. In the Old World Polish nobles enjoyed the right of patronage (*jus patronatus*) and could not only appoint parish priests, but also exercise control over parish affairs. In the New World, the people wanted to transform "the old world individual patron into a more democratic form of collective patronage."[20] But the bishops and clergy, many Polish priests included, would not go along. For them, the clergy, not the people, should run parish affairs and hold title to all church property. The Polish people did not give in on this issue. They resisted strongly and even accepted excommunication rather than go along with the tradition of clerical control in parish affairs. Such resistance was a fact of life in Polish parishes across the country, and parish battles, complete with street riots, church demonstrations, and appeals to Rome, were commonplace. In fact, conflict over the issue of ownership of church property and lay involvement in the government of the local church was the cause for the first major schism in American Catholic history.

Schism in the American Catholic church had occurred throughout the nineteenth century. Generally it involved dissident parish congregations who chose to separate from the Roman Catholic Church because of a difference of opinion with their bishop over the issue of ownership of parish property. Most often, time healed the wound and the people rejoined the church. Things did not go so smoothly among the Polish, however. During the 1890s schismatic independent churches began to emerge in Chicago, Buffalo, Scranton, and other cities in the Northeast. Then, in 1904 Rev. Francis Hodur, leader of the Scranton independents, called a meeting of several independent parishes; this gathering was the formal beginning of the Polish National Catholic Church. A key issue in the dissidents' platform focused on democracy in the government of the local church. Hodur became the bishop-elect of the new denomination and headed it until his death in 1953. Though it never reached more than 5 percent of the entire Polish population, the existence of the Polish National Catholic Church served as a continual reminder of the struggle for democracy that took place in the Polish Catholic community.

Immigrant Catholics from other parts of Eastern Europe followed a pattern similar to the Polish in the organization of their churches. Like the Polish they too sought to democratize an Old World tradition, namely the right of patronage of a local noble, and to gain control over parish affairs. This would mean ownership of church property, an elected board of trustees, and even removal of uncooperative pastors. In their mind the rationale for this was quite simple and clear-cut: "The people have built the churches," wrote a Lithuanian immigrant, "therefore the people are the owners of the churches; and not the will of the bishop or of the Pope, but that of the people must be the rule in the parishes."[21] As with the Polish, conflict broke out in these communities and parish battles were frequent. Some Slovak and Lithuanian parishes went into schism and formed independent churches rather than give in on this question of ownership of church property. Among the Ukrainians, Eastern-rite Catholics who followed a different tradition of worship than Latin-rite Catholics, the issue of democracy in the local church was a major reason why many Eastern-rite Catholic clergy and laity left the Roman church in the pre–World War II period.

The loss of hundreds of thousands of Eastern-rite Catholics, along with thousands of Poles, Lithuanians, and Slovaks, illustrates how critical the issue of lay involvement in parish government was. Insistence of Catholic immigrants on preserving their authoritative role in managing local church affairs was such that they would accept excommunication, rather than give in on this point. At the same time the Catholic hierarchy, along with the majority of the clergy, were so adamant that they were willing to allow thousands of laypeople to leave the Roman Catholic church, rather than give in to their demands on this issue.

An irresistible force had met an immovable object, and the encounter produced bitter and prolonged conflict. Nationality differences certainly intensified the conflict, but more than just cultural differences were involved. Fundamentally it was a conflict between two radically differing views of the church. One view advocated a model of church that emphasized a democratic functioning of authority with an emphasis on local autonomy. According to this model, laypeople and clergy would work together and share responsibility for the organization and government of the parish. The other view supported a monarchical model of the church; championed by the hierarchy, this emphasized the authority of the clergy over the laypeople, with the bishop exercising supreme authority over everyone, priests and people alike.

The one nineteenth-century immigrant group most identified with the monarchical view of the church was the Irish. In the republican period the Irish were very much in support of the trustee system, but as the church developed institutionally the mission church of the 1820s was transformed into a large, bureaucratic organization that was able to recruit the personnel needed for an expanding constituency. This was especially true for the English-speaking community, and large numbers of these clergy came from Ireland, where the attitude of deference to clerical authority was growing stronger during the nineteenth century. Because of their numerical dominance among clergy and laity, the Irish tradition of deference became a standard that others were expected to follow. Of course not everybody followed the Irish in this regard, and that was when conflict would erupt.

Throughout the nineteenth century Roman Catholicism was steadily moving toward a more monarchical, less democratic style of church government. The Vatican Council of 1870 decisively pushed the church in this direction when it proclaimed the infallibility of the pope and encouraged the centralization of the church in Rome. Such centralization of authority filtered down throughout the church, enhancing the authority of both bishop and pastor. The Third Plenary Council of Baltimore in 1884 mirrored this development by making the will of the bishop supreme in all local church affairs. A directive issued by the archdiocese of Milwaukee in 1907 clearly articulated such a way of thinking: "The Church is not a republic or democracy, but a monarchy; ... all her authority is from above and rests in her Hierarchy; ... while the faithful of the laity have divinely given rights to receive all the blessed ministrations of the Church, they have absolutely no right whatever to rule and govern."[22]

The shift from a model of church that endorsed the involvement of the laity in the government of the local parish to a monarchical model in which the clergy were the supreme authority took place gradually. It was first noticeable in the Irish communities during the 1820s and 1830s; by the 1850s most Irish parishes had accepted the hierarchical concept of the church. Other immigrant groups resisted the trend, with some being more successful than others. Though there never was unanimous agreement among all ethnic groups on this point, resistance was widespread enough to cause conflict and even schism. By the 1920s, however, the clergy controlled the parish, and the tradition of laypeople participating in the organization and government of the local church had come to an end.

Clerical control of the church, most specifically episcopal control, remained the norm throughout the first half of the twentieth century. It reached its apex during the pontificate of Pius XII (1939–58) and very few people questioned such dominance. In these years the church was the clergy. In a very telling comment to a gathering of clergy Bishop Walter Foery of Syracuse, New York, spoke for many Catholics when he stated that "the history of the Catholic Church is essentially the history of the priesthood...."[23] Such an understanding of the church left little room for lay involvement in the government of the local parish. The priest was lord of the manor, and in places like Boston the parish was his personal benefice. This meant that all income from the parish belonged to him; in effect, the pastor legally owned the parish even though his name did not appear on the title to the land. Clerical control did not get any more absolute than that.

History shows, however, that the monarchical, clerical model of church was not the only model that existed. From the earliest years of Christianity the spirit of democracy has found a home in the church, and this tradition has endured to the present day, rising and falling in popularity depending on the prevailing attitudes of the day. Even in the brief history of American Catholicism a democratic model of church enjoyed wide support for a number of years, and such a historical tradition demonstrates that the monarchical model of church was not the only way that Catholics understood the meaning of church. Catholic laity wanted to be involved in shaping their spiritual destiny, and one way that they sought to achieve this was through a more democratic style of parish government.

This desire for democracy in the church has resurfaced once again. Behind this new surge of democracy is a theology of church that is much more populist than the monarchical, clerical model of church that has prevailed since the mid-nineteenth century. This new theology has produced such phenomena in the church as collegiality, parish councils, and pastoral letters written in an open, consultative manner. In the last several years, however, Pope John Paul II and others have tried to limit such openings toward democracy in the church. Indeed, they have tried to restore a more monarchical model of church reminiscent of the days of Pius XII.

History teaches us that this does not have to be. A democratic model of church has had a venerable tradition, and now more than ever before Catholic theology has endorsed such a populist understanding of church. As the Second Vatican Council put it, the church is "the people of God." A generation of people raised with this understanding naturally expect to have a voice in shaping their own spiritual destiny. To deny them this is to risk alienating an entire generation of Catholics. Indeed, it will mortgage the future of Catholicism to a model of the church that is both theologically and historically out of date.

Notes

1. Rhys Isaac, *The Transformation of Virginia 1740–1790* (Chapel Hill: University of North Carolina Press, 1982), 64.

2. Sean Wilentz, *Chants Democratic: New York City and the Rise of the American Working Class 1788–1850* (New York: Oxford University Press, 1984), 61.

3. Nathan O. Hatch, *The Democratization of American Christianity* (New Haven: Yale University Press, 1989), 9.

4. Patrick W. Carey, *People, Priests, and Prelates: Ecclesiastical Democracy and the Tensions of Trusteeism* (Notre Dame: University of Notre Dame Press, 1987), 108.

5. Mathew Carey, *Address to the Rt. Rev. Bishop Conwell and the Members of St. Mary's Congregation*, February 14, 1821, 3–4; Mathew Carey, *Address to the Rt. Rev. Bishop of Pennsylvania, the Catholic Clergy of Philadelphia, and the Congregation of St. Mary in this City by a Catholic Layman*, 1822, V, privately published by Carey himself.

6. Quoted in Carey, *People, Priests, and Prelates*, 156.

7. Quoted in Patrick W. Carey, "Republicanism within American Catholicism, 1785–1860," *Journal of the Early Republic*, 3 (Winter 1983): 416.

8. Ibid., 417.

9. Ibid., 421.

10. Quoted in Carey, *People, Priests, and Prelates*, 161.

11. Ibid., 163.

12. Sr. Mary Ramona Mattingly, *The Catholic Church on the Kentucky Frontier 1795–1812* (Washington, D.C.: Catholic University of America, 1935), 139.

13. Quoted in Jay P. Dolan, *The American Catholic Experience: A History from Colonial Times to the Present* (Garden City, N.Y.: Doubleday and Co., 1985), 116.

14. Ibid., 166.

15. Ibid., 164.

16. Ibid., 168.

17. Ibid., 181.

18. Ibid., 182.

19. Ibid., 183.

20. Ibid., 183.

21. Ibid., 185.

22. Ibid., 181.

23. Quoted in David O'Brien, *Faith and Friendship: Catholicism in the Diocese of Syracuse 1886–1986* (Syracuse, N.Y.: Diocese of Syracuse, 1986), 343.

PHILLIP BERRYMAN

– 7 –

Other Experiences, Other Concerns: Latin America and the Democratization of the Church

In the original conception of the editors, I had a rather straightforward task: to reflect on the possible contributions of the Latin American Christian base communities to a process of democratization within the Catholic Church. Proposals for democratization have made sense to me for many years. No doubt many Latin American church people would assent to the general notion that the church should be more democratic — especially if the democracy in question were understood in opposition to monarchy. They are quite familiar with instances of top-down authority from both the Vatican and their local bishops.

However, as I began to consider the question I was struck by how little resonance the notion seems to have within the Latin American church. For example, I do not recall the notion coming up in the course of many interviews in preparation for a book on the churches in Central America during the 1980s. A recent book on the "challenges" facing the Catholic Church in Guatemala does not even seem to broach the issue. Leonardo Boff's *Church: Charism and Power* is instructive. On the one hand it is far more direct in criticizing the abuses of the institutional church than virtually any other writing by a Latin American theologian — at one point even comparing it to the (pre-Gorbachev) Kremlin. However, as suggested by the title itself, Boff seems to argue that the antidote for abuse by those who hold power in the church is that "charism" should be its "principle." He does not translate his proposal into procedural norms, and (at least in a hasty rereading) does not even suggest that the church learn from modern democracies.[1]

To be sure, the Latin American church has offered some glimpses of alternative models, most notably in base communities. Nevertheless, as will be noted, even where successfully implemented, base community work

128

reaches only a tiny minority of Catholics. Moreover, to the best of my knowledge, that experience has not led to proposals for democratization of the church. Hence my observations here are largely an attempt to account for why that is so. If I end up doing something more ambiguous than what I was asked to do, it may nonetheless be useful. Democratization of structures and procedures in the Roman Catholic Church will occur only as the result of an international movement. My modest observations on recent Latin American experience can be of some help to this enterprise with which I sympathize.

Hopes and Frustrations of a Generation

In a recent letter from Brazil a longtime observer writes that Latin America is changing. "Liberation theology is in a crisis which reflects the state of crisis in all social movements on the continent, including Marxism. . . . I think the situation of crisis is widespread although the people themselves do not say so. Partly it reflects repression from Rome, and partly it is the discouragement of pastoral workers who after twenty years have not seen any change in the political and social situation."

This letter confirmed what I have been sensing in recent years. I can recall the high hopes of the immediate post–Vatican II period: the meetings and conferences, the statements and manifestos, and the 1968 bishops meeting at Medellín, whose documents seemed to launch the church in new directions. In Latin American countries one had a sense that radical change was on the horizon, though not necessarily through armed revolution.

In the 1960s base communities were a new idea; indeed the term had just been coined. Nevertheless, the idea of lay-led communities made eminent sense sociologically, theologically, and pastorally for parishes where there were ten thousand or more people per priest. Moreover, it seemed only a question of time until celibacy would be ended and married men from among the people could be ordained. (The question of women's ordination had not really been raised and certainly not in Latin America.)

At first issues of church reform and social change seemed to be linked together, and Latin American clergy initially felt in tune with the contestatory spirit in Europe and North America. Public controversies between priests and bishops erupted in some countries. Secularization theory (casting doubt on popular religion) and Marxism were part of the mix. Perhaps the highwater mark of the period I am talking about was the Christians for Socialism conference held in Chile in 1972, with delegations from around the continent.

Even at that point, military dictatorships ruled in Brazil, Bolivia, Uruguay, and Central America and would soon do so in Chile and Argentina, as the progressive military rule in Peru turned conservative. In this context some who had been swept up in the anti-institutional spirit of the late

1960s were moved to reassess their view of the institutional church, which in some instances was the only institution that could offer some public resistance to the pretensions of national security regimes. In base communities people could express some hope and affirm their dignity as children of God.

During the 1970s a conservative backlash among the bishops brought Archbishop (later Cardinal) Alfonso López Trujillo to the leadership of CELAM (Latin American Bishops Conference). Liberation theology and the new pastoral approaches were put on the defensive. The new situation became all the more clear when Pope John Paul II, then in office only a few months, came to the Puebla meeting (1979) and left his imprint on it.

A few months later the Sandinista revolution, with strong Christian participation, overthrew the Somoza dictatorship in Nicaragua. Once more expectations were raised for both societal change and new pastoral forms. Realistically, however, the Nicaraguan revolution — and the possibilities of similar regimes in El Salvador and perhaps Guatemala — could not offer models to the larger, more complex countries of the continent. At most they could offer a sign that change might be possible.

Elsewhere in the early to mid-1980s military regimes were giving way to civilian governments, whether through a phased withdrawal of the military as in Brazil, or forced out by events as in Argentina, or largely through civilian pressure as in Chile and Uruguay. "Democracy" and "democratization" became part of the political lexicon, even of the left, for whom the term had previously always carried the adjective "bourgeois." Whether these new governments — plagued by the worst recession since the 1930s and saddled with seemingly unpayable debts — were democratic in anything but a formal sense was an open question. In any case, the Catholic Church's political profile was lowered.

In Central America the original high hopes spurred by the Nicaraguan revolution failed to materialize as the U.S.-sponsored contra war forced the Sandinista government to sacrifice development to defense. With massive U.S. aid, the Salvadoran military was able to withstand the FMLN insurgency and the civilian government achieved some legitimacy. Ambitious revolutionary aims were scaled back, although the revolutionaries themselves said they were only adjusting realistically to changing conditions.

Hence the sense of crisis — though not necessarily made explicit — alluded to in my friend's letter. The high hopes of twenty or twenty-five years ago for significant social change have been disappointed.

Questions about Base Communities

Although mass migration to the cities was well underway twenty-five years ago, most Latin Americans were still rural, typically peasants or laborers on ranches and farms. Today, the typical Latin American lives in a city or town.

Even El Salvador is today more urban than rural. With few new industrial jobs, these people often have to fend for themselves as street vendors, or doing odd jobs in the burgeoning "informal sector."

Again my friend writes from Brazil that the Catholic Church is "helpless" in the midst of the new urban masses. It is "closed in tiny traditional minorities and does not reach the masses. The younger clergy are quite indifferent since they live in the sacristies and church offices and go around distributing sacraments. The liberationists feel lost because they are separated from the masses. Their rhetoric separates them." Among the urban masses it is Pentecostal Protestantism and the Catholic charismatic movement that are having some success.

This was not supposed to happen. At Medellín the bishops seemed to give their blessing to making the base community the new model of church work. Certainly at that time traditionalist priests felt threatened and resisted, but it seemed only a question of time until base communities proved their worth and became the normal model of the Catholic Church. However, even by the time of Puebla, there seems to have been some backtracking as the bishops no longer saw them as *the* structure at the village or *barrio* level, but as *a* legitimate and useful pastoral method.

My friend in Brazil writes, "Basic Christian communities are being co-opted by the system, which makes them subdivisions of the parish." This observation squares with the findings of Daniel Levine in a number of places in Colombia, where typically the base community is regarded as the lowest unit of the church, and is part of a top-down structure where the priest or sister provides guidelines for activities to be carried out by local people, who have little initiative. On the other hand, Levine found that in some base community experiences, particularly in Venezuela, the emphasis is on empowerment of the people to act on their own.[2] I believe those findings can be generalized on a broader scale, that is, that in Catholicism there is a tension between coopting and empowering uses of base community pastoral methods.

It should be kept in mind that base communities encompass only the tiniest fraction of Latin American Catholics. As a rough rule of thumb perhaps one tenth of the parishes of a country may use this approach, and in those parishes only a fraction of the population participates. In a rural parish of thirty thousand people scattered over sixty communities, an average of fifty adults in each of them might participate (i.e., 10 percent of the population and 20 percent of the adult population). In urban areas such work is more difficult, and success in numerical terms is far more modest. I have in mind an area in Guatemala City, for example, where a team of ten people (priests, sisters, and seminarians) feel they are doing well when they can have group meetings involving several hundred people in a *barrio* of sixty or eighty thousand.

In this same area, however, there is an almost equal number of charismatic Catholics who seem to do well with only marginal contacts with priests or sisters. There are also a couple of dozen Protestant chapels, and the team members themselves estimate that a third of the *barrio* are evangelicals. Similarly, a study in Chile found that approximately 1 percent of nominal Catholics and 2.5 percent of practicing Catholics (i.e., those who attended Mass with some regularity) were participants in base communities.

These quantitative observations are intended only to make it clear that Christian base communities cannot be regarded as *the* form of the Latin American church, but only as one form. It is my impression that some Latin American Catholic defenders of base communities are nevertheless now raising some questions.[3] Some of my interviewees, for example, wondered whether the strong stress on consciousness-raising might not be one-sidedly rational. Pastoral workers are beginning to drop easier explanations for the growth of evangelicals and to acknowledge that these churches have genuine appeal and seem to touch something deep in popular culture.

Base community work can be credited with a number of accomplishments under difficult, often dangerous, circumstances. Such communities have furnished a place where people can come together in an atmosphere of confidence. There they have been able to articulate their own thoughts and to come to know and experience directly the power of the Scriptures, to internalize them, to make them their own. They have gotten a new sense of Christianity as a vocation lived in community. Base community work often spins off into community projects. Their members may become involved in community development projects or struggles for human rights.

This method of pastoral work has provided many sisters and priests with a way of becoming present among the poor in a nonpaternalistic way. As impressive as the witness and service of these people often is, it leaves largely unresolved the question of how the Catholic Church can develop effective outreach among the poor.

The upshot is that, although most Latin Americans call themselves Catholics, they have only fleeting contacts with the institutional church. Their Catholicism comes through channels of family, culture, and tradition and only marginally from the church institution. It is my sense that this gap between the broad masses of people who call themselves Catholics and the church institution — parishes, dioceses, etc. — is an urgent problem and affects questions of democratization. If, as many hoped fifteen or twenty years ago, base communities had become the normal church structure in most parishes, they would constitute the grassroots level cells for new democratic structures. However, in practice, they are simply one kind of pastoral approach — alongside a number of others, as well as traditional sacramental administration.

Democracy comes more or less naturally to churches whose basic unit is the local congregation, say, a Baptist church. Where Catholics have a high level of identification with a parish, as in the United States where 50 percent of Catholics attend Mass with some frequency, there might already be a basis for more democratic structures because there is already something of a constituency. Latin American parishes, however, are not congregations, but territorial administrative units of the church, which is still somehow identified with the national culture. A large majority of people will identify themselves as Catholics, but on any given Sunday only a small proportion — sometimes 3 percent — may attend Mass.

By no means do I wish to argue that Catholicism with a higher Mass attendance is in any way more "Christian," but rather that the lack of a congregational basis may be one of the reasons why democratization of church structures and procedures has not become a live issue in Latin America. Given its quite different sociological basis — high Catholic identity but very low level of contact with the church institution — the circumstances of Latin American Catholicism are less propitious for such a development.

The growth of evangelical churches will probably spur a stronger interest in outreach among Catholics. For example, a priest in Guatemala City candidly told me that he had been impelled to action by the nineteen active Protestant chapels in his parish. He needed something that could give results and had opted for the SINE (Integral System for Evangelization), a pastoral method developed in Mexico, which combines outreach through house visiting, a kind of evangelistic mission through house meetings, a weekend retreat, and the establishment of ongoing house communities. Although, with its use of Scripture and friendly atmosphere, it is somewhat similar to base communities, there is a rather authoritarian top-down and doctrinal feel to it. During the 1990s such new approaches to evangelization may multiply in Latin America. However, their participants and clerical leaders are unlikely to perceive the lack of democracy in the Catholic church as problematic.

To my knowledge, it is in Brazil that base communities have sought systematically to have input into the church, particularly through nationwide meetings held periodically during the last fifteen years. Nevertheless, given their relatively small weight in the Catholic population and the crisis I have been suggesting, I have the impression that at this point their contribution to democratization is limited.

Church Authority: Uses, Abuses, and Limits

Many years ago when I met a Mexican bishop visiting seminarians, what struck me was the contrast with U.S. bishops. This bishop had no secretaries scurrying around, no crammed schedule to keep, and seemed very approachable in contrast to the distance that until then had seemed to be part of being a bishop. This impression has since been reinforced. A U.S. bishop must be capable of administering a corporation-like entity with millions of dollars in cash flow — or have smart people to do the administering. A Latin American bishop simply has no empire to rule. In the countryside he may have a couple of dozen priests in the diocese and his cash flow in dollar terms is less than that of a poor U.S. parish — often money from foreign church aid agencies. In a large city an archbishop may have a hundred or so parishes, but again his administrative tasks are relatively simple. He does not need anything like the staff housed in the ten-story chancery office building in Philadelphia.

I am not talking about a difference in character. Latin American bishops can be personally pompous and self-important. Archbishops and cardinals can convince themselves that their breakfasts with presidents and generals are their "ministry." Nevertheless, they are far less impeded by bureaucracy and administration than their North American counterparts.

Thus at their best many Latin American bishops have found ways of operating with a high degree of consultation, even if they do not use the language of democracy. An outstanding example is Archbishop Oscar Romero of San Salvador, whose greatest virtue was perhaps his ability to listen and to work collegially. He established human rights monitoring services under the roof of the chancery office itself with official status. His Sunday sermons were worked out by a team of priests, sisters, and laypeople, although ultimately he took responsibility for them. His acts of courage were not impulsive but were generally a response to considerable dialogue. This was not formal procedural democracy, however.

Some might regard the behavior of the Nicaraguan bishops and especially Archbishop Miguel Obando y Bravo during the Sandinista revolution as quite antidemocratic. In their effort to make the church structure a bulwark of resistance to the Sandinista revolution, they systematically sought to have priests and sisters sympathetic to the revolution transferred. In the early 1980s there were a number of incidents in which parish groups protested. Tempers flared so much that some pro-Sandinista groups roughed up bishops. Was this an instance in which the "authoritarian" bishops were resisting the will of the people, who spontaneously showed desire for a more "democratic" church? I would be loath to go so far. Data indicate that church personnel were split over the revolution, as was the population at large. In their enthusiasm the Sandinistas and pro-revolutionary Christians often assumed that "the people" were overwhelmingly Sandinista, whereas the real, empirical people were always somewhat more divided. In other words, it is by no means assured that procedural democracy at the parish level would always have supported revolutionary priests.

In Latin America religious orders constitute something of a countervailing structure in a way that at first sight may not be obvious. Again in Central America, approximately half the parishes are staffed by religious order priests. Thus their primary commitment is to their religious family, and it is their religious superiors (not local bishops) who transfer them, often even to another country. The family spirit generally carries over into the way authority is exercised, with a good deal of consultation. (Since bishops chronically need priests, they can interfere with religious order priests only for matters they regard as very important.)

On the level of everyday work parish priests feel they can operate with a degree of freedom. Exceptions such as the policies of Cardinal Obando aside, most priests do not find chancery offices to be an obstacle to their work with people. Again, this may help explain why democratization of church structures is not a demand articulated from the ground up.

Some rural dioceses in Latin America operate with a fairly high level of collegiality, especially where a religious order may supply most of the personnel in the area. Their efforts to draw up pastoral plans and to cooperate in programs of leadership training and liturgy may have something of "democracy" about them, although the participants are primarily full time church personnel and by and large they are not questioning patterns of power and authority at higher levels in the church.

In Central America in recent years many dioceses have undertaken consultative approaches, holding synods, councils, and so forth. Pastoral agents working together may draw up two- or three-year pastoral programs, involving meetings with people. In Guatemala, progressive church people, just emerging from years of the "dirty war," frankly told me they were working within the framework of the archdiocesan synod and using its discussion guides, fully conscious that deep down their pastoral vision was quite different from that of other church people. On one level such exercises bring people together in an ostensibly open forum, but in fact the underlying differences in pastoral vision remain.

There is yet another reason why proposals for democratization within the church have not arisen in Latin America and may not meet with wholehearted enthusiasm. In the United States its proponents generally assume that the undemocratic use of church authority and its allegedly theological warrants are the main element of the logjam currently blocking further advance along the way opened at Vatican II in matters such as the role of women, ministerial models, dissent and authority, and papal pretensions. Those who raise such questions are generally sympathetic to peace and justice issues and feel a kinship with liberationist tendencies in Latin America. Yet they may experience less reciprocity from the Latin American side than they might expect. Leonardo Boff, for example, is the only Latin American male theologian I can recall who has taken on the issue of women's ordination directly. Issues of sexual ethics are very little discussed in Latin American church literature. Abortion is largely undiscussed, although the practice is widespread, and is in fact a leading cause of death among women of childbearing age. Despite the cases of Boff and other theologians, issues of academic freedom do not arise in the same way, since there is no large body of university theologians.

The cases of Hans Küng and Leonardo Boff may be paradigmatic. Küng took a principled stand against Vatican pretensions, even though it cost him his title as "Catholic" teacher. In fact, however, he retained his true constituency, Catholics in Western countries who had already gotten some distance from Roman absolutism. Boff, on the other hand, accepted the terms of his year of silence (in 1985 and again in 1991), no doubt using the time profitably. As desirable as institutional changes in the governance of the Catholic Church might be, for now and for the foreseeable future church progressives (largely clergy and religious) feel it is important to remain a Catholic in good standing in order to bring the weight of the church institution onto the side of the poor as much as possible. I suggest that the different reactions reflect underlying attitudes that affect how proposals for the democratization of the church are viewed.

Democracy Evolving

Twenty years ago the word "democracy" did not spring readily to the lips of the generation of church activists I am talking about. Latin American countries seemed to be condemned to oscillate between periods of abusive military rule and weak civilian rule. Candidates courted votes in populist fashion, but elections did not offer real choices for the poor majority. Except for a few opportunists, most people in *barrios* and villages were cynical about politicians. The left spoke contemptuously of bourgeois democracy.

If structural change was needed — and at Medellín the bishops themselves had called for "sweeping, bold, urgent and profoundly renewing changes" — somehow an overwhelming popular movement had to take state power and to begin to make institutional changes, such as land reform, and, more generally, make the economy work for the poor majority. Only on the basis of such an economy would political democracy be really meaningful.

As has been noted, expectations have been scaled back. Those who a generation ago hoped for revolutionary transformation are now playing within the existing system — the only one that exists and is likely to exist. Procedural democracy looks better when compared to government by military decree. As a veteran Brazilian political scientist, an advisor to the Workers Party, told me, "We're not talking revolution; we're working for democracy."

Today I hear people on the left self-critically confess that they overemphasized the importance of political struggle, whose aim was to take state power (electorally or through other forms of struggle). By the same token they now recognize the significance of other kinds of organizing aimed at meeting people's more immediate needs — such as soup kitchens, small-scale development projects, housing construction, and women's groups. For the most part these groups explicitly seek to avoid "politics," that is, alliances with particular parties or organizations. Nevertheless, taken altogether they constitute an upsurge of organizing often together called the "popular movement." They are often seen in Gramscian terms as building up "civil society."

The dream of making basic changes after seizing state power is gone. The left, including the church left, has been coming to the conclusion that complete seizure of state power in order to implement an overall revolutionary program is perhaps impossible — especially in more complex urban societies. Or to put it another way around, even if a left coalition should control the government, it will confront a strong private sector, other political tendencies, and (except in the unlikely case of a guerrilla victory) an existing military. Thus, even if it were possible to march triumphantly into the capital, it might not be desirable; that is, the longer route of consensus and compromise, and trial and error, might in the end lead to a more satisfactory society.

In other words, I have a sense that Latin Americans are in a process of coming to a new view of what democracy might mean. One lesson is that of coexisting with people and organizations whose view of society is vehemently opposed to one's own. Another is the ability to accept halfway measures, whose virtue may lie in their reflecting more accurately the state of public opinion.

This apprenticeship in democracy is also taking place in countless local organizations. Indeed it is in the citizens' groups not directly tied to political parties that the real democratization of recent years is taking place. While there is little direct evidence yet, it is possible that the gradual development of a more democratic culture may be one of the seeds of a future concern for democratization within the church.

In early 1991 a group of Central American analysts connected to the popular movements held their annual meeting, which issued a fifty-page analysis of regional developments published in *Envío*.[4] The publication was dedicated to Ignacio Martín-Baró, one of the Jesuits murdered in November 1989, and Mirna Mack, a Guatemalan researcher murdered in September 1990, both of whom had been members of this group. That personal loss could serve as a symbol for their view of larger trends in the region: in what was being called a "new world order" of ascendant U.S-supported (or imposed) "democracy," murderers could operate with impunity.

Yet the analysts, while reflecting a new mode of realism, made democracy one of their major themes. Their final section was on the "popular" alternative to the economic models being imposed in Central America by new conservative governments and international agencies. Their final series of proposals was for "democratization" of power, of the state, of the market, of culture, of international institutions, and of nongovernmental organizations. Under the heading of democratization of culture, they noted,

"Democracy within the Central American Catholic churches, i.e., moving from slogans to the real, fully egalitarian participation of their members in the churches' tasks and functions, has been one of the most difficult tasks. The complexity of Archbishop Romero's religious life, prototype of this possibility, attests to the difficulty."

Concluding Remarks

These observations can be summarized briefly.

1. When Latin American Catholics reflect on what direction the church should take, they do not readily discuss the need for democratization.

2. The agenda of those arguing for democratization, especially relating to opening the ordained ministry, to the role of women, and to sexual morality, is largely not shared by Latin American church people — or is seen in somewhat different terms.

3. The relative lack of personnel, real estate, and money often reduces the distance between the hierarchy and ordinary people.

4. While base communities offer a glimpse of a more lay-led church, they represent only a tiny portion of Latin American Catholics. That model of pastoral work may be entering a crisis. Effective outreach among the masses largely eludes the institutional church.

5. Although the return to elected civilian governments is at best ambiguous, there are other signs of democratization, especially the growth of grassroots citizen groups of poor people. Contact with these movements may contribute to raising issues of democracy within the church.

Notes

1. Luis Samandú, Hans Siebers, Oscar Sierra, *Guatemala: Retos de la Iglesia católica en una sociedad en crisis* (San José: DEI, 1990); Leonardo Boff, *Church: Charism and Power — Liberation Theology and the Institutional Church* (New York: Crossroad, 1985). Kremlin comparison, chap. 5, n. 17, 171–72.

2. Daniel H. Levine, "Colombia: The Institutional Church and the Popular," in Daniel H. Levine, ed., *Religion and Political Conflict in Latin America* (Chapel Hill, N.C.: University of North Carolina Press, 1986).

3. See José Comblin, "Algumas questões a partir da prática das comunidades eclesiais de base no nordeste," *Revista Eclesiástica Brasileira*, 50, fasc. 198 (June 1990).

4. *Envío* (Instituto Histórico Centroamericano, Managua) 10, no. 117, 54–55.

PEDRO A. RIBEIRO DE OLIVEIRA

– 8 –

Conflict and Change in the Brazilian Catholic Church

It is no longer necessary to compile evidence to demonstrate the reality of changes that have occurred in the Catholic Church during the last twenty-five years. Although there is much diversity in the rhythm and intensity of this process of change, it is undeniable that in the Latin American countries this process brought about an institutional profile unimaginable in the decade of the 1950s. The changes were so large in number and scope that an observer who had not followed the entire process would certainly doubt that they could have occurred without profound institutional ruptures.

It is in this context of rapid change that the sociological debate concerning this process of change in the Catholic Church is situated. This raises questions such as: What is the nature of this process of change? Are we talking about a process of internal reforms, or is the ecclesiastical structure in question? Is there a schism being developed, or is this institution that has survived for thousands of years simply preparing itself to survive for another thousand?

Theologians are not alone in this intellectual debate: more and more scientists do participate in it. It is as a social scientist that I present my contribution to the development of the discussion. I am aware of the difficulties as well as of the complexities of this topic. For this reason I propose the elaboration of this essay by beginning with the presentation of an empirical case study and then continuing by approaching the theoretical questions concerning the process of the institutional change.

My arguments seek to demonstrate that the nature of the conflicts is primarily an *ecclesiastical* one: the parochial structure versus the structure of CEBs (a Portuguese abbreviation that corresponds to "base ecclesial communities"). However, this ecclesiastical conflict expresses a much more fundamental conflict, namely, the class struggle for religious hegemony. Once this perspective is accepted, we are obliged to take into account the principle of the *relative autonomy* of religious institutions. In the first part of this work, its autonomy will be accentuated; in the second part, its relativity in the context of the class struggle. I know that such an approach is not endorsed by all social scientists. Nevertheless, I do believe that this kind of approach will be able to help us understand the nature of the conflict that directs the process of change now happening in the Catholic Church.

Parish vs. CEBs: Conflict of Ecclesiastical Model

In order to evaluate the importance of CEBs in the Catholic Church, it is essential to consider just what the parish represents in the church since the reign of Pope Pius IX. Vatican Council I and the Latin American Plenary Council (1899) determined the centralization of religious power. The pope and the Roman curia became preeminent at the top level, while at the local level this power was given to the bishop and to the parish priest. In this model, the parish is considered to be the basic organization of the ecclesiastical structure. Functioning within it there are several internal organisms, such as the religious and charitable associations for the laity, chapels, service organizations, youth and family groups. In spite of their importance, these groups are not autonomous nor do they formally constitute part of the basic ecclesiastical structure.

In other words, the parish is fundamental because a diocese cannot exist — except in rare cases — unless it is subdivided into parishes, each of them having a priest as its head, to whom the bishop delegates part of his ministries and power. Although the internal organisms of the parish are important and effective elements for the pastoral vitality of the church, they do not have their own autonomy. A parish may terminate one or all of these groups without effecting any structural change. It would not be an exaggeration to characterize the romanized form of Catholicism by taking the ecclesiastical parish as a model. Romanized Catholicism can be characterized by its emphasis on the sacraments, parochial organization, and the indispensable presence of the priest.[1]

After Vatican Council II, the CEBs appear as a "new way of being church" — to use an expression consecrated by the official documents of the Brazilian National Bishops Conference. This signifies that the CEBs have come to modify the proper foundations of the ecclesiastical structure, taking the place previously occupied by the parish. In this ecclesiastical model, the parish does not disappear, but it loses its dominant position. It turns into a center for mobilizing pastoral action and for providing bureaucratic services, but loses its function as a commanding and decision-making center. The CEB model, which has been the object of several theological debates, has its origin in the very conception of church as "people of God," as well as in criticisms of the parish by the Episcopal Conference at Medellín. We are not talking here about a model that is finished and institutionalized, but of a dynamic constellation that has been initiated and put into action based on pastoral experiences, the results of which cannot yet be fully determined.

We have, consequently, *two models of church*. The first one, inspired by the Council of Trent and standardized by Vatican Council I, has the parish as its structural base and is still alive in the Latin American church, although coexisting, in many dioceses, together with the alternative model of the CEBs. In fact, the CEB is not already an institutionalized model. It is an experimental construction inspired by Vatican Council II. Its concrete reality comes from the experiences of popular pastoral work with the poor in Latin America. Therefore, the conflict that exists between these two models can be placed at the theoretical level — the ecclesiology of Trent vs. the ecclesiology of the CEBs — as well as at the pastoral grassroots level.

It is the conflict that emerges at the grassroots pastoral level that we are going to analyze here by examining the nature of this conflict and its possible development, as well as its social and political implications. But, in order to do this, we will make use of a case study: the archdiocese of Vitória in Espírito Santo state in Brazil.

The choice of this archdiocese is not accidental. The archdiocese of Vitória was chosen for three important reasons. The first is a methodological one. This study analyzes ecclesiastical models, so the scope of the study cannot be smaller than that of the diocese, because the diocese in itself is the fundamental unit of the Catholic Church. It would also be desirable to analyze the relationship between the local church and the universal church, including its relationship with the Holy See. Unfortunately, the empirical data necessary for this type of analysis is beyond our reach due to the limits of the research done. The choice of a supradiocesan level, whether that of the National Bishops Conference or of CELAM (Latin American Bishops Conference) — which would have to be undertaken if the object of the study were the relationship between the church and society or the church and state — is inadequate for the analysis of ecclesiastical models.

Another reason for the choice of the archdiocese of Vitória is its exemplary character. The processes of religious and organizational change that have occurred in Vitória had national and international repercussions because of its pioneering spirit and because of the support given by its bishops and by the greater part of its clergy and pastoral agents. These repercussions were also motivated by the fact that this archdiocese had been the sponsor of the first and the second inter-ecclesiastical CEB encounters held in 1975 and 1976, respectively. It is a medium-size archdiocese, with extensive rural areas, an advanced industrial sector, and heavily populated low-income urban neighborhoods. These characteristics make Vitória an excellent object for a case study.

Lastly, the choice of Vitória is a practical one. From 1984 up to 1987, this church went through an extensive pastoral self-evaluation. Included in this evaluation was a series of sociological surveys in which a team of sociologists of the Institute for Religious Studies/ISER — to which I belong — played an important role. A census was taken of the pastoral resources, such as the people involved and the existing groups and organizations in each community and parish. A questionnaire was filled out by everyone who attended the Sunday liturgical celebration on a certain week-end, and the opinions of approximately forty thousand people were collected during small group reflections. These reflections were made on ten themes relevant to the pastoral evaluation. The data collected from this extensive survey were voluminous, the benefits of which are yet to be exhausted. For the purpose of this essay, however, this data provides us with more than enough empirical information.[2] This data also shows the reality of one of the dioceses where the CEB structural ecclesiastical model has been so well implanted as to bring to light the conflict between the two models, the traditional parish and the CEBs.

The Archdiocese of Vitória

The archdiocese of Vitória has approximately twelve hundred CEBs (included in this are fifty parish centers) for an overall population of 1.5 million inhabitants or more. Therefore, there are about 250 families for each CEB. Obviously, in the rural zones the size of the communities is much smaller than in the intensively populated urban and poor neighborhoods where it is not unusual to find communities with more than five hundred families. Nevertheless, there are no provisions being taken to divide the larger communities nor to create new communities in any significant number. The data indicates that the number of CEBs is near its limit, and that its growth is already following a natural rhythm.

It is worthwhile mentioning that the number of CEBs created in the period from 1980 to 1985 was 40 percent less than in the previous five years. Half of these have a stable membership, while almost another half still show indications of growth. But only a few of them are decreasing in membership. This data gives the impression that the CEBs are established and consolidated in the Vitória archdiocese. As a matter of fact, this is the truth for some of the pastoral areas; there are regions where the CEBs are just beginning to be implanted and still have to be consolidated.

Another series of data corroborate this impression of the consolidation of the CEBs. One of these is the fact that almost all communities have a chapel or their own place for meetings and gatherings. Another significant fact is the existence of community councils in three-fourths of the CEBs. With rare exceptions, these councils are opportunities for the laity to participate in discussion and decision making at the grassroots level. In 90 percent of the communities, council leaders are elected by their own members and are periodically changed. In 80 percent of them, meetings are held at least once a month. The decision making of the CEBs can, therefore, be seen as being effectively carried out by its own members.

Another important datum to be noted is the existence of homogeneous *groups within each CEB*. The most important of these groups is without a doubt the biblical reflection group. Although it is impossible to define the exact number of these groups because some of them have a very ephemeral existence, we estimate there are at least three thousand of these biblical study groups. It is not an exaggeration to say that they are the soul of the base communities. It is within these groups, during their weekly or bi-weekly meetings focused on biblical readings, that the connections between religious faith and day-to-day life are made. These reflections generate the energy that impels the CEBs and brings their members into active social and political engagement.

Also important are numerous service groups of various types. They assume the responsibility of organizing and performing weekly community celebrations, catechetics, and preparation for reception of the sacraments, doing financial maintenance and cleaning of the community's chapel. There are on the average about six of these groups per community and this number also includes the groups and committees geared toward specific pastoral or social work: e.g., youth, factory workers, families, women, black people. This data shows that the CEBs are not small homogeneous groups, but communities with a great deal of internal diversity and a certain complexity of organization. They articulate the specific internal groups, the traditional churchgoers, and the masses of Catholics who only sporadically go to church.

This data really points to the existence of a "new way of being church," i.e., a church based on the CEBs. They are not small groups that interact among themselves, like movements and associations. Indeed, they are religious groups to which every Catholic should turn for his or her membership in the church. To the extent that the CEBs become more effective as a *community* — that is to say, collectives united by the same identity and by the links of solidarity which admit a diversity in their internal groups and in which there is space for the participation of the Catholic population as a whole — they will become the base of a new ecclesiastical structure, substituting for the parish. The foundation of this structure is the particular community and not the small groups within the community, because only at the community level do we have a stable assembly of the faithful, an assembly that can legitimately claim the title of *local church*. It is in this sense that the CEBs can be a new way of being church, a church built on the CEB structure and not along old parish lines.

However, we should examine other data that alert us to the possibility of exaggerating the importance of CEBs. The total number of people actively involved in CEBs is certainly not great. Even in one diocese in which persons were asked to fill out a questionnaire during the Sunday celebration, this number did not reach seventy thousand persons. The archdiocese in question does not have more than thirty thousand persons paying the monthly contribution. The groups that participated in the "Great Evaluation" were, at the maximum, forty thousand persons. One estimation, a very optimistic one, holds that there are fifty thousand active Catholics in the church of Vitória. In a population of more than 1.5 million inhabitants in the whole area of the diocese, however, the number of those participating in CEBs is not that significant.

Apparently, the CEBs bring to the ecclesiastical organization what could be called "a popular religious elite,"[3] which is distinct from the great mass of nonpracticing Catholics. This larger group of nominal Catholics, however, do not seem to relate to the CEBs. Rather, they generally go directly to the parish to fulfill their religious needs. To conclude, the CEBs seem to service active Catholics — principally those of the poor strata where the parishes serve — and a part of a "pious elite" from the middle and upper strata. The conflict between these two ecclesiastical models creates in the church two parallel structures.

It is exactly here, in the existence of these two parallel structures, that there lies the crucial problem in the process of change occurring in Brazil. This conflict, of course, deserves to be more closely analyzed, and this will be done next by using other sources for analysis than that of the archdiocese of Vitória.

Lay Participation in Ecclesiastical Decisions

The participation of the laity in ecclesiastical decisions is, without a doubt, the most salient element in the renewal process in the post–Vatican II church. This participation can be seen not only as a result but also as a cause of this renovation process. The post–conciliar renewal opened the door for the laity to participate in the ecclesiastical decision-making process, principally via CEB and grassroots pastoral groups, which can be considered the main agents for ecclesiastical renewal. As a matter of fact, laity had a participating role in church activities before Vatican II, particularly through Catholic Action. But lay movements had more direct influence in wider public issues of society than in the internal decisions of the church. They were important in the process of change, but they did not manage to produce a new ecclesiastical model as has occurred with the CEBs.[4]

The research data on Vitória shows that the participation of laity in church decisions and, in particular, in the expansion of the religious space where laity assumes very active functions (for instance, liturgy, catechetics, evangelization) is designated as the most positive result by the majority of those people questioned. To this data we can add the results of the questionnaires given to the "animators of the CEBs" (laypeople who play organizational and leadership roles in the communities) at the inter-ecclesiastical assemblies in Itaici (1981) and Trindade (1986). In both situations the most cited "struggle" was the "struggle to transform the church."[5]

It is not necessary, we believe, to bring forth more evidence to demonstrate that the awareness of "being church" is already a reality for the great majority of CEB members. The question is not that of just being an active Christian, but of having a feeling of belonging to the "people of God" and of having the right to participate effectively in the decisions of the institution. This personal conviction reinforces the objective link that unites institutionally the CEBs to the hierarchy of the church. These *institutional links* make the CEBs truly *ecclesial* from a sociological point of view, resonating even to the top of the hierarchy what is happening at the grassroots level and vice-versa.[6]

Although the CEBs have a certain autonomy as achieved forms of the local church, they cannot isolate themselves institutionally from the diocese if they do not want to lose their ecclesial character. Herein lies the importance of the priest, of the religious sister, or of the pastoral agent as representative of ecclesiastical authority on the grassroots level. If this ecclesiastical link were to be broken or if the CEBs were to interact among themselves without passing through diocesan authority, they would become a movement or volunteer association, ceasing to be the base of an ecclesiastical model.

Therefore, the ecclesiality of the CEBs necessarily raises the question of the laity's participation in the decision-making process or, if we will, the question of ecclesiastical power.

The survey done in Vitória shows that the laity has not questioned the actual *religious power of bishops*, priests, or pastoral agents, so long as the sacred remains their exclusive domain. Contrary to what one might think, the majority of people consulted still preferred celebrations offered by persons consecrated for this specific purpose, although they also accepted celebrations by laypeople.

In this situation what is put in question is *ecclesiastical power*, that is, the capacity to govern the religious institution. In the Roman Catholic Church the power of governance and the power of spiritual ministry are joined together in the same persons. The holders of religious power also become governing authorities of the institution, thus becoming a "hierarchy" (sacral rule) in the literal sense of the word.

It is exactly this "confusion" that the members of the CEBs question when they demand their participation in institutional decisions such as the naming of persons for ecclesiastical positions, the transferring of priests and pastoral agents, the financial administration and direction of religious organizations. This is a thorny question that generally gets camouflaged under the veil of ministerial theology and gains prominence to the extent that CEBs become centers of local power in the ecclesiastical sphere. When this happens, there arises a conflict between the power of decision on the local level and the decision making of the clergy on the parochial and diocesan levels.

The decentralization of ecclesiastical power to the CEBs would imply the participation of the CEBs' representatives in parochial and diocesan decision making. This would affect the exclusivity of and control by the clergy. This problem becomes clear at diocesan assemblies. At these assemblies, the CEBs' representatives always constitute the majority of the voters with the exception, of course, of conservative dioceses where the base groups do not have the right to vote. This participation of CEBs brings about a sharing of ecclesiastical power.

The solution of the conflict through the sharing of ecclesiastical power would clash, however, with the existing power in the universal church. If a local church would come to the point of breaking its bonds with the universal church, it would immediately be isolated. What has occurred is the tactic of bringing to diocesan assemblies only those decisions in which there is a consensus or at least an agreement between those at the base and the hierarchy. In this way, the two parties avoid potentially divisive arguments.

In fact, the participation of the laity results in an insoluble contradiction: the sharing of ecclesiastical power at the base level does not have anything corresponding to it in the hierarchical institution, where the decision-making power is concentrated in the hands of the clergy, especially in the hands of the bishop. At a first glance, this contradiction is imperceptible because the CEBs are primarily concerned with local problems. However, to the extent that they begin to widen their scope of action, their demands for ecclesiastical power will also increase and spread. Hence the conflict becomes inevitable. It seems that this is the stage in which some dioceses find themselves, especially those where the CEBs' ecclesiastical model is more developed. They have done their best to become *CEB churches* only to discover that this very model of church is incompatible with the existing parochial structure in the *universal church*.

The only goal that the CEBs can realistically reach is to be a *church with CEBs*, trying to combine the parochial structure with the CEB structure. Herein resides the fundamental ecclesiastical conflict, namely, one diocese with a double structure: the parishes on one side and the CEBs on the other side. And even the dioceses that attempt in good faith to put into practice the alternative CEB model as their only structure would have their project obstructed by the structure of the universal church. The recent Vatican admonition of Dom Pedro Casaldáliga, bishop of São Félix in Mato Grosso State, and the recent episcopal nominations to key dioceses have made it quite clear that the Holy See is protecting the parochial structure against the advances of the CEBs.

Because of this, it is impossible for us at this time to predict the outcome of this tension. Either the CEBs will be reduced to "movements" or volunteer lay associations and, as such, be assimilated by the parochial structure, or else one day they will succeed in establishing and consolidating themselves as a new ecclesiastical structure.

Ecclesiastical Conflict and Class Struggle

The expression "class struggle" may have an excessively strong connotation to be applied to the internal conflicts of a religious institution. Nevertheless, if this sociological category is used in the same way as it was by Otto Maduro, following the interpretation of Antonio Gramsci, it can be a valid instrument for the study of religion.[7] By the concept of class struggle, we understand more than just political and economic struggles. In our view, the concept refers also to the effort of a social class to imprint its intellectual and moral direction upon the social arena. In other words, the struggle for social hegemony is one dimension of the class struggle. And it is in this sense that we are considering it here.

Latin American culture is religious throughout the very fiber of its being. Being a "threshold to consciousness," religion selects and presents the categories used by vast sectors of our population to give sense to the cosmos and society.[8] For this reason, the control over religious symbolism is far from being politically indifferent. The class or social group that is able to imprint in the religious code of the people its values and ethics will have social hegemony.[9] "Liberation theology" and the "pastoral option for the poor" are expressions of popular class interest, in the same way that "theology of individual salvation" and "sacramental pastoral programs" are expressions of bourgeois Catholicism.[10] Starting from this hypothesis, we will consider the dimension of the class struggle in the present ecclesiastical conflict.

It is an incontestable fact that the CEBs have been satisfactorily developed only within the poor classes, whether in urban or rural zones. There are only a few and rare exceptions where CEBs have been established in middle-class neighborhoods.[11] This connection is so strong that in current literature about CEBs, "base" has become synonymous with "poor," "the simple people," "the oppressed," referring to the people that we find at the bottom of the social pyramid. One international congress of theology has suggested that the expression "base ecclesial communities" be replaced by the expression "popular Christian communities."

Although there are eminent theologians who support this latter interpretation, it is, to our understanding, an equivocal attitude, equivocal because, if the CEBs were exclusively reserved for the popular classes, there would be no room in such ecclesial groups for those who are not poor. And this would go against one of the basic principles of Catholic identity, which is its universality.[12] This ambiguity comes from thinking of the relationship between the CEBs and popular classes as fixed, and not as an "elective affinity." The CEBs are meant to be for all Catholics; in fact, they want to be a "new way of being church," including its universality. Nevertheless, it is among the popular classes that they have received their greatest receptivity and there that they have developed.

The explication of the development of the CEBs among the popular classes can be found in the chosen affinity between their spiritual and pastoral approach and the interests of the popular classes. Its ideal — better called utopia — of an egalitarian society can be encountered in such examples as the peasants' religious protest movements during the period of agrarian capitalistic implantation, the most outstanding examples of which in Brazil are Canudos, Juazeiro, and Contestado.[13]

This egalitarian vision that still lives on, guarded and celebrated by the popular culture,[14] will come to the surface and will become explicit to the extent that the church is capable of welcoming it and of giving space for it to develop. One study about the successive stages of this process — which is the process of "consciousness-raising" — shows that it is a dialectic: the church helps the popular classes to become self-conscious and, at the same time, the church becomes popular by the action of the popular classes on the structure. Here we will look at some data that will help us to continue our analysis of the "popular church."

The Emergence of the Popular Church[15]

The category *povo* (people) fulfills a key position in the process of "consciousness-raising": through it the subordinate class, which has historically been an unorganized mass, becomes conscious of itself as a historical subject with its own identity, organization, and direction.

In the first stage of this process, *povo* denotes the undifferentiated category of poor inhabitants in rural villages or urban slums. The following expressions are indicative of this mentality:

- "Here is a place where the people work the field; most of them work for others."

- "Here live the marginalized people who build large buildings but don't have a decent house to live in."

- "Here live people who build buses but remain without transport."

What is being expressed here, therefore, is a category that designates a collectivity, a group of people that have a common social experience of living in the downtrodden sector of society.

The category *povo* becomes more explicit when it is opposed to the various categories of the ruling elite. The following quotations should concretize this discussion:

- "The municipal authorities haven't yet done anything to improve the situation of the poor workers."

- "The boss dominates when people remain unorganized."

- "How can we confront the decisions of the businessmen or of the mayor if we're weaker than they are?"

- "The traditional church doesn't believe in the people; it is afraid of us."

- "The city has nice neighborhoods but not for us to live in, because they are for the upper class."

- "All of this is the result of the situation created by the big wigs."

- "There are leaders of the people who are on the side of the oppressors."

In all these quotations, the adversaries of the people are marked as the "big wigs," as those who control the power, whether it comes from politics, ownership of the land or capital, religion, police force, or from any other kind of existing power in the society.

Consequently, the "big wigs" do not live in the same world as that of the "little ones." When seen in this light, the category *povo* no longer merely connotes those who belong to a certain class; rather, it stands for those groups that stand up against the ruling classes or dominating elite, since they have already acquired their own social identity.

The following testimonies show that the people achieve social strength only when they, in some way, manage to organize themselves so that they can determine their own destinies. As long as there is no popular organization, the people do not constitute a historical subject:

- "It is the people themselves that do not believe in their own leaders."

- "The majority of the people still believe that God wanted it this way."

- "The people think that they are incapable."

- "We are a portion of dispersed beings, not a *povo*."

When people are motivated to fight to improve their living conditions, they let go of their social passivity and begin to confront their problems with their own strength. And, at this moment, they become a *popular movement*.

Popular movements may be of different kinds: work teams, similar to the old-fashioned barn-raising; neighborhood organizations demanding public services; workers demanding organization of authentic labor unions; citizens organizing themselves in defense of their rights; people organizing rural cooperatives; landless peasants fighting for agrarian reform; people leading and mobilizing public health organizations; and many other different types of popular struggles and campaigns. What is important in these movements can be shown by the following statement: "People who become conscious of their dignity and their rights overcome individualism so that, via collective action, they unite to confront their difficulties and problems and to assume responsible control of their own action." Or, as another statement shows: "The commission saw that it was necessary to strengthen the groups at the grassroots level so that the neighborhood dweller could continue the struggle." After all, as another statement says, "the struggle concerns the people, and without people there can be no victory."

In this way, grassroots popular groups — among which the CEBs maintain a prominent place — behave as catalytic agents, mobilizing segments of the masses for a collective action, and in this process the *masses* become *povo*. This process can be slow or rapid depending upon the local conditions and the kinds of struggle, but it always produces the same effect: in the momentum of the struggle, people gain the self-awareness that, by uniting and organizing, they get more and more strength to influence their own destiny. Undeniably, this is therefore one process of popular political self-education.

Lastly, we can say that the category *povo*, in the sense here presented, takes on an axiological dimension: the people can discover their own values and develop their own historical project without having to borrow it from the dominant cultural elites. The following statements are examples of this new value awareness:

- "We should always begin with our own interests and not with the interests of those in power."

- "When we recognize the wisdom of the people, when we begin to believe in the lesser ones, then we are cutting the very roots of oppression."

- "The ambient of the *povo* is different; the way that we conduct ourselves is different from the upper class."

- "The *povo* will not be a pawn of power plays; we will choose our own goals."

As we can see, in this stage of popular consciousness, the people not only realize that they are *povo* but feel good being *povo*. Their values, culture, art, and religious expression are no longer considered by them as inferior to those of the elite and therefore they have a motive for being proud of themselves. To be *povo*, to behave as *povo*, to have the popular aesthetical sense and to practice the religion of the *povo* is not a dishonor or something of which to be ashamed. On the contrary, it is reason to be proud, especially for those who identify themselves as different from the elite and, as such, as carriers of their own values.

The relationship between the church and the popular classes has a dialectical character in which two stages clearly stand out. The first stage happens because of the impact of the church in the process of consciousness-raising and organization of the people. There is no doubt that the Christian churches — and not only the Catholic church — are leaving their mark in this process. Nicaragua was the most prominent example: there, one could clearly perceive the Christian mark on the revolutionary process, not under the form of neo-Christendom or anything like it, but under the form of an ethic that gave direction to the popular political practice. It existed as a spirituality that gave life to the popular projects.

In this way it would not be difficult to list many other examples of the ethical, spiritual, and symbolic impact of the Christian churches on the popular movements. The current debate concerning partisan political militancy of Christians underlines exactly the Christian contribution. This contribution is made by way of the current political practice stemming from their option for the poor, which includes a participative and egalitarian option, beginning with the oppressed themselves.[16]

The second dialectical stage of this relationship between the church and the popular classes is the impact of the active presence of the *povo* in the church. It is a well-known fact that in Latin America the poor have always been in the church, but in an anonymous and passive manner. They received the sacraments and learned the catechism, but did not participate effectively in the life and decisions of the institution. They were allowed as "customers" of religious services. Today the participation of the poor has taken a new direction. In the CEBs, in the specialized pastoral groups, and even in parochial and diocesan assemblies, the poor people are no longer just an anonymous mass of "customers." Now they are an organized laity, capable of dynamic participation in ecclesiastical life. In this way the *povo* is imprinting its mark on the church, giving it a new form, a new way of being.

The *popular way of being church* can be clearly perceived at the religious celebrations of the CEBs. We will not find there the ascetic or the rational expression of bourgeois Catholicism but, rather, a noisy, lively expression of popular Catholicism. The popular classes bring to the church their cultural baggage and feel at home in their celebrations and assemblies. We will not find there a contemplative climate where each "soul" has its private encounter with God. We will find a festive one in which the community as a whole celebrates, laying before God its problems, its struggles, and its joys. Instead of the monotonous repetition of preestablished formulas, we find spontaneous prayers, popular songs and poems, using bodily expression along with the rediscovery of religious traditions.

In summary, the *povo* brings to the church its way of self-expression and of interrelationship between neighbors and God. In this way, it confers on the church a "popular way of being," just as feudal nobility gave it an aristocratic way and the bourgeoisie gave it a liberal form.

And it is not just from a cultural point of view that one can speak of the constitution of a "popular church." Christians active in popular movements also bring to the ecclesiastical institution their experiences of participation and decision making that are a characteristic of the popular classes. The experience of the popular movements — where no one rules alone, where solidarity is the fundamental principle, where everyone has equal weight in decision making, and where any authoritarian behavior is held suspect — is transferred to the religious institution, bringing to it popular forms of power with broad-based participation and engagement of all participants.

Such forms of power are incorporated well into the flexible structure of the CEBs whose theological foundation values communion and participation.[17] As such, the CEBs and the popular pastoral groups are becoming ecclesiastical unities where popular structures of power are being experienced. The term "democratic" can also be used here, if one understands it to mean equal participation. However, this form of popular power does not fit into the prevalent hierarchical structure, either at the intermediate or at the top levels. On these levels, the power has a bureaucratic form — to use a Weberian category — which defines the exercise of power by the assignment of specific competence to functionaries, hierarchically organized with separation of persons from their function.[18]

The conflict between a democratic type of power of the "popular church" and a bureaucratic kind of power prevailing in the institution is, therefore, the key in the explanation of the conflict between the two ecclesiastical models.

The Structural Conflict in the Church

Having arrived at this point of our analysis, we can look once again through the question posed in the beginning of this essay concerning the nature of the current process of change in the Catholic Church and the consequent conflicts that can derive from this process.

The analysis of the data brings us to the question of ecclesiastical power. What is in question is not just a model of church, although one cannot discard the importance of the debate between liberation theology and salvation theology. The parochial model that sustains *hierarchical power* of the bureaucratic type is *incompatible* with a decentralized, *democratic model* where the laity share power as in the CEBs and in popular pastoral programs. The contradiction is unsupportable and its development could lead to an institutional rupture.

This structural contradiction is not a recent phenomenon in the Christian churches. Ernst Troeltsch, in a classical work, has already pointed out that the internal structure of the Christian churches is conditioned by the relationship between the religious community and the society.[19] When the religious community is a minority and occupies a marginal position in society, it tends to structure itself in the form of a participative, united, and egalitarian sect that can resist unfavorable social and political pressures. When, to the contrary, a religious community aspires to be coextensive with society, it tends to structure itself in the form of a church that is internally diversified in a way that it is able to contain all social classes and groups under the centralized government of those who carry out the sacred functions. Evidently, we cannot classify CEBs as sects. Nevertheless, it is undeniable that they present many common elements with the Pentecostal groups that can be classified as sects.[20] So we can ask whether the "popular churches" would break with the Catholic ecclesiastical structure.

Such a question clearly appears on the horizon of any social analyst who studies the Latin American Catholic church. And, of course, we cannot avoid it. Although our analysis points to a structural conflict in which antagonistic class interests are influential, we have not yet seen concrete symptoms of an institutional rupture. The case of Nicaragua is a paradigmatic one. In spite of all the pressure that the local hierarchy put on the popular base, practically instigating a rupture, neither side took the first step to force the issue.

In reality, the conflict seems today to be going in the direction of the CEBs' ecclesiastical subordination. Given its structural contradiction within the current parochial model and with no institutional rupture anticipated, the most viable alternative would be — as Troeltsch pointed out as having happened to the mendicant orders in the Middle Age — absorption, subordination, and institutional confinement.[21] The CEBs and the popular pastoral programs could no longer be a "new way of being church" and would find their space as specific movements.

If this happened, Catholics who wanted to express their religious beliefs in a popular way could become members of CEBs, just as others choose to follow the ideals of Opus Dei, Charismatic Renewal, or the Communion and Liberation movement. The parochial structure, without a doubt, has the capacity to absorb the CEBs and even to preserve their theological and pastoral autonomy, as long as the CEBs accept the relinquishment of their definition of themselves as the *basis* of the ecclesiastical structure. And perhaps this would be the only way that the popular church could survive if it lost its episcopal support. But, as long as bishops identify themselves with this "new way of being church," the conflict of two ecclesiastical structures inside the Catholic Church will persist.

Notes

1. This analysis of the Catholic Church before Vatican Council II is grounded in R. Aubert et al., *Eglise dans le monde moderne (1848 à nos jours)*, vol. 5 of *Nouvelle Histoire de l'Eglise*, ed. R. Aubert, M. D. Knowles, and L. J. Rogier (Paris, 1975), and in H. Küng, *Structures de l'Eglise* (Paris: Desclée de Brouwer, 1965). An essay of structural analysis was done using empirical research collected between 1966 and 1972 and can be found in C. A. Medina and Pedro A. Ribeiro de Oliveira, *Autoridade e Participação* (Petrópolis: Vozes, 1973).

2. The sociographic data can be found in Pedro A. Ribeiro de Oliveira, C. A. Steil, and S. S. Rodrigues, *Relatório sobre dados da grande Avaliação da arquidiocese de Vitória*, vol. 2 (Rio de Janeiro: ISER, 1985–87 [dactilo]).

3. This fact has become more and more clear in Brazil, and today the pastoral of the masses is already a frequent theme in the CEBs. In respect to this, see Pedro A. Ribeiro de Oliveira, "Comunidade e massa: Desafio da pastoral popular," *Revista Eclesiástica Brasileira* (June 1984): 287–98.

4. Concerning this theme, see Scott Mainwaring, *The Catholic Church and*

Politics in Brazil 1916–1985 (Stanford, Calif.: Stanford University Press, 1986), especially chaps. 4 and 6. Various other aspects of our analysis converge with those of Scott Mainwaring in this book; however, our theoretical focuses are different.

5. See Pedro A. Ribeiro de Oliveira: "Oprimidos: Opção pela Igreja," *Revista Eclesiástica Brasileira* 164 (December 1981): 643–53. The data that refers to the encounter in Trindade was not published; the results of the questionnaires can be found at ISER, Rio de Janeiro.

6. The definition of the constitutive elements of the CEBs is not yet a resolved question among the different pastoral theologians involved. What is a *community*? Is it a small group? Is it a primary group relationship? Or is it a collectivity on a territorial *basis*? What confers *ecclesiality* on the CEBs? Is it the Christian faith? Or is it the eucharistic ecclesiastical unit? Although generally accepted, the definition of CEB as "popular Christian communities" as defined by the Fourth International Theological Congress held in 1980 is still a polemical and questionable issue. See Pedro A. Ribeiro de Oliveira, "Comunidade, Igreja e Poder," *Religião e Sociedade* 13, no. 3 (November 1986): 48–52.

7. Although Otto Maduro, *Religión y lucha de clases* (Caracas: Editorial Ateneu, 1979), and "New Marxist Approaches to the Relative Autonomy of Religion," *Sociological Analysis* no. 38 (Winter 1977), uses few of Gramsci's categories, it is understood here that the convergence of perspectives between these two is quite significant. For the concepts of Gramsci used here, see *Gramsci dans le texte*, recueil realisé par F. Ricci (Paris: Editions Sociales, 1975), 560–607.

8. The expression is from F. Teixeira: *A Fé na vida* (São Paulo: Loyola, 1987), chap. 2. On this subject, see also C. R. Brandão in *Os Deuses do Povo* (São Paulo: Brasiliense, 1981), and R. C. Fernandes in *Os Cavaleiros do Bom Jesus* (São Paulo: Brasiliense, 1982). In these publications the authors call our attention to the importance of religious categories in popular thought.

9. See P. Bourdieu, "Genèse et structure du champs religieux," *Revue Française de Sociologie* 12, no. 3 (July/September 1971): 295–334.

10. The hypothesis that links Romanized Catholicism to bourgeois hegemony can be found in Pedro A. Ribeiro, *Religião e dominação de classe* (Petrópolis: Vozes, 1985), chap. 7. For an accurate analysis of the theme, see J. B. Metz, "Religião messianica ou religião burguesa?" *Concilium* 145, 1979/5, 78–93.

11. The only example that I know of a well-off CEB is the community of Santa Clara de Assis in the archdiocese of São Paulo. As far as the concept of "popular classes" goes, it is certainly not precise, but we would rather use a concept that is less precise than a classic concept that is inadequate for the Brazilian reality. Concerning this, see L. A. G. Souza, *Classes populares e Igreja nos caminhos da História* (Petrópolis: Vozes, 1982), chap. 4.

12. Scott Mainwaring, *The Catholic Church and Politics in Brazil 1916–1965*, 2, takes this principle as the central thought of institutional analysis.

13. See D. T. Monteiro, "Um confronto entre Juazeiro, Canudos e Contestado," in B. Fausto, ed., *História geral da civilização brasileira*, 3/2 (São Paulo: DIFEL, 1977), 38–92.

14. This is one of the favorite themes of E. Hoornaert in his many works, e.g., *Verdadeira e falsa religião no Nordeste* (Salvador: Beneditina, 1973).

15. This is a part of the text published in *Concilium* 196, 1984/6: "O que significa analiticamente 'povo'?" 108–12.

16. See Clodovis Boff et al., *Cristãos, como fazer política* (Petrópolis: Vozes, 1987).

17. See Yves Lesbaupin, "A Igreja Católica e os movimentos populares urbanos," *Religião e Sociedade* 5 (1980): 189–98.

18. See Max Weber, *Economie et societé* (Paris: Plon, 1971), 1:223–27.

19. See Ernst Troeltsch, *The Social Teaching of the Christian Churches* (New York and Evanston: Harper & Row, 1960).

20. C. L. Mariz: "Religião e pobreza: uma comparação entre as CEBs e as igrejas pentecostais," *Comunicações do ISBR* 30 (1988): 10–19.

21. See Troeltsch, *Social Teaching of the Christian Churches*, 240–45.

WALTER GODDIJN

– 9 –

Toward a Democratic Ideal of Church Government in the Netherlands, 1966–1970: A Sociological Analysis

Scope of the Inquiry

The Netherlands, or Holland as it is called, was one of the few countries to create a national pastoral council in the late 1960s. Dutch Catholics were poised to grasp at once the implications of Vatican II and were extremely energetic in putting them into practice. The Dutch Pastoral Council met in six sessions between 1968 and 1970. It was watched with great international interest and with growing suspicion in Vatican circles. The focus of attention was not so much the controversial nature of the themes discussed, which, in any case, were already at that time subject of heated discussion in the church at large (such as priestly celibacy and the position of women in the church), but rather its effort to construct a model of church government that would satisfy the needs and aspirations of the Catholic community.

The Dutch endeavors could be regarded as an inspirational model for others and a threat to Roman centralism. It is perhaps for this reason that the Dutch Pastoral Council was greeted with such hostility in Rome and in other countries, which showed a marked unwillingness to be seen following in the Dutch footsteps.

It is ironic that only very recently some four hundred American theologians published a report (CTSA) in which a number of proposals (among which was the issue of married priests) are discussed that nearly thirty years ago were exhaustively treated in the Dutch Pastoral Council.

Although countless books have been written to explain what Vatican II did, there has been little detailed analysis of the impact it made on different Catholic communities. Yet the shock waves are still reverberating around the world, and their results are highly ambiguous, uneven, and, in some cases, ignored or forgotten.

156

In this state of affairs, at a time of curiously mixed impulses, perceptions, and attitudes, it seems necessary to ask committed Catholic experts in various academic and practical disciplines to present for general reading the self-images and prospects of Catholicism in different countries in the world church.

The American sociologist Gerhard Lensky, whose classic study of Detroit, *The Religious Factor*, appeared in 1961, remarked with some irony a decade later that Vatican Council II had barely received detailed attention from the international community of scholars. He offers an especially telling contribution:

> Vatican Council II was a major religious revolution. It legitimated dissent within the church, thereby reordering the whole structure of authority, both organizationally and intellectually, and thus sweeping the Catholic Church swiftly into the mainstream of contemporary life. In effect, it was a kind of belated consummation of the Protestant Reformation. Because of this, I am inclined to think that such differences as existed between Catholics and Protestants a decade ago have been seriously eroded and are likely to diminish even more in the decade ahead.[1]

The purpose of this essay is to give neither a detailed account of all the events and ideas that went into the making of the Dutch experiment, nor to offer a satisfactory explanation for its success or failure, but to focus attention on what may be called its most valuable contribution, namely, in the area of decision-making processes and lay consultation. It is in this area that conflicts between Rome and Dutch Catholics arose.[2]

The present author was deeply involved on both a personal and professional basis in the fortunes of the Pastoral Council. The author of this article was director of the Pastoral Institute in Rotterdam (September 1963–September 1972) and, after 1966, secretary general of the Pastoral Council. Being so close to the genesis of the council, witnessing its struggles, hopes, and fears, he is aware that complete detachment and consequently a "value-free" approach is not possible.

In these matters one has to resign oneself to the use of less precise and less satisfactory methods of observation and participation. It is hoped that this study will encourage others to pose new questions and rework old answers in the light of recent developments in the church.

Hans Küng suggests that all of us have to rethink our positions and go beyond acquired convictions about the future of the church.[3] Our story may reveal some unexpected corners and niches in the church in which the Spirit leaves its traces of hope and confidence.

Working toward the Pastoral Council

The trend forward to a more democratic form of church government gained considerable force after the Second World War. After the Netherlands had been liberated from German occupation, Dutch society as a whole had to remold its social and economic institutions after a period of stagnation. Differences between Catholics, Protestants, socialists, and non-Christians became less obvious in a time when Dutch people were forced to cooperate with one another in making a stand against German forces, creating a more flexible and tolerant attitude to different forms of authority.

At that time the pace of industrialization was accelerating and the increasing differentiation between individuals and intellectual and social collectivities was almost imperceptibly altering the relations of elementary and traditional systems, such as the family, the working community, and the parish as local unit for religious groupings. Population mobility today ensures that people are confronted with ways of life that differ from their own, although the anonymity of urban existence may dilute this experience. People accept modernization very easily, and it is a less conscious reality than attachment to traditional cultures. Part of the process of industrialization anywhere in western Europe was the emphasis on the ideal of equality before the law and the accessibility of all to every occupation.

The transformations in Dutch Catholicism were not all at once apparent, but a clear sign of changing attitudes was undoubtedly the famous pastoral letter (Bisschoppelijk Mandement) issued in 1954 by the bishops. They urged Catholics in this letter to remain loyal to the Catholic institutions of the past. Dutch sociologists, historians, and theologians believe that 1954 was an important hallmark in the evolution of Dutch Catholicism. It is relevant to mention here that Dutch society as a whole had become increasingly "pillarized" from the middle of the nineteenth century onward, a process by which secular institutions became segregated on denominational lines. This type of "vertical pluralism" — called *verzuiling* — lays stress on religious differences between socioreligious groups, without affecting in a marked degree their social position, in terms of income, occupation, and status.

The Catholic "pillar" in particular was remarkable for its control over its members. A plethora of interlocking institutions had been set up under the tutelage of the church, all designed to preserve a Catholic identity. The metaphor of "pillar" is somewhat inappropriate, suggesting compactness and separateness, while in any society specific social groupings are interacting with one another in a process of give and take. As has been shown in many studies on this subject, religion often becomes an important vehicle of mass cultural identity, and religious loyalty becomes a crucial means of reaffirming one's loyalty to cultural values that are under threat.

Nevertheless, the corporate model encouraged among Catholics a religious and mental encapsulation. But we cannot infer from this that the functions for the individual are the same as those for the group. Seeds of dissent among intellectuals, Catholic politicians, priests, prominent leaders in trade unions, and educationalists had long been smoldering under the surface of conformity.

The response to the pastoral letter of 1954 was negative among all sections of the Catholic population. Their leaders were no longer satisfied with the corporate model and showed signs of unwillingness to work on confessional lines. More important, the Roman Catholic Church, like other major denominations, no longer had the power to present social issues or conflicts entirely within its own frame of reference. The notion of Catholic identity appeared now to be in decline; no need was felt for a vehicle of such conscious difference.

Meanwhile, a new Catholic middle class had been growing up; it had greatly benefited from post war occupational advancement and generally had little desire to remain encapsulated in the old way of thinking and acting. The more radical leaders among clergy and laity felt that decisions in the church should be legitimated by reason and argument and not on the basis of obedience and tradition. They believed that social integration no longer occurs through organized religion, but through the omnipresent welfare state, and that the social bonds offered by the church must be reworked to fit into an adequate order in which religion would provide spiritual values.

All this was not all at once clear. But suddenly the whole outward structure of Catholic culture was coming apart in an inexplicable fashion. It seems as if essential features disappeared almost overnight, even to the great surprise of Protestants. There was no way of instilling the desired new values or forms that were to replace the old system. The church in the Netherlands was, for the first time, confronted with contrary and often contradictory demands for renewal.

The history of society is always the history of a succession of accumulated choices. Dutch Catholics had a great number of institutional resources at their disposal in meeting the challenge of modernization. The bishops shared the same outlook in assessing the possibilities for renewal and were fairly united in the course of action to be taken. In fact, they were well informed about what went on among the laity and priests. They were assisted in this by such resources as, for example, a number of research institutes, the Catholic University of Nijmegen, highly professional Catholic media, the KRO (Catholic Radio and Television Broadcasting Corporation), and a progressive elite.

The Catholic Demographic Society (KSKI), a professional body established in 1946, had provided the church over a long period with statistics and sociological surveys on the state of Catholicism. A striking feature of these research institutes was that they enjoyed an independent status, and their findings could not be manipulated for other purposes, unlike, for example, the Newman Demographic Society in England, a professional body disbanded by Cardinal John Heenan, who did not like its findings.[4]

Meanwhile, Pope John XXIII had issued his clarion call for *aggiornamento*, the updating of the church. His call did not fall on deaf ears. Vatican II had begun to work out the whole structure of the church. Vatican II was literally "God-sent" for Dutch Catholic leaders. The bishops realized at once that the proposals for church renewal would give them a *legitimate* basis for doing something similar for their own church. Some of the conciliar texts proved to be crucial in understanding the legitimate position of a particular church. An important insight of Vatican II was precisely to locate the primary reality of the church in the local church. Speaking of the local churches, the council fathers declared: "It is in these and formed out of them that the one and unique Catholic church exists" (*Lumen Gentium,* no. 23).

As the saying goes, "Make hay while the sun shines." On December 24, 1960, the bishops issued a pastoral letter informing the faithful that they wished to apply the ideas of Vatican II to the Dutch situation. The principal author of the text was Professor Edward Schillebeeckx at the University of Nijmegen, but the bishops took full responsibility for the text.

A plea was made for relating the monarchical rule of the pope to other levels of the church and for allowing a greater measure of autonomy for the local church. Emphasis was laid on the principle of "collegiality": the pope rules together with the bishops. This would not violate the basis of the Petrine-papal doctrine, that all bishops, priests, and faithful must be in communion with one another and with the Holy See. This letter, translated in many languages, attracted worldwide attention. It certainly set the Dutch on a definite course.

Another important factor in shaping the bishops' attitudes was their experience of Vatican II itself. At the council, the church appeared not to be uniform, but presented itself as a world organization of local churches, representing different cultures and nationalities. For the first time the younger churches in the Third World were represented by brown, black, and yellow bishops. It was certainly an exhilarating experience. Hitherto, bishops had been their own promulgators and counselors with or without advice. Now they were forced to look beyond their own horizons, to listen to others, and to intermingle with a great variety of people, both formally and informally.

The bishops also had to rely on experts in articulating their views. There were over four hundred *periti* at the council, most of them canonists, historians, and theologians. The expectations of the church had changed, but so had the expectations of the theologians, who were no longer content to defend acquired convictions but sought to effect change in the church itself. They pleaded for freedom of research and expression. "Pluralism" had become a fact of theological life.

The lesson was not lost. The bishops decided in 1963 — when the Vatican Council was still in full swing — to set up the Pastoral Institute of the Church Province in the Netherlands in Rotterdam to facilitate lines of communication between church leaders and to process valuable information. This institute merged in 1972 with the Secretariate of the Church Province in the Netherlands. Its chief purpose was to coordinate lay commissions and diocesan councils and to prepare reports for the use of the bishops. Its professional status was recognized, and its findings were publicized for reflection and debate.

Meanwhile, formal and informal discussions on the internal transformation of the church were bound to produce conflicting opinions. It was out of the question to start from scratch. Large institutions are slow to change, believing that continuity with the past is more important than revolutionary breaks. Although everybody was convinced that decision making in the church ought to be a collaborative work among several persons of appropriate rank and ability, undertaken in a spirit of consensus with those likely to be affected, it was by no means clear how this task should be undertaken. The bishops were not given any directives as to how Vatican II proposals should be implemented. Nor were the ordinary faithful consulted.

The important contribution in this area of "democratization" was made by G. de Vet, bishop of Breda, the youngest in the episcopate. He was deeply interested in sociology and the principles of industrial organization. In addition, he enjoyed the confidence of Cardinal Bernard Alfrink. On November 16, 1965, Bishop de Vet delivered a speech in the presence of seventy Dutch-speaking missionary bishops who, together with their advisors, had attended the sessions of Vatican II. He raised some critical questions: would Rome be willing to encourage plural forms of government within the church, and would episcopates be inclined to support such developments? He noted that the faithful at the grassroot levels were not sufficiently informed by the spirit of Vatican II and that their earlier sentiments might well have evaporated.

The spirit of the council, de Vet insisted, is chiefly pastoral, ecumenical, and open. In this address the term "democratization" is referred to as "ordered process of democratization" in the practical government of the church (*De episcoporum munere*, 27, 37vv). The substance of this speech was reproduced in a joint pastoral letter on December 8, 1965. There is still mention of a "provincial council," but it was hoped that its work would lead to a more comprehensive compendium for dealing with Vatican II proposals. It was felt that efforts in this direction should not be haphazard and based on subjective impressions.

As a consequence, the synod of bishops requested on January 18, 1966 the Pastoral Institute in Rotterdam to make preparations for the Provincial Council. Bishop de Vet advised the cardinal about the feasibility of such a project. Cardinal Alfrink consented, permitting the establishment of a preparatory commission that would not be clerically dominated and controlled. But on March 16 Bishop de Vet announced that the term "Provincial" should be dropped and be replaced by the term "Pastoral," mainly because the Pastoral Institute had already obtained a great deal of information about the pastoral activities of the dioceses. It was believed that a common strategy should be devised in coordinating diocesan activities on a national level, in the hope that as many people as possible would be involved in the church's decision-making processes.

Strenuous efforts were made to build toward the Pastoral Council from the parish and diocesan level. The next step was to announce post office boxes to which the people could write. In addition, the Catholic media were employed to clarify central issues. Special programs were prepared for radio and television to inform the public. It was the first time that outsiders also got a fascinating glimpse of what was going on in the Catholic community.

One result of the proliferation of consultative bodies was that experts were given great influence. It was suspected that members of the middle class were predominant on the lay commissions and that the ordinary faithful were not sufficiently represented. The manner of appointment to membership of the commissions reflected, of course, a person's previous role in the life of the church. Some members might be appointed for their technical expertise in a particular area, while others might be "elected" or "nominated" as representatives of certain group interests. The net result was that the membership of the commissions tended to consist largely of people who were committed to a type of reform that suited their own purposes. This danger was averted because the organizing committees took care that decisions were to be open to public discussion and that deliberations were available for inspection.[5]

A more crucial question was to what extent lay participation could be built into decision-making processes. No one at the time was suggesting that the church is or ought to be a democracy, or that important decisions could be made on the basis of popular consent. According to the popular view, the democratic process is regarded as a summation or indexing of individual preferences, and, for many people, democracy simply means "majority rule." But, of course, the majority never rules, for a majority decision is simply a setting of terms under which discussion and discourse go on indefinitely for the lifetime of the organization.

Cardinal Alfrink put it this way:

> The Pastoral Council is neither a mere talking shop leading nowhere, nor is it a parliament that can make legislative decisions, for if it were a mere talking shop, it would not take the laity seriously and if it were a parliament, it would not take the bishops seriously.[6]

The church, moreover, apart from being an organization, is also an expression of values and beliefs. As Cardinal Joseph Ratzinger recently said: "The church is no democracy, because she cannot allow her eternal truths to be adapted to the changing morals and opinions of the majority."[7]

Whatever internal organization was contemplated, it was obviously not on the same level as revealed truth. The role of the lay experts was agreed upon in a stormy session on January 19, 1967 in Rotterdam. They were encouraged to formulate ideas, to put forward proposals, and so on, but their voice remained consultative, on the condition that the bishops could not just give their advice without some justification. It was an outstanding feature of the Pastoral Council that attention to lay expertise was taken very seriously, and properly channeled, enhancing in this way the responsibility of the laity.

It was realized that, if bishops cede power, it will not simply ebb away, but will pass into other hands. Furthermore, some members of the Pastoral Council were chosen not for their professional skills, but in the hope that they would be able to represent the viewpoint of the nonexpert, the "person in the pew." Yet much misunderstanding arose between the Dutch and Rome on this point.

The Pastoral Council was meant to be a consultation of a special kind in which voting procedures were used for the purpose of getting more exact assessments of the various opinions, and not at converting these into policy decisions. Furthermore, a decision was seen as a partial resolution of a conflict, or, to put it differently, a democratic process in the understanding of the bishops was punctuated by decisions that are essentially temporary in nature, since they do not close the discussion but constantly modify the proposals. The fact is that the Pastoral Council was a serious attempt to manifest a new way of expressing church authority in a modern world in which structural change is a widespread phenomenon.

Peter Berger has suggested that there are three options confronting cultural and religious traditions in this situation. The deductive option is the refusal to communicate with the surrounding world. It is in effect cultural encapsulation, a reaffirmation of past certainties. Such a course dooms a culture or a religious tradition to irrelevance. It is an option that aptly characterized the corporate model of prewar Dutch Catholicism. The reductive option implies drift and an acceptance of cultural relativism. Finally, the inductive option implies dialogue. It takes given traditions seriously and tries to rework them to clarify the Christian faith.[8]

Cardinal Alfrink contrasted two views of authority in the church — the *dominating* view of authority, which he believed had gone from modern conscience, and the *dialogical* approach, which he continued to hope would be liberating on the road to future developments. "The Dutch intention," he explained, "was not to create a parliament, but to set up dialogue in which all, at their own level, had their share of responsibility."[9]

The Collapse of the Experiment

The Dutch Pastoral Council met in six sessions between 1968 and 1970. But in 1968 *Humanae Vitae* was published by Pope Paul VI. There is little doubt that the encyclical had an adverse effect on Catholics all over the world. The American sociologist Andrew Greeley, for example, maintained that the encyclical retarded developments, initiated by Vatican II, which in his view were accepted by American Catholics as a whole.[10]

Humanae Vitae generated the most passionate and extensive debate that the postconciliar church has known. The encyclical had not been put forward under the formal label of "infallible," but it did not stipulate what was to be done about those who disagreed. For the ordinary Catholic in the Netherlands, as elsewhere, the best thing to do was to look for solutions outside the church.

A graver issue was that moral rules had been completely cut adrift from the moral values they were designed to defend. The crisis in the moral authority of the church aggravated the situation of dissenting Catholics. What, in any case, became clear was that institutional forms do not necessarily create the conditions for a personal experience of faith.

Another source of conflict was the publication of the *New Catechism* in 1966. The *New Catechism* caused controversy among progressives and conservatives as well. What alarmed Roman authority was the tenor of the views put forward. The starting point was that faith could not be commended by simple assertion and that God's saving grace could not be confined exclusively to institutional channels. Faith was not a matter of learning the catechism by heart, but a quest for God that unfolds with life and is never finished.

The catechism became a best-seller. It appealed to some who wished to take refuge in the private sphere; to others because of its emphasis on personal commitment and religious experience. There is little doubt that the new catechism strained the relationship between Rome and the participants of the Pastoral Council. It looked as if the Protestant ethos, laying stress on the individual's responsibility before God, was slipping in through the backdoor.

Signs of disapproval soon clouded the Dutch sky. By April 1969 Cardinal Alfrink had shown himself sensitive to Rome's objection that the bishops seemed to have abdicated their responsibility. In 1970 he declared: "In our country we are still learning the difficult art of dialogue. The bishops will do everything in their power to keep that dialogue open and to win understanding for what the church in Holland is trying to do."

At its final plenary session on April 8, 1970, Cardinal Alfrink declared that its work, which so far had been provisional and experimental, would be continued in a *permanent* Pastoral Council. The idea behind this was to allow the local church and the national conference of bishops to exercise their own authority on a regular basis. In *Christus Dominus* (no. 38) the decision to erect episcopal conferences was left in the hands of the participating bishops, although canon 449 reserves the decision to the Holy See.

By August 31, 1971, the statutes of the new organism were published.

They explained its purpose in these words: "The scope of the Permanent Pastoral Council is to foster the cohesion of all Dutch Catholics in the development of a common pastoral strategy." It added: "This council is a *strategic* body, and therefore *more* than a consultative body" (italics ours). The last phrasing caused Roman suspicion, and reactions were soon forthcoming.

The answer was loud and clear: the church's government and pastoral policy were not a matter for discussion; they were to be kept firmly in the hands of the bishops. Everybody else was granted merely a consultative voice. Rome objected to the fact that the role of the bishops had been whittled down and that only a semblance of episcopal authority was left. The Dutch had little choice. Any hint of disloyalty to Rome in such grave matters was abhorrent to the cardinal. As a result the bishops gave way and announced on December 2, 1972, the setting up of a new body to be called the National Council for Pastoral Deliberation, which was but a shadow of its predecessor.

Disappointment and surprise grew when it became known how the appointment of Bishop A. Simonis to the diocese of Rotterdam had come about. The resignation of Bishop Martin Jansen in 1970 gave the diocese of Rotterdam a chance to experiment with the new system of consultation. There was a strong desire to involve all the people of the diocese in the choice of a new bishop. The people of the Rotterdam diocese, after they had received questionnaires, wanted a bishop who was able to listen, take advice, and work with others for the good of the diocese.

On December 30, 1970, Bishop Simonis's appointment was announced without any sign of consideration for the longstanding and elaborate procedures of consultation. Even the traditional procedures were deliberately set aside at the drop of a hat. The maxim of Pope Leo the Great was rejected: "On no account is anyone to be a bishop who has not been chosen by the clergy, desired by the people, and consecrated by the bishops of the province with the authority of the metropolitan." Cardinal Alfrink, the primate of the Dutch church, was evidently not asked to approve this appointment.

Rome's policy became even clearer when, in rapid succession, one conservative bishop after another was appointed from 1972 until 1985, involving changes in personnel by removing people from official posts who differed from the new bishop's line of thought. The arbitrariness of the appointments were even more startling. A missionary bishop, Hendrik Bomers, for example, was plucked from Ethiopia to Haarlem, although he had no personal experience of the Dutch situation.

Bishop Simonis became archbishop of Utrecht and a cardinal, and Bishop Gysen became auxiliary in Roermond. The Salesian Jan ter Schure, of the same cast of mind, was transferred to the largest diocese in the Netherlands, 's-Hertogenbosch and has shown himself to be unable to bridge the gap between himself and clergy and laity. As the author has said, Rome's *bulldozer*[11] did its work effectively, so that all the things for which the Dutch had worked so hard went for nothing. As a result, the Dutch ecclesiastical landscape was radically transformed. One of the negative effects was that the faithful were to witness a hierarchy who were not able to resolve their internal differences on common policies.

Reactions to these structural changes are difficult to assess, for the best of all possible structures are only as good and as effective as the people who run them. There can be no doubt that many fruitful ideas were nipped in the bud. It is ironic that some of the Dutch proposals on priestly celibacy and the position of women in the church should now figure on the list of American bishops.

In the Dutch church there was a resolution concerning celibacy in 1970. Some of the details deserve to be remembered. It stated that, for future priests, celibacy should no longer be a requirement for admission to the ministry. Priests who intend to marry or have already been married should — under certain conditions — be given the opportunity to remain in office or to be readmitted to it; married people should be given the opportunity to be admitted to the ministry; compulsory celibacy as a condition for ministerial work should be abrogated.

It should be pointed out that the bishops did *not* vote on this resolution concerning celibacy. But on January 19, 1970, only twelve days after the council meeting, they published a press communiqué in which they admitted that not all the faithful share the same views on celibacy and that this topic should be further discussed with the Holy Father, informing him about the exact situation in the local church. The bishops did state their view that their religious community would be better off if, beside a celibate priesthood clearly chosen in freedom, married priests should be admitted to the Latin church; i.e., if married people could be ordained priests, and if, in special cases and under certain conditions, priests who have married could return to the ministry.[12]

But the bishops added a caution:

> But no single church province can do this alone, without consulting the Holy Father and the world church. A deliberation of the entire church about such important and urgent matters, which regard the whole church, would certainly be beneficial for the church.

On July 30, 1970, the Dutch bishops published a comment: Cardinal Alfrink had frankly discussed the problem of celibacy with the Holy Father, who showed great sympathy, but, in the end, no definite agreement was reached. Both sides had expressed the wish that the discussion between the Dutch episcopate and the Holy See be continued.

The resolution on women in the ministry also was farsighted. It said that it is necessary, as soon as possible, to enlist women in all those fields of church activity in which their appointment is possible under present church law. Further developments should go toward admitting them to all ecclesiastical functions, presiding over the eucharistic celebration not excluded. As can be surmised, this resolution was shelved and was not open to further discussion in Rome.

We do not know, on an empirical level, whether this abrupt change in leadership has retarded the spiritual forces initiated by the Pastoral Council and to what extent it is affecting or has affected the spiritual vitality of the Catholic community in the Netherlands. The wrangling about the appointments of bishops does not show in great depth that a shift has occurred from engagement to indifference among committed Catholics. It would be dangerous to assume that the progressives are always betting on the right horse and that traditionalists always miss the boat.

What we do have, rather, is a degree of incomprehension between the generations as time goes on. The vision of a "participatory community" has receded, and the young distance themselves from the old vision. This vision has lost its power to inspire younger people. Conformity to a prepackaged image, enforced upon the majority of the faithful, is not likely to be acceptable.

We must be aware of defining a blurred picture too precisely. Religious innovations can justify change and reform, as well as social conservatism or dissent. We cannot simply assume *a priori* in any social situation that because a reorganization of church structures is proposed, all the groups in a community will support or reject it. Although the Catholic community in the Netherlands appears fairly homogeneous in outlook and behavior, it may be easily forgotten that *regional* differences may play a much greater part in perceptions and attitudes than is generally supposed to be the case.

History, as we have said, is an accumulation of choices, and people are not free to distance themselves from their own cultural inheritance. The predominantly Catholic "South" (including the provinces of Brabant and Limburg) has a history of development different from that of the North. The Catholic South has never known the full impact of the Protestant Reformation, whereas Catholics in the North have been assimilated into the wider society over a long period of time.

Even in a densely populated country like the Netherlands, now highly industrialized, differences in mentality persist below the surface.[13] It is an ironic twist of history that it is precisely the Catholics in the diocese of Roermond (some 80 percent Catholic) in Limburg, who have always looked with suspicion and lethargy in the past on a strongly centralized authority, whether secular or religious, who are now, once more, saddled with a bishop they do not really want.

Some Lessons to Be Drawn from the Dutch Experiment

The proposals of Vatican II had induced Dutch Catholics to do something similar for the local church. It should be remembered that the preparatory work for holding their own council took place when Vatican II was still in full swing. The council fathers were, at that time, still wrestling with the new insights, and the conciliar texts were as yet not fully understood. In retrospect the Dutch tended to regard the Vatican Council somewhat optimistically, as an expression of a truly multicultural church, in which national episcopates would be entitled to have a share in decision making. The conciliar texts pointed to the primary reality of the church as residing in the local church. The local church is the Catholic Church in a particular place (*Lumen Gentium,* no. 23).

The Dutch interpreted some of these texts to their own advantage, without realizing that other interpretations were possible. There were those who interpreted them selectively and those who would whittle them away to suit other purposes. In this respect the Dutch underestimated the *curia Romana*, who interpreted the new insights in terms of canon law. Vatican II did not, on this point, effectively resolve the question of who has *legal* authority in terms of canon law, which, despite revisions, continues to enforce a monarchical form of government. This raises afresh the question of universal norms, in particular the 1983 Code of Canon Law. It should be obvious that pastoral insights cannot be exhaustively translated into judicial terms. The Dutch effort revealed that "collegiality" was not allowed to be brought into the authorized structures of the church. The principle of collegiality became, as a result, very inadequate in handling local differences. While in principle local differences were admitted, it appeared in practice that they were not to be decided locally, but in Rome. Apparently, there is no law enforcing the recommendations of Vatican II, so that they can be ignored or only partially applied, leaving the initiative to local episcopates. As the appointment of conservative bishops between 1972 and 1985 over the heads of the people has revealed, the very notion of episcopal collegiality has become largely illusionary.

This is perhaps one of the reasons that the Netherlands in particular has been singled out for harsh and corrective treatment by the pope, who seems to think that the Dutch have taken collegiality too seriously. But, in the end, the hard-line proved to be counterproductive. The negative effects of this policy brought about in the Netherlands still further divisions among the faithful and weakened the position of the hierarchy. Its internal unity was shattered, and, what is worse, the bishops were not able to resolve their own problems.

The Dutch hierarchy failed to communicate sufficiently with the internuntius in the Hague and to call upon him to render his services to the Pastoral Council. The nuncio, pronuncio, or apostolic delegate is, so to speak, the intelligence service of the Holy See. He has to send in reports on matters of interest, to keep track of dissident theologians, to scrutinize the goings-on of bishops, priests, and the faithful. The worldwide network of Vatican diplomats means that the Holy See has highly trained people on the spot to provide it with information. The exaltation of the role of the internuntius and the playing down of the local hierarchy is a favorite game of the curia.

The Dutch bishops were a little naive in supposing that their proposals would be acceptable in Rome on their face value. Yet it is known that in collective decision-making areas in churches, and in any institution of whatever kind, the feeling is often quite overtly articulated that problem solving is rarely properly handled in the formal arena of discussion. So what normally happens is that the persuading, bargaining, and coalition building has to be done *outside* the formal arenas, beforehand.

The Dutch were, in this respect, ill-equipped in dealing with the cat-and-mouse game in Vatican diplomatic circles. They represented only a tiny fraction of the world episcopate of the Vatican Council. Powerful professional interest groups among them acted as lobbyists for causes that had little to do with Dutch concerns. Apart from this, the Dutch were not able to lobby for their ideas in countries like France, Germany, and Great Britain, with the consequence that they became isolated after the first wave of victory was spent. Furthermore, they underestimated the manipulative power of groups of influential Dutch Catholics, mostly of a conservative stamp, who got a sympathetic hearing in Rome. They put the Dutch undertaking in a bad light. This isolation discouraged the Dutch from projecting their self-image to the outside world.

When I delivered a lecture on October 29, 1975 at the University of Tübingen on "Konflikte in der Kirche," Hans Küng remarked that "it was the greatest scandal in the history of the church in the twentieth century that France and Germany have left the Dutch church to cultivate their own garden."[14] In a broader perspective, the whole question of an appropriate form of church government has since then received a new impetus in the light of developments in Latin America, Africa, and throughout the Third World. Inevitably Vatican II took, as starting point, the vote of the Christian churches in industrialized Western society. This was one of the major problems that bedeviled the attempt of the council fathers to offer an analysis and program for the whole world.

The Vatican II declarations dealing with the social and cultural aspects of the church are valuable. But the European-American limits of the social self-analysis were not realized until later. Reflection did not keep pace with the new awakening of Christianity in various countries in the Third World. It has been observed that in the year 2000, most of the world's Catholic population will be living in Latin America. Before long, the numerical center of gravity of the Catholic Church will be in the South. Christianity will no longer be the monopoly of Europe, although this Europe, the North, is still making the decisions on how Christian communities should be structured.

In any case, the issue of what form of church government is likely to develop in these countries will be outside Rome's control. There are now some one hundred thousand basic Christian communities in Latin America that, in their desire to restructure the Christian life, are less willing to maintain the imported model of church government.[15] It is often said that people make history without knowing it. It may well be that the Dutch example will bear fruit in some place or in some time unknown to us. The new ecumenical spirit and the respect that representatives of the great religions have lately shown toward each other attest perhaps to a conversion to the universalist spirit at the heart of Christianity.

Notes and References

1. Gerhard Lensky, "The Religious Factor in Detroit, Revisited," *American Sociological Review* 36 (1971): 48–50.

2. The genesis and aftermath of the Dutch Pastoral Council is recorded by the author, Walter Goddijn, in *The Deferred Revolution: A Social Experiment in Church Innovation in Holland 1960–1970* (Oxford, New York: Elsevier, 1977), and in numerous articles. See also Walter Goddijn, "Pastoral Concilie en Kerkelijk leiderschap," research project by H. Wewerinke and F. Mommers, theological faculty at Tilburg (Baarn: H. Nelissen, 1986); Walter Goddijn, "Het geheim van J. P. II" (The Secret of John Paul II), science fiction about the abdication of Pope John Paul II in 1995 and the church in the year 2000; Walter Goddijn, "Das Dilemma des Niederländische Katholizismus: Für oder gegen Rom?" in Norbert Greinacher and Hans Küng, eds., *Katholische Kirche: Wohin, Wider den Verrat am Konzil* (Munich-Zurich, 1986), 269–85; and Philippe Stouthard and Gérard van Tillo, eds. *Katholiek Nederland na 1945* (Baarn: Ambo, 1985).

3. Hans Küng, *The Church Maintained in Truth* (New York: Seabury Press, 1980), 82–83.

4. A. E. C. W. Spencer, "Demography of Catholicism," *The Month*, March 1975.

5. In May 1980 a National Pastoral Council was held in Liverpool, but its decisions were not open to public discussion and lay membership of the commissions was almost entirely middle class (Michael Hornsby-Smith, *The Month* [March 1975]).

6. *Alfrink en de Kerk, 1951–1976* (Baarn: Ambo, 1976), essays dealing with Alfrink's views on collegiality and authority.

7. Cardinal J. Ratzinger, cited in *Intermediair*, December 21, 1990, 23.

8. Peter Berger, *The Heretical Imperative* (Garden City, N.Y.: Anchor Press, 1979).

9. Walter Goddijn, "Alfrink, een gedistantieerd hervormer," in *Alfrink en de Kerk, 1951–1976*, 254–73.

10. Andrew M. Greeley et al., *Catholic Schools in a Declining Church* (Kansas City, Mo.: Sheed and Ward, 1976), chapter 5.

11. Walter Goddijn, "Rome's Bulldozer," *The Tablet*, February 23, 1991.

12. Walter Goddijn, *Rode October: Honderd dagen Alfrink* (Baarn: Ambo, 1983).

13. T. L. Koopsmanschap in J. Wynen, *Hoe Katholiek is Limburg? De Kerk en het Bisdom Roermond* (Maasbree, 1981). A regional analysis.

14. Walter Goddijn, "Konflikte in der Kirche: Dargestelt am Beispiel der Katholische Kirche der Niederlande," *Theologische Quartalschrift* (1976): 15–27.

15. Leonardo Boff, *Ecclesiogenesis: The Base Communities Reinvent the Church* (Maryknoll, N.Y.: Orbis Books, 1986).

Translated by Dr. T. L. Koopsmanschap

MARIE AUGUSTA NEAL, S.N.D.

-10-

Democratic Process in the Experience of American Catholic Women Religious

One of the major findings of the Sisters' Surveys of 1967, 1980, and 1989 is that "blind obedience" is no longer accepted in faith as holy by Catholic sisters.[1] Deep respect for and appreciation of those who are willing to accept positions in the administration of religious groups have replaced that former unquestioning call to obey lawful superiors in all situations short of manifest sin. The search for God's will in reflective meditation is very strong. It includes: reading the signs of the times, listening to the community gathered to deliberate solutions to problems, hearing the cries of the poor and recognizing God's presence where the poor organize to claim their rights as human beings. What has changed is the assumption that God speaks more directly to those in charge than to the members whose commitment is to carry out the mission.

The new emphasis on participating in the decisions that affect one's life has been experimented with in various forms over the past quarter century since the Second Vatican Council. Although it is far from perfected to date, the effort to teach the democratic skills needed for responsible and accountable participation at every level of decision making is the object of prayerful meditation, contemplative reflection, community experimentation, and cooperative action in formation programs for new members and in ongoing formation and reformation of other members. This conviction that God speaks in and through the community and not only to those delegated to administer is a radical transition from pre–Vatican II institutionalized customs and mystiques, one symbolized by the dropping of the title "reverend mother."

What is the historical origin of the radical change in the faith position of Catholic women in institutes of religious life regarding authority and obedience in the late twentieth century, and what are the implications for the immediate future of the Catholic Church in the United States? These are the questions pondered in this essay.

172

The relationships that develop historically between religious institutions and behavioral practices are intricate and complex. They are also historically specific in their invention and function. To capture this linkage into a research design requires careful and systematic observation of the historical process, as well as the creation of well-defined variables that operationalize the concepts that the researcher hypothesizes account for the phenomena being investigated.

I became aware in the mid-1950s of the fact that dedicated Catholic actionists and theologians were calling Catholics to address the injustices in race relations in the United States. At the same time, they were chiding us as a church in the mid-twentieth century for our blind obedience to customs and systems that allowed many of us in a world church to fail to see the related evil in the Holocaust, the atomic destruction at Hiroshima and Nagasaki, the repression of native populations in Latin America, and racial segregation in our city schools and in the job market. All these were institutionalized evil that prevented felt responsibility by members of one community for what was being experienced in others.[2]

The writings of post–World War II theologians — Henri de Lubac, Yves Congar, M. D. Chenu, Karl Rahner — and others involved in action for change of unjust structures — Gary MacEoin, William Ferree, John Cogley, Gordon Zahn — were calling attention to these social problems.[3] At the same time powerful forms of enculturated definitions of the situation prevented us as a group from seeing what needed to be done, even when those needs were presented in dramatic forms of protest, as in the civil rights marches. A number of theologians speaking persuasively to these issues were silenced, such as de Lubac, Chenu, Congar, and Rahner, lest an aroused public destroy an entrenched order of church and society.

Two agendas in particular manifested themselves to the church in the decade before the Second Vatican Council: the plight of the poor of the world unjustly repressed by powerful structures of governance and economies, and the blind obedience demanded of those who proposed changes in social conditions to reform those structures. The two agendas were manifest in the activities of the United Nations wherein study was being done to make the Declaration of Human Rights, adopted as part of its charter in 1948, into covenants binding in international law. The human rights under examination divided thematically into what came to be known as the Covenant on Political and Civil Rights, on the one hand, and the Covenant on Economic, Social and Cultural Rights, on the other.[4]

Because the capitalist countries related directly to the political and civil rights and the socialist countries to the economic, social, and cultural rights, the commission working on the covenants had to divide into those two themes in order to get their work done, so great was the disagreement between the two ideologies. Their task, begun in 1953, was not completed until 1967, and the covenants were not voted into adoption by the United

Nations until 1976.[5] In the encyclical *Pacem in Terris*, published in 1963, the Catholic Church officially recognized the entire set of rights, including also the right of all peoples to "self-determination and to use freely the resources of their land," a right added to both covenants in 1967.

Understanding this human rights struggle as background to the church's attitude toward models of governance that are fully participatory, allowing each individual person the right to participate in the decisions that affect her or his life, is essential in discussion of the historical movement toward a democratic church. This issue of democracy is a part of the historical development of Christianity since the Protestant Reformation, which begins with a challenge to the authority of the pope, perceived by the year 1517 as requiring a conformity contrary to what is called for in the gospel. Having sacralized structures adopted from medieval monarchy when exercising discipline, the Roman Catholic Church so scandalized some groups of Christians in the newly established nations of Europe that they changed their relationship to the church.

After breaking away from the Roman Catholic Church, various Protestant denominations then developed different structures of governance, experimenting with new modes of participation that would in time reorder relationships among church members. These new structures varied widely, ranging from belief in authority as residing in the members (Congregationalists), in the elders (Presbyterians), or in the bishops (Episcopalians), to there being no authority at all (Society of Friends).

The more participatory forms came in time to be associated with nations that adopted successfully a capitalist economy. This pattern manifested itself so clearly that one of the earliest classics in modern sociology is an analysis of this association written by a founder of sociology, namely, Max Weber's *Protestant Ethic and the Spirit of Capitalism*.[6] At the same time, the nations that remained more traditionally feudal, honoring landlords' control of estates, with semifree serfs bound to work them according to the lord's will, also retained the traditional style of church government based on the same dependency model. Hence, these Catholic nations preserved hierarchical state and church structures. They also adopted a decidedly weaker work ethic, one decried in the nineteenth century as based on a philosophy of *carpe diem*. It included a workday/playday pattern following the planting and harvesting timetable and was not well adapted to the round-the-year work week called for by the transition from an agricultural economy to an industrial, technology-driven one.

It was easy to see the contrast in the two work ethics: a growth to a responsible, self-determining quality in the Protestant ethic, and a more docile, childlike character of dependency in the older, more traditional, and longer institutionalized workday/playday pattern. The latter, carried over from the old feudal-structured society, became in time associated with the Catholic Church, which had not broken with the old regimes and forms.

The language of community came to characterize the Protestant ethic, while the "Catholic" ethic kept the language of family, with fathers as patriarchs, lording over the farm workers as children and enforcing their wills in the order of life, work, and even religion.

When these farming peoples, however, came to the United States as immigrants seeking a livelihood and brought their families and churches with them, they maintained the dependency patterns in the labor market for a time, until they organized into unions and experienced the power and responsibility codetermining for their wages, hours, and conditions of work. But some were more comfortable with the family model, and the concept of accountability, linked to representative forms of government adopted earlier by the Protestant groups, was alien to them. They introduced the family model into the work place and the work ethic, thereby unwittingly generating the Mafia and/or other disruptive structures in the work system. All these factors and many more of like origin raised the question, many times over, of the proper form of governance to be exercised by adults, or peers, in situations clearly calling for change because the existing structures had become manifestly ineffective for their intended use.

When models of one type of relationship within organizations are imitated in another setting simply because they are familiar and have been sacralized by use over many generations, there comes a time when their dysfunction becomes manifest and their encultured rationalization questionable. The mid-twentieth century came to be that time for the Catholic Church in the United States. The model of the Roman family, an absolutist social and political model, wherein, by Roman law fathers had the right of life and death over slaves (workers of the time), children, and wives is the case in point.

Education to literacy and calculation, down through the centuries, has freed sons and daughters alike from the need to be dependent on family for support. With the advent of technology, dependence on the agricultural seasons and on the land control of feudal lords was no longer the only source of subsistence for succeeding generations of progeny. This same education revealed to both daughters and sons why and how progeny were, in fact, generated. Thus, daughters learned their vulnerability to their master's will in the exercise of the master's sexual capacity to generate progeny.

The movement in the mid-twentieth century for responsible control of world population size, in recognition of the resources needed to sustain life adequately, led inevitably to a review of the conventional rules of marriage promulgated by churches even to the mid-twentieth century. By these rules of the marriage vow, women were made subject to the will of their husbands with respect to family size and decisions about the life and death of their progeny, be it in family setting or in the arena of war. These same unexamined, hence unchallenged, norms extended to other structures of society equally questionable today. For example, the law's assumption of the legitimacy of male dominance was the rationale for husbands' control of homes through male ownership.

Review of these and many other factors of control over their lives taught women and men alike that the rules for institutionalization are generated by both interests and values that are historically defined. But they learned further that whatever the balance of the one or the other, i.e., interest or value, sacralization occurs and is applied both to legitimate decisions already in place and to justify those yet to be made. But with this insight into the uses and abuses of customs, including religious ones, comes also the realization of responsibility for choices to be made and accountability for those already made.

Earlier, the limited education of women and their incorporation into the unpaid and underpaid work force in the nations of the world set critical limits on what they could be expected to do and to become. But when the reason for the existence of a rule no longer holds, then the rule loses its moral authority or power. With the abrogation of the dependency relation of the wife on the husband for example, the marriage vow can no longer authentically ask women to be subject to their husbands. Women begin to question the husband's demands to accept what cannot in conscience be done by women educated to recognize what may be dangerous to their health or exploitative of their children.

This new responsibility not to obey arises with her education because she becomes primarily a human person, not just a wife, just as a husband is perceived by himself and his peers as a person and not just as a husband. So too, if one who exercises authority in any administrative system asks for an obedience that violates reason, justice, or compassion, obedience cannot be accorded by an informed and aware woman or man in good conscience.

The most general way to summarize these points is to say that the age of the masses is over. There are no longer "classes" of adult people who fall into the category of children, in the sense of needing a guidance they cannot provide for themselves. The peoples of the world are coming to understand their rights as human beings. Failure to provide relevant education now is a violation of a person's human rights. No one may be deprived of those rights by those in power who allege physical or psychic limitations of dependents.

Clearly, however, the world has not yet grown up to full realization of the responsibilities entailed in having the right to participate in the decisions that affect one's life. Many people may still prefer not to have or to exercise those rights because they are not ready to accept the corresponding responsibilities for the outcome of decisions in which they share. Still, those rights are not privileges of the crown to dispense or to withhold at will, as law claimed in an earlier age in Britain. Today, societies that fail to honor the rights and responsibilities of women and men alike are subject to critical review and demands for change.

The Sisters' Survey
and Responsible Decision Making

How does this reflection on rights and duties relate to the life of women in institutes of consecrated life today in the Catholic Church? For women in religious institutes, the transition from "blind obedience" to responsible participation in decision making accompanied their formal education for mission. The upgrading of sisters to the category of highly educated women followed their responsible implementation of the encyclical on education of 1927. This document of Pope Pius XI mandated women in apostolic congregations to provide themselves with the training available and necessary to take advantage of the scientific, as well as the classical, education needed to carry out effectively the works of charity, mercy, health, and education that the church had adopted by the early twentieth century as ways of responding to human needs. Modern technology, rapidly developing, made this formal upgrading of preparation for ministry among women essential. What we are examining here is the effect that upgrading had on the structures of governance in the various religious institutes.

The remainder of this essay is limited to two aspects of the question of authority and governance and their legitimation: (1) the faith position(s) held by Catholic sisters regarding religious authority to which the following questions are addressed: What faith position do Catholic sisters affirm regarding religious authority in their own governing structures? How is this faith position related to their preferred and actual forms of government? How satisfied are they with the structures of governance in their own institutes? and (2) the expectations sisters have toward a fuller participation in the decision-making process in the church. The questions here are: What attitudes to authority characterize how Catholic sisters view the authority structure of the institutional church? How are these views related to their views on women in church and society and, specifically, to women in church roles.

When the decrees of Vatican II were promulgated, one of those documents, the Decree on the Appropriate Renewal of Religious Life, mandated religious institutes of men and women to revise their constitutions, to update them, in order to make them relevant to the carrying out of the mission of the church in these rapidly changing times. A complete review of their existing governing systems was part of that mandate. When the revisions were in, it became evident that rethinking their reasons for existing led numerous congregations of Catholic sisters to restructure their government in such a way that the line of authority, instead of being modeled on the hierarchical structure of the institutional church, looked more like the model of the Congregational Church. Authority had been relocated to the membership.

One formulation of this shift is this article from a revised constitution: "The entire Congregation through the General Chapter, entrusts the government group with the exercise of authority in accordance with these Constitutions." "These" constitutions then mandated the government group of five elected members to operate as a team. Prior to making any major decisions, they were not only to inform the entire membership but also to include in their deliberations, before even forming a proposed policy, those whose lives would be affected by the policies made.

This process came to be called "authority in the membership," and it was inspired by the mission of liberation of the poor and the oppressed of the world "from every oppressive situation." It is the mission the church gave itself in the famous synod on Justice in the World, which was called by Pope Paul VI to implement *The Call to Action. The Call to Action*, whose Latin title is *Octogesima Adveniens*, was written on the occasion of the eightieth anniversary of the encyclical *Rerum Novarum*. Paul VI wrote *The Call to Action* to further the justice work that the Vatican Council had begun and that he had explicated in 1967 in an encyclical letter called *The Development of Peoples*, or *Populorum Progressio*. Working earnestly within this "option for the poor" to which they were making a faithful response, sisters were confused, even scandalized, to find that the structures they were proposing for their religious life in mission were not acceptable to the Roman authorities responsible for approving their constitutions and thereby granting them official recognition in the church.

The Roman authorities rejected the proposed changes in government structures because they did not follow the hierarchical model, even though, in fact, institutes of religious life are not part of the hierarchy of the church. They play no official role in church governance. These institutes are founded by women and men inspired to follow the gospels and to bring to their Christian commitment a special charism in solidarity with others who choose to join them. The members take vows of poverty, chastity, and obedience to apply the Scripture-based beatitudes in their historically developed way of life. The vows assure a stability to their commitment to live simply and share their resources with those in need (poverty), to concentrate their commitment to mission by promising to remain uninvolved with sexual partners (chastity), and to commit themselves forever to the carrying out of a mission that requires stability to be effective (obedience). Determining how those three "counsels of perfection" become institutionalized is the prerogative of each institute. It accepts or recognizes the calling of those who seek membership and presents them with the challenge of participation in the implementation of the institute's charism as it has been developed and changed in the long tradition.

Down through history, there has periodically been friction between the call to mission within religious institutes and the contractual mandates associated with formal church acceptance of the lifestyles and specified missions of the various institutes.[7] The new challenge facing religious congregations of women today stems from their desire, on the one hand, to incorporate the structure of their own governing system into their witness of participatory decision making that the church has recognized as essential to the development of people[8] — and, on the other, their growing consciousness of the less than peer relationship that all women are experiencing in church and society today.[9]

The Sisters' Survey of 1989 provides some evidence concerning these questions and issues. It is based on a random sample of 3,000 sisters representing 90 percent of all apostolic religious institutes of women in the United States, contacted in 1989 as a follow-up to a similar study completed in 1967, just after the Second Vatican Council ended.[10] The response rate to the 1989 survey was 74 percent. Among the 363 questions asked, 14 have reference to governance and sixteen to women's roles in church and society.

Prior to the renewal sponsored by the Second Vatican Council, training for the taking of the vow of obedience included the assumption that God spoke directly to a sister through the voice of her superior whose will represented God's will for the sister. The following item was introduced to determine how many sisters actually believe that God speaks directly to them through the voice of their superiors. This item, used in all three surveys, reads:

A truly obedient religious need seek no source other than her Rule and the will of her superiors to know what she should do.

Here is the response range from the original survey, responded to by 139,691 sisters in 1967 and two follow-up random samples in 1980 and 1989.

	1967	1980	1989
1. Yes, I agree	31%	9%	11%
2. No, I do not agree	59%	75%	72%
3. Undecided or uncertain	5%	7%	6%
4. Topic irrelevant	1%	4%	6%
5. Statement too annoying to answer	1%	5%	6%
(Item 310)			

Note that even in 1967 those agreeing with the personal authority belief is low, only 31 percent saying yes. But note particularly the 9 percent and 11 percent similarity of response for 1980 and 1989 and its relationship to the item discussed below.

In the survey in 1980 and again in 1989, this question regarding preferred forms of governance was posed:

Women in religious institutes have experimented with structures of govern-ment over the past 20 years with varying effects. Given your experience, which of the following alternatives would you prefer your institute to have at this time?

1. A government that places decision-making ultimately in the hands of lawfully chosen superiors who in turn accept responsibility for the outcomes and to whom the members are accountable.

    1980 1989
    10%   11%

2. A government that places decision-making in an assembly of the whole which then delegates authority to administrators who are account-able to the members in assembly, which is then responsible for the outcomes.

    1980 1989
    45%   44%

3. A government that places decision-making in the hands of lawfully chosen delegates, who, in turn, lawfully choose administrators to whom they delegate responsibility and who are responsible to the members who represent themselves through delegates to the next assembly.

    1980 1989
    45%   43%

(Item 357; this item was not included in the 1967 survey.)

There is a consistency in the choice of type of government preferred and the belief about God's will being channeled through the will of the superior in item 310 just above. Cross-tabulation of these two items in the 1989 data reveals that, in fact, those rejecting the religious qual-ity of blind obedience to superiors are not necessarily the same people who believe that all the members should share the responsibility for governance.

In order to compare preference and actual practice, the following item was included in 1980 and in 1989:

Which of the following methods of administration is characteristic of your province, or congregation if you have no provinces?

1980	1989		
9%	26%	1.	The major superior makes the decisions with the advice of her council where required by canon law.
7%	8%	2.	The council makes all decisions collegially.
22%	16%	3.	The council consults the membership and then makes decisions.
12%	18%	4.	Committees or delegated groups research the issues, and report to the council which then makes the decisions.
38%	24%	5.	The council administers decisions made by an assembly and is accountable to the members for all decisions made between assemblies, either to their delegates at the next assembly or to all the members if it is an assembly of the whole.
12%	10%	6.	Other

(Item 168)

What is interesting about this distribution is that the first response has increased since 1980. I think this is due to the fact the Congregation for Institutes of Consecrated Life (CICL), responsible for the acceptance of constitutions of Catholic institutes at the Vatican, has required changes in constitutions that did not have this structure of government, and some groups have acceded to their demands.[11] This is, at present, an untested hypothesis from my research. What is of further interest is that various forms of participation in decision-making have become more the practice in the institutes.

On the practical side, in another item, in a section described as "philosophy of Government," the sisters were asked whether or not they agreed that

The decisions that we need to make about our life and work are highly specialized and require a degree of knowledge that takes too much time to accumulate for all to participate: therefore, I think full participation in decision making is unwise.

The responses took this form:

	1980	1989
No	41%	45%
Probably no	15%	16%
Not sure	13%	12%
Probably yes	18%	16%
Yes	12%	11%

Note that the yes response at 12 percent and 11 percent, respectively, are remarkably consistent with responses to items 310 and 357 above.

The sisters were asked to express their opinion on who should govern in an item with this wording:

A small representative group should be elected and delegated to become informed and make the decisions for us.

The responses were distributed as follows:

	1980	1989
No	46%	54%
Probably no	15%	15%
Not sure	11%	10%
Probably yes	16%	11%
Yes	11%	10%
(Item 163)		

Note again the remarkable consistency of about 10 percent only accepting the dependency model. Note also, from the item numbers, how widely separated these items are in the survey instrument. This consistency is all the more remarkable due to this factor of recall.

To an item that read: "All members should participate in the process of decision-making," 90 percent responded with an unqualified yes. Note again the consistency in response.

Related to the hypothesis about the faith position that subsumes these choices and actions, another belief item in the 1980 and 1989 surveys took this form:

Since the will of God becomes manifest to us in Church, in Scripture, and Sacrament, in our Constitutions and the institute's decisions, in the signs of the times and the needs of the people, our vow of obedience requires of us an ongoing effective reflection on these sources.

Here are the responses:

	1980	1989
Yes, I agree	91%	87%
No, I do not agree	1%	2%
Undecided or uncertain	5%	6%
Topic is irrelevant	2%	3%
Statement is annoying	.4%	.7%
(Item 304)		

These responses are again consistent with the preferred forms of governance expressed above. Carrying that belief commitment to one more item, we can see that, although new directions in thinking about authority and obedience are varied, there remains that consistent 10 percent only who accept as right and good, for them, what has come to be called personal or religious authority in the church, that is, obedience to the will of the person in charge, whether it be in the local house or community, the province or other unit, or to a general moderator of the entire institute.

The old faith position that the will of the superior, by reason of "grace of office," represented for the individual the expressed will of God, unless the expected behavior qualified immoral, has declined to about 10 percent in religious institutes of Catholic women in the United States. This does not mean that anarchy reigns. The present reality demands no less respect for the person(s) in charge, no less consideration of the ideas decided upon in responsible decision settings, but rather, a wider vision of how God speaks to the membership, which is responsible for searching out God's will and to whom and by whom accountability is to be rendered.

Item 305 suggests what the content of this wider vision includes:

> Our vow of obedience unites us to the Church and its mission in a way that dedicates our lives to the redeeming work of Christ through the decisions we make and bind ourselves to fulfill as a religious institute. Our accountability is determined by our particular form of government.

Here are the responses:

	1980	1989
Yes, I agree	66%	63%
No, I do not agree	9%	11%
Undecided or uncertain	17%	17%
Topic is irrelevant	7%	6%
Statement is annoying	.8%	2%

Notice that now the "no" response takes on the 9 percent to 11 percent pattern already expressed in item 310 (see above p. 179). Note also the consistency of the 1980 and 1989 responses.

Other responses add some ambiguity to the pattern. For example: despite the preference of 87 percent for self-governance, 56 percent of the sisters agree that they are satisfied with the kind of government they have now and another 20 percent say they are probably satisfied (item 104), even though almost 90 percent have said they want self-government and 25 percent that they do not have it now (see above page 181, item 168). In item 105, 34 percent claimed that they had to change their constitutions to comply with the prescription from the Congregation of Institutes of Consecrated Life in Rome (CICL) regarding their government.[12] As of October 1989, 67 percent of groups responding had already submitted their constitutions to CICL and 59 percent were satisfied with these submitted constitutions (item 167). There must then be only a minority not satisfied with current governing arrangements, even though the government they have is not the government they want. Perhaps government is not that important to some to make an issue of it when the form it takes is so controversial in the church at the present time.

Thus far we have looked only at statements of belief about obedience to authority and preferred and actual structures of government that characterize the government within the institute of which the respondents are members. To determine if there is a link between participation in government and commitment to the mission of taking a special option for the poor, the following item was included:

Participation in decision-making is a skill the poor must learn in order to take command of their own lives. Therefore, sisters must try to develop this skill so that they will use it well in their ministries wherever they may be. So, for us now, government is for mission.

	1980	1989
No	2%	5%
Probably no	2%	4%
Not sure	12%	21%
Probably yes	28%	31%
Yes	55%	39%

(Item 165)

This item attempts to measure what has come to be called "government for mission," meaning that sisters should govern themselves according to the model they are trying to work out with the poor who are organizing to take what is rightfully theirs.[13] This policy of deciding to model the government of the institute on the form of participation being practiced is being explored in numerous religious institutes in their chapters.[14] This happens when community developers are working with local groups in poverty, helping them to develop responsible decision making forms for changing the conditions of their lives of deprivation and oppression. This item exemplifies the dilemma of authority and obedience sisters experience when the expectation the institutional church has for them in governing their life in the religious community contradicts the model the church itself also mandates to guide their attempts to learn to work effectively with the poor who are struggling to develop models of effective decision making, as in the base community movement.[15] The implications of this dilemma are not always clear to the sisters themselves.

We move now to the second question, that is, the attitude of sisters toward the authority structure of the church and whether or not they are interested in the possibility of its being changed over time to include the full participation of women. I will include here the larger question of the ordination of women for full pastoral participation because ordination is required for entrance into the hierarchy wherein the magisterium of the church makes decisions for the whole church. At this time, because of the link to ordination, all decision makers for the church not arbitrarily selected are men. This accounts for the form the following item takes:

> Would you affirm your congregation's exercising leadership toward full participation of women in the life of the Catholic church, including all levels of decision-making?

The responses are:

No	8%
Probably no	8%
Not sure	14%
Probably yes	21%
Yes	49%
(Item 159)	

The implication here is that 70 percent of the women responding would consider ordination for women. Asked specifically: "Have you ever seriously considered ordination for women?" the sisters gave the following responses:

	1969	1989
Yes, but not for myself	11%	40%
No	85%	52%
Yes, and for myself	3%	7%
(Item 232)		

What these responses indicate at the present time with respect to democracy in the church, it seems to me, is that Catholic sisters and nuns devoted to a mission of societal transformation are growing in awareness of the responsibilities entailed in its realization. They are moving toward accepting the structural changes that the realization of this mission entails for the church, but they still clearly separate their own calling to religious life from the call to priesthood.

Conclusions and Interpretation

In *From Nuns to Sisters* I used the image of a tortoise shedding its hardened carapace to describe the course sisters have taken down through the ages to meet the challenges to their mission and to respond to what they clearly experience as a calling to do apostolic ministry in the church. Sixty-two percent of sisters experience this call with a clear "yes" response and another 25 percent with a "probably yes" in answer to the question:

As you look back on the last twenty years, would you say there is a special quality of commitment that distinguishes the religious vocation, something that you know you have, even if you cannot define it? (Item 361)

Sisters also recognize the unique charism of their own institutes, 85 percent agreeing that their "order has a distinct spirit that distinguishes it from all other orders" (item 103). Yet, across their differences, they unite in their beliefs that this is a time of special call through the voices of the poor, 78 percent agreeing that:

inherent in the developing understanding of mission is the belief that God, who continues to speak to us in diverse ways today, calls to us with special insistence through the voices of the dispossessed and the materially poor as they organize themselves to claim their rights as human beings. (Item 344)

While 77 percent "agree" or "probably agree" with this formulation of faith, only 49 percent give an unqualified "yes." This means that sisters are divided within their institutes on a variety of issues, one of which is what is the best mode of governance and another is why one prefers one mode to another. For those for whom government is for mission, there is a passion in their commitment to their own responsible participation and to the accountability of administrators to the members. For those for whom governance is seen and felt as a prerogative of their trained competency, lack of it is experienced as alienating and threatens withdrawal. For those for whom it is a segment of the struggle of women for their human rights, it is larger than life. For some it is all three. For others it is none of these because awareness of the issue has not reached consciousness yet.

As with the role of women in church and society across the world at the present time, this issue of responsible participation in the decisions that affect our lives is a function of our commitment or lack of commitment to human liberation "from every oppressive situation," as well as our concern to implement effectively the gospel in our times.

Notes

1. In 1967 the Conference of Major Superiors of Women Religious (CMSW) mandated a survey of all sisters in the United States to determine readiness for the renewal requested by the Decree on Renewal of Religious Life of the Second Vatican Council. Since that time there have been two updates also sponsored by the Leadership Conference of Women Religious (LCWR), the new name for the CMSW. See note 10 for further details.

2. Marie Augusta Neal, *Values and Interests in Social Change* (Englewood Cliffs, N.J.: Prentice-Hall, 1965), 44.

3. Henri de Lubac, *The Drama of Atheistic Humanism* (New York: Sheed and Ward, 1950); Yves Congar, *Lay People in the Church* (Westminster, Md.: Newman, 1957); M. D. Chenu, O.P., "Toward a Theology of Work," *Cross Currents* 7, no. 1 (1957): 175–87; Karl Rahner, S.J., "Reflections on Obedience," *Cross Currents*

10, no. 4 (1960): 362–74; Gary MacEoin, "Ireland, Vacuum of National Purpose," *America* (November 14, 1959): 185; William Ferree, *The Act of Social Justice* (Dayton, Ohio: Marianist Publications, 1951); John Cogley, "Is the Church a Power Structure?" *Information* (August 1959): 17; Gordon Zahn, *German Catholics and Hitler's Wars* (New York: Sheed and Ward, 1962).

4. See *The International Covenants on Human Rights and Optional Protocol,* United Nations Information Center, 1976; this document was later published as the United Nations Bill of Human Rights, 1978.

5. The United States has yet to vote in the covenants. The State Department still defines as "myths" the Covenants on Economic, Social and Cultural Rights, as "goals to be achieved" rather than as what they are, namely, rights to be honored. See United States Department of State, *40th Anniversary: Universal Declaration of Human Rights,* United States Department of State, Bureau of Public Affairs, December 1988, 11, and Paula Dobriansky, "U.S. Human Rights Policy: An Overview," Washington, D.C., United States Department of State, Bureau of Public Affairs, Current Policy No. 1091, 1988, 3.

6. Max Weber, *The Protestant Ethic and the Spirit of Capitalism* (New York: Charles Scribner, 1980; originally published 1905).

7. See Marie Augusta Neal, *From Nuns to Sisters* (Mystic, Conn.: Twenty-Third Publications, 1990).

8. See John Paul II, *Centesimus Annus* (Hundredth Year Letter) (Boston: St. Paul Books, 1991), nos. 46, 47.

9. See the second draft of the Catholic bishops' pastoral on women entitled "One in Christ Jesus: A Pastoral Response to the Concerns of Women for Church and Society" and the Center of Concern's commentary and critique of it in *Center Focus,* no. 97, July 1990).

10. Marie Augusta Neal, "The Relationship between Religious Belief and Structural Change in Religious Orders," *Review of Religious Research* 12, no. 1 (Fall 1970): 2–16; 12, no. 3 (Spring 1971): 153–64. This survey is the second follow-up study to a population survey returned by 139,691 sisters in 1967 sponsored by the LCWR (at that time CMSW). See note 1 above. See also Marie Augusta Neal, "A Theoretical Analysis of Renewal in Religious Life," *Social Compass* 18, no. 1 (1971): 7–25; Marie Augusta Neal, "The Sisters' Survey," *Probe* 10, no. 5 (May/June 1981); Marie Augusta Neal, *Catholic Sisters in Transition from the 1960s to the 1980s* (Wilmington, Del.: Michael Glazier, 1984), and Neal, *From Nuns to Sisters.*

11. See Congregation for Institutes of Religious Life, "Directives on Formation in Religious Institutes," *Origins* 19, no. 42 (March 22, 1990).

12. The item numbers are included here for cross reference for those who have copies of the survey instrument. The full report on this survey, including the instrument itself and the complete distribution of responses, was completed in 1991. It can be ordered from The Sisters' Survey, Emmanuel College, Boston, MA 02115. Attention: S. M. A. Neal.

13. Marie Augusta Neal, *The Just Demands of the Poor* (New York: Paulist Press, 1987).

14. Consultation with over fifty of these groups yields this evidence.

15. See Phillip Berryman, *The Religious Roots of Rebellion: Christians in Central American Revolutions* (Maryknoll, N.Y.: Orbis Books, 1984); Madeleine Cousineau Adriance, *Option for the Poor: Brazilian Catholicism in Transition* (Kansas City, Mo.: Sheed and Ward, 1986); Jeanne Gallo, S.N.D., "Basic Ecclesial Communities: A New Form of Christian Organizational Response in the World Today," unpublished doctoral dissertation, Boston University, 1988.

– 11 –
Spirituality and Justice:
Popular Church Movements
in the United States

The Second Vatican Council had a particularly dynamic effect on the United States Catholic Church. The council came at a time when what had been largely an immigrant church, which felt itself both religiously and ethnically marginalized by the Anglo Protestant majority, was moving into the mainstream of American life. By 1960 Catholic America was becoming predominantly middle-class and college educated. In 1960 the last barriers to political achievement were broken with the election of an Irish Catholic to the United States presidency. John F. Kennedy represented U.S. lay Catholics come of age. Harvard-educated, wealthy, urbane, and politically liberal, Kennedy was quick to make clear to the wider U.S. public that lay Catholics in politics were no pawns of the ecclesiastical hierarchy, foreign or domestic.

The election of John XXIII as pope in 1958 and John Kennedy as president in 1960 signified for many American Catholics two revolutions in their identity that happened almost simultaneously. In their religious world view the long spell of defensiveness toward the modern world was dispelled. *Aggiornamento*, or bringing the church up to date, was the term that the pope coined that gave approbation to this new rapprochement with modernity. Modern ideas in philosophy, history, and the social sciences, long dangerous territory for Catholics, were thrown open to their exploration with the encouragement of the highest Catholic authority, or so it seemed.

Openness to the modern world also meant a new freedom to admit that the church had not always been right. For many Catholics this meant a fundamental shift from an authoritarian model of truth, dictated from above, to the notion that truth is something that people search for together, in a process that is never final and perfect. In effect, liberal Catholics were shedding the mind-set of infallibility, although few were prepared to confront this issue directly in relation to papal teaching authority. Freedom to admit mistakes and to search for a consensual truth also meant a continuing process of church reform, a rediscovery of the idea of *ecclesia semper reformanda*.

That same tumultuous decade of the 1960s also saw U.S. Catholics, along with other Americans, experiencing sharp blows to their nationalist triumphalism. The assumption that the United States was a beacon to the world, a model of justice and prosperity at home and the promoter of democracy and economic development abroad, was being questioned on both fronts. African-Americans emerged in a national civil rights movement to expose centuries of racist beliefs and legal discrimination. Other nonwhite groups, such as Hispanics and American Indians, would follow their example in national movements for both justice and reclaimed particularity of culture. A new feminist movement was born, throwing off the 1950s ideology of the feminine mystique. The exposure of widespread poverty gave the lie to the myth of U.S. economic fairness.

The myth of America the Good was also challenged in the realm of foreign policy. The Vietnam War not only gave Americans the first taste of military defeat, but also raised the question mark over the whole pattern of U.S. foreign policy since the Second World War, and before. Were the various interventions in Asia, Africa, and Latin America by the U.S. government, with its military and economic power, really about the defense of democracy, as Americans had been led to believe? Or was this rhetoric a cover-up for the United States takeover of the defense of Western neocolonial hegemony against the legitimate aspirations of the peoples of Asia, Africa, and Latin America for political and economic self-determination?

These sweeping challenges of the 1960s to both American and Roman Catholic hegemonic consciousness took place in an atmosphere of resurgent optimism. Many Americans felt stimulated by the challenges to national reform as an appropriate new stage in the realization of the "American dream." Many American Catholics shared this optimism and welcomed the opportunities to build both a better church and a better society. The liberal community appeared to dominate public culture, providing a base for still more radical groups to surface, expanding the agendas for social transformation, and challenging the moderate reformism of the liberals.

In retrospect this confidence in the capacity of either the Catholic Church or American culture to tolerate rising expectations of social transformation was naive. Already in the latter half of the 1960s, immediately after the Second Vatican Council, the leadership of the Roman curia was laying plans to counteract the demands for greater participation in decision making at the national church and local levels. Vatican II theologians, democratizing religious orders, new intellectual freedom in Catholic universities, liberation theology, and base Christian community movements in Third World churches would all become targets of Vatican reaction. The pontificate of John Paul II in the 1980s would see the fuller implementation of this movement of retrenchment.

In American society rising expectations of justice were quickly met by rising repression. The FBI, together with new "red squad" sections of local police forces, would target the movements for peace and for racial and economic justice as "enemies" of the American society. Many of the gains in civil rights legislation were consciously eroded in the 1980s. Under the Reagan administration, continued in the 1990s in the Bush administration, it became the stated goal of the U.S. government to defeat the "Vietnam Syndrome," i.e., the questioning of the righteousness of U.S. military intervention against Third World liberation struggles.

It was in this context of rising hopes for social change in both the church and in society of the 1960s, then the slowing of the momentum and increasing reactionary repression in the 1970s and 1980s, that one must situate the grassroots movements for church reform and social justice that arose among American Catholics during this period. In this essay I will discuss two parallel types of popular American Catholic movements: peace and justice organizations, which would see women's rights as one agenda among others in their vision of a new church and society, and feminist movements, linked to racial, economic, and peace issues, but with women's experience as the defining perspective.

Peace and justice protest represented a new stance of U.S. Catholics toward their society. There had been a Catholic presence, both on the official level and much more on the lay level in the American labor movement in the first half of the twentieth century. But generally Catholic conservativism, and also the sense of embattlement as a religious group, kept Catholics from being a part of the reform movements of earlier periods. The 1960s saw a change in this as Catholic priests and nuns linked arms with Protestant ministers and Jewish rabbis in marches for civil rights and for peace. With the Berrigan brothers and their circle, Catholics even seemed to take the lead in radical forms of direct action protest against the Vietnam War.

In 1975 the U.S. Catholic bishops launched a church renewal movement that was intended to coincide with the American bicentennial of 1976. The bishops' Call to Action mandated each diocese to choose delegates from leaders among priests, women religious, and laity who would come together to discuss the issues that the church in the United States should address, both internally and in terms of its mission to society. Some bishops embraced this agenda enthusiastically. Others, such as Cardinal John Cody of Chicago, did so reluctantly, recognizing the expectations for popular participation it would release.

Many progressive Catholics came to this assembly in Detroit. Some managed to become official delegates of their diocese. In other cases, leaders of new popular movements came without official endorsement and were able to obtain credentials or otherwise make their presence felt in the assembly. The result was a series of resolutions, approved by the majority of the delegates, that were considerably to the left of what the bishops themselves were able to accept.

More than two hundred resolutions were passed at the assembly. Among these resolutions were demands for optional celibacy for priests, broader participation of women in church ministry, including consideration of ordination, acceptance of birth control, diocesan financial accountability to the people, the right of divorced Catholics to remarry, democratic participation in decision making in the church, and challenges to racism in the church. The U.S. bishops were stunned by these results.

Although some bishops appointed Call to Action groups in their dioceses to follow up on these resolutions, these were soon officially dropped when the American bishops as a body voted to scrap the process and to reject those resolutions of the assembly that pertained to church reform. However, many of the delegates, and other Catholics who had not been present but had been inspired by this process, attempted to continue. In some cases these people were able to be recognized as official peace and justice organizations of the diocese. In other cases peace and justice groups were founded without links to the hierarchy, depending on lay leadership and/or backing from men's and women's religious orders.

Parallel to the development of popular peace and justice groups, a feminist movement was rising in U.S. Catholicism. This was quite a new development, since American Catholic women had had no presence in the earlier American women's suffrage movement, which was predominantly middle class and Anglo Protestant. The Catholic bishops also took a negative view of women's suffrage in the first decades of the twentieth century. A small British organization, the St. Joan's Alliance, had begun in 1910 to promote women's suffrage among Catholics, but the American branch of that group was founded only in 1965.

Several influences converged to promote a feminist movement among U.S. Catholics after the Second Vatican Council. The most important was the renewal of the feminist movement in American society in the late 1960s. The better educated and more middle-class Catholic women were now ready to participate in this movement. Feminism was also having a new kind of impact on the Protestant churches. From 1956 into the 1970s more and more Protestant churches were ordaining women, and their numbers were increasing in seminaries. An ecumenical Catholicism was now much more in communication with these Protestant developments. Increasing numbers of Catholic women were also getting advanced degrees in religious studies and raising feminist questions about Christian theology and practice.

Another source of feminist ferment in Roman Catholicism came from the renewal of women's religious orders. In the 1950s American Catholic nuns were engaged in a struggle with the hierarchy to improve their education level. This struggle also implied a more independent-thinking religious woman. Some leaders of women religious (most notably, Sister Mary Luke Tobin of the Sisters of Loretto, then head of the newly formed Leadership Conference of Women Religious) also endeavored to be represented when women auditors were allowed to attend the Second Vatican Council. They attempted to bring the concerns, not only of nuns, but of women in general before this body.

When the Second Vatican Council invited nuns to renew themselves by reexamining the charisms of their founders, many American women's orders took this as a mandate to democratize their communities. They modernized or discarded altogether the religious habit that set them apart from other laywomen and began to create new ministries with the poor that were not under the control of the hierarchy. Awareness of women's problems, both in the church and in society, grew among this sector of nuns. In 1972 LCWR (the Leadership Conference of Women Religious), which represented 90 percent of women's religious congregations in the United States, adopted a stance of solidarity with the issues of women's liberation. This was understood in the double sense of working for justice for women in society, and also examining their own identities as women in the church.

Study materials were prepared by which each congregation could study these women's issues in terms of their own lives and mission. These study books assumed a critical stance toward the role of the church as an agent in promoting the inferiorization of women and the denial to women of roles appropriate to their gifts. In the 1974 assembly of the LCWR it was voted to support the principle that all ministries in the church be open to women and that women should have active participation in all decision-making bodies in the church.[1]

In July of 1974 the struggle in the Episcopal Church for women's ordination reached a critical stage, in which several retired bishops agreed to ordain "irregularly" eleven seminary-trained Episcopal women. These developments had a strong impact on Catholic women, and, in December of 1974, a group of Catholic women began planning a national conference on the ordination of women in the Catholic Church. Although the conference was planned to include lay and religious women equally, religious orders took the major role in funding and organizing the conference.

The interest in this conference exceeded all expectations. Originally planned for six hundred, registration was finally closed at twelve hundred people. The conference planners defined their goals, not simply as the inclusion of women in ordained priesthood traditionally defined, but as the "renewal of priestly ministry," by which they meant a substantial redefinition of the authoritarian pattern of clergy-lay relations, to bring it more into line with the understanding of the church as a participatory community. The clergy role, as traditionally defined, was symbolically and structurally patriarchal and misogynist. This was seen as the major block to the inclusion of women in it.[2]

This conference in Detroit launched the Women's Ordination Conference as a national movement, with both a national office and local chapters. In 1978 a second national conference was planned. However, when this equally large gathering assembled, there had been a shift in perception of the goals. Increasing conservativism in the Vatican, expressed in the 1976 Vatican declaration rejecting the ordination of women, disposed the gathering to see the longer term struggle to democratize the church as the priority goal, with the inclusion of women in ordained ministry possible only when that had been achieved.

Many Catholic women were disposed to begin to take their own spiritual and worship life into their own hands, forming autonomous feminist base communities empowered to do the Eucharist for themselves. This direction came to predominate among the Catholic women's groups involved in the movement. Thus, when the third national conference was assembled in Chicago in 1983, the purpose of the gathering had been transformed. The focus on women's ordination had faded away, as both a distant and a questionable goal. Instead the conference organized around the theme of "women-church."

Women-church was understood to mean that women themselves, gathered in faith communities, were church, exemplars of the "people of God," not in the sense of excluding men, but in the sense of being empowered as women to define their own religious needs and experience and to move to organize communities to serve these needs. They were not dependent on the male hierarchy to mediate the presence of God to them. The conference organized itself around the three collectivities of "spirituality," "sexuality," and "survival."

Under the category of "spirituality" there were workshops on topics such as feminist theology, counseling, retreats, spiritual direction, and liturgy. Under "sexuality" were considered topics such as sexual lifestyle for heterosexual and lesbian women, married, celibate, divorced, and single, reproductive rights, sexual violence, pornography, and prostitution. Under "survival," questions on poor women and children, church workers, aging women, welfare, unemployment, refugees, militarism, networking, and organizing were considered. The conference tried to be inclusive of racially and economically marginated communities and was bilingual (English and Spanish).

The 1983 Chicago conference established the women-church idea as an expanding theme that began to include Protestant women and women who had given up on any kind of organized Christianity. The idea also began to spread internationally, with groups in England, Holland, Germany, and Latin America forming their own networks. In 1987 the Women-Church Convergence, a coalition of Catholic feminist groups, sponsored an even larger conference in Cincinnati, with numerous workshops, plenaries, and experimental liturgies. A third international gathering is planned for April 1993.

By 1991 the Women-Church Convergence had grown to thirty-five groups. This includes three types of women's organizations: national organizations, such as the National Assembly of Religious Women, the National Coalition of American Nuns, the Conference of Catholic Lesbians, WATER: the Women's Alliance for Theology, Ethics and Ritual, LAS HERMANAS USA, New Ways Ministry, and the Catholics for a Free Choice; local organizations, such as Chicago Catholic Women, Boston Women-Church, Massachusetts Women-Church, St. Louis Women-Church, Women-Church Baltimore, and the Women of the Spirit of Colorado; and feminist sectors of larger organizations, such as the Adrian Dominican Commission for Women, the Women's Issues Group of the Eighth Day Center for Justice, the Loretto Women's Network, the Grail Women's Taskforce, and the BVM Network for Women's Issues.

In order to illustrate the types of ministries, the modes of participatory organization and the ecclesial self-understanding of these popular U.S. Catholic groups, I have chosen to profile five such groups well known to me, all in the Chicago area. These five groups are Chicago Call to Action, the Eighth Day Center for Justice, the National Assembly of Religious Women, Chicago Catholic Women, and Mary's Pence.

These organizations fall into three main groups. The first two organizations are multi-issue peace and justice organizations, in which women's issues in church and society are seen as one type of issue among others. The second three groups take women's experience as their central context, but understand women's issues as crossing all the other social issues, such as racism, classism, poverty, structural violence, and war. Mary's Pence falls into a distinct category. Feminist in perspective, its purpose is to raise money to help fund other Catholic feminist grassroots organizations.

The Chicago-based Call to Action (CTA) arose out of the failure of the bishops' Call to Action process described earlier. After the Chicago delegates returned from the 1976 Detroit meeting, it was evident that Cardinal Cody disliked the whole idea and intended to do no follow-up on the assembly. Consequently a number of Chicago Catholics, representing organizations such as the Association of Chicago Priests, Chicago Catholic Women, the Leadership Conference of Women Religious, the Eighth Day Center for Justice, Dignity (an organization of predominantly Gay and Lesbian Catholics), the Chicago Archdiocesan Teachers Association, the National Assembly of Religious Women, and others decided to survey their membership to locate which issues among the more than two hundred resolutions from the Detroit meeting were seen as most important.

As a result of the survey eight areas were designated as those of greatest concern: (1) the arbitrary closing of inner-city Catholic schools (by the cardinal), (2) archdiocesan financial accountability, (3) divorce and remarriage, (4) decision making in the church, (5) racism, (6) married priests, (7) marriage and family life (especially birth control), and (8) women in the church. It was decided to have a major forum on these issues. Some 450 people assembled at a St. Scholastica High School for the first forum. In addition, the decision was made to create a Call to Action Newsletter, and a couple with long experience in journalism agreed to edit it.

As Chicago Call to Action was launched as a local peace and justice organization, it was initially conceived of as an umbrella group that would represent the various constituent bodies. However, soon some of the groups, such as the Archdiocesan Principals' Association, dropped out. Other groups, such as Dignity, continued as supporters, but the leadership of such groups were fully occupied trying to keep their own organizations afloat. So Call to Action, with the support of the founding organizations, was restructured after a few years into a predominantly lay group, with its own staff, which sought to be a resource and sounding board for the concerns of Chicago's progressive Catholics.

A couple, Sheila and Dan Daley, took on the primary work of being the staff, together with several other close associates. In accordance with U.S. regulations for not-for-profit groups, a board of directors of ten to twelve people supports the work of the staff. Thus the basic genesis of Call to Action as an organization follows the lines of what might be called the "movement" type. This means that a small group of self-designated people gather around a basic set of needs and agree to dedicate a major portion of their time to serving these needs.

A small core group of five or six people are salaried. There may also be an office worker or two that work as volunteers. The management of the office and the decisions about programs evolve through a constant consensus model of discussion among this core staff and board. The core group also set up the structure of the board, inviting willing and compatible people to serve on this board. The basic support for the staff and its office comes from a membership fee, which also brings the member a copy of the newsletter, published bimonthly. Grants and donations are sought for specific projects.

In the first five years of its existence (1977–82), Call to Action focused primarily on church reform issues raised by the leadership of Cardinal Cody. Cardinal Cody's "corporation sole" style of leadership alienated many Chicago Catholics and thus brought together a large spectrum of discontented people. Protests around the closing of schools, (lack of) financial accountability, and refusal to consult with his own priests provided a large pool of dissent for which Call to Action provided the forum. Annual meetings with workshops, a major speaker, and a participatory liturgy, together with the newsletter and participation in various anti-Cody protests, were major activities.

The coming of Cardinal Joseph Bernardin as archbishop of Chicago removed some of the more glaring forms of intrachurch conflict. In the next five years (1983–88), Call to Action moved into the area of social justice in support of episcopal initiatives. The U.S. bishops' pastorals on peace and on the economy provided foci for organizing, primarily in the form of creating workshops to help Catholics in the parish study these pastorals.

Call to Action took on the task of organizing a peace pledge among Chicago Catholics in support of the bishops' pastoral. They also formed a spirituality and justice center, with staff members and a team of volunteers, that gave parish workshops. Reprints of key articles on the interconnections of spirituality and justice were provided for subscribers among CTA members. A women's issues group also was formed, with an annual women's retreat and small discussion groups.

In the process of developing workshops on the peace pastoral and the economics pastoral, CTA somewhat unexpectedly became involved in theater. Several associates interested in theater decided to write a musical drama to illustrate the ideas of the pastoral on economics. Later other musicals were added, one on the peace pastoral and another on women in church history. These theater pieces became the major means by which CTA took church and social issues to parishes, schools, and conferences.

The musicals have attracted audiences that might not have listened to a lecture. After the presentation, the players engage the audience in discussion on the themes presented. The CTA Performing Arts Ministry now travels around the country, although the Chicago office still provides all management, fundraising, and financial accountability for it.

During the mid-1980s CTA also became involved in several forms of networking with other peace and justice projects. Among these was the gathering of humanitarian aid for Nicaragua, as the Midwest coordinator of the Quest for Peace. This was a project developed by the Quixote Center, a Catholic peace and justice center in the Washington, D.C., area, to counteract U.S. aid to the Contras. CTA has also worked with various coalitions concerned about racism and social legislation in Chicago and in the state of Illinois.

The end of the 1980s saw CTA become increasingly national as a membership organization. It also returned to some of its earlier focus on church reform. A network of Catholic women's and justice groups met in 1989 in Washington to discuss the reactionary trends of the Vatican. A series of demands for democratic reform of the church was formulated. These included demands for married priests, women's ordination, election of bishops, financial accountability, academic freedom in Catholic seminaries and universities, and consultation with the laity on teaching on human sexuality and in church decision making.

CTA agreed to become the main sponsor of an ad campaign for the national Call to Reform. The campaign gathered some twenty thousand signatures for an ad, which was published in the *New York Times*, listing eleven demands for democratic reform of the church. A follow-up conference was held in Washington at the time of the annual bishops' meeting. As a result of this campaign over 50 percent of the current five thousand dues-paying members of CTA are now from beyond the greater Chicago area.[3]

The Eighth Day Center for Justice is a second major peace and justice center in Chicago. Unlike CTA, however, Eighth Day is sponsored by religious orders, and its staff and major funding come from these sponsoring orders. They also depend on subscriptions, donations, and grants. Eighth Day Center arose when a number of religious orders, each of which was concerned to commit itself to peace and justice work, got together to pool their resources. Contributing religious orders fall into two categories: sponsoring orders, who contribute both support and a staff member, and friends, who contribute to the center, but do not have a staff member from the order.

The current sponsoring members of Eighth Day are the Adrian Dominicans, the Dominican Fathers and Brothers, the Claretians, the Missionary Oblates of Mary Immaculate, the Priests of the Sacred Heart, the School Sisters of Saint Francis, the Sisters of St. Joseph of the Third Order of St. Francis, the Sisters of Charity, BVM, the Sisters of Mercy, and the Sisters of Providence. Ten other orders contribute as friends of the center.

The first organizing issue of the Eighth Day Center was hunger, sparked by the experience of several of the members of religious orders who had worked in poor parishes in urban ghettos in the United States or as missionaries in Third World countries. Soon, however, it was felt that the center must also focus on the interconnections with other issues, particularly militarism, which is both a major cause of hunger and destitution and the means by which the wealthy repress the protests of the poor.

For a time the center dedicated itself to a major information campaign on injustice in South Africa, urging boycott of the Krugerrand. In the mid-1980s much of its efforts went into solidarity work with Central America, especially Guatemala, El Salvador, and Nicaragua. It also turned to questions of corporate fiscal responsibility, providing information packets to religious congregations to guide their investments and their use of the power of the shareholder to pressure corporations toward conversion away from weapons production and/or racist and sexist employment and consumer practices. It also helped create an alternative investment fund from which low income people could receive loans for self-development projects.

Eighth Day, with a somewhat larger core staff than Call to Action, currently organizes itself around four working groups, which presently work in coalition with over ninety international, national, and local organizations. Some staff relate to more than one of these groups. The four groups are:

1. poverty, with links to both antipoverty legislation and grassroots organizing among poor and homeless people themselves;

2. peace and human rights, which focuses on issues both internal to the United States, in projects such as the Sanctuary Movement, and also on solidarity work with South Africa and Central America as well as demilitarization and anti-interventionism. As a result of the recent Gulf crisis, Eighth Day has developed new ties with the Arab Community Center in Chicago and Palestinian human rights groups. They have also made major commitments to activities concerned to demythologize the 1992 celebration of the conquest of America by Columbus;

3. economic justice, which works on such projects as fair wages and working conditions for *maquiladoras* (women workers) on the U.S.-Mexican border. They are also working to expose the devastating effects of the "fast track" free trade agreement with Mexico. This group also develops analyses to help constituent groups understand economic trends and investments;

4. women's issues. This group is committed to research and educational projects to raise consciousness on the needs of women in both church and society. Activities include workshops on undoing sexism, an educational packet on changing structures from a dominating to a partnership model, alternative nonsexist worship services, and a participatory process by which women can safely discuss abortion.

Each working group has the authority to make decisions on its own ongoing projects. The whole staff of some twelve people meets weekly. During this staff meeting they pray together, evaluate their work, share information, and decide on new projects. Decisions are made by consensus. In addition, the staff meets three times a year for two or three days for retreats. One of these retreats does planning for the coming year, the second evaluates the current work, and the third provides spiritual resourcing and renewal.

Thus the Eighth Day Center functions as an activist community, which consciously recognizes and expresses the spiritual basis of its commitment to justice and peace. It has constituents and subscribers in forty-six states and twenty-six other countries. It provides them with quarterly analyses of the issues, the *Eighth Day Report*, a monthly legislative action sheet, and, for Illinois residents, a monthly calendar of events. Eighth Day also is the major organizer of the Good Friday March for Justice, a procession of witness and prayer modeled on the Stations of the Cross. It is joined in this march by many other Chicago-area justice and solidarity groups, each of which provides a "station" that witnesses to their particular concerns.[4]

The National Assembly of Religious Women started earlier than Call to Action or Eighth Day. Its first gathering, under the name of the National Assembly of Women Religious, took place in 1968. Its original concern was to provide a network for women in religious congregations who wanted to respond to the Vatican's call (as they understood it) to both internal renewal and to renewed mission to the poor in society. In 1970 NAWR was formally organized, with a national office in Chicago. In 1975 the name of the organization was changed to the National Assembly of Religious Women (NARW) in order to include laywomen equally in the membership. Currently (1991) there are 2,800 dues-paying members, 53 percent lay, 47 percent in religious congregations. ninety-three percent identify themselves as related to the Catholic tradition.

NARW sees itself as a feminist organization that addresses a broad range of justice issues from the perspective of women. The organization offers resources and programs that focus on education and action to bring about systemic change. NARW has made a major commitment to work inclusively, as women from differing racial, ethnic, and economic backgrounds, taking into account, in both its social analysis and its process, the diversity of perspectives of women from different cultural and social contexts. It also sees itself as working out of a faith commitment and lived spirituality.

Among the major activities of NARW are the preparation of resource packets on particular issues, such as women and homelessness, and the offering of skills-training workshops to help both women who are economically exploited and service providers analyze the problems and organize for change. NARW also offers an annual conference in which the connections between social analysis, faith reflection, and strategies for action are demonstrated. The conference consciously models cross-class and racial/ethnic women's leadership. It draws about three hundred participants yearly and has become a major means of networking its constituency as well as drawing in new members.

NARW also sends out a bimonthly publication, *Probe*, to its dues-paying membership. *Probe* publishes major analytical articles on social justice issues in the church and society, as well as information on coming events. Other activities of NARW are emergency action responses. These include working with exploited women workers on the U.S.-Mexican border and also networking with other solidarity movements, in relation to Central America, Haiti, Puerto Rico, Peru, Chile, and South Africa. NARW also endeavors to identify women experiencing particular repression for their leadership efforts and their work for systemic change and seeks to give them a national forum and support.

One example of an emergency action project took place in April–May of 1991. NARW sponsored a national caravan in fifteen cities across the United States that did teach-ins and press conferences and gathered medical supplies and donations for medical aid to war-devastated Iraq. A team of five women took the aid to Iraq in May, and also visited the occupied territories of Palestine. The team brought back first-hand information on conditions in these areas to communicate to people in the United States. Connections between the Gulf war and poverty in the United States was also drawn throughout this process, and part of the medical supplies were donated to homeless shelters in the United States.

NARW is supported by its dues-paying membership, donations, and grants. As a membership organization its seeks to consult and obtain feedback from its constituency. It does periodic surveys of its membership to find out who they are and what they want the organization to be doing. NARW members carry out the organization's programmatic efforts at the local level. The membership is also invited to nominate members for the board of directors. A slate of candidates is then prepared by the existing board and national team and voted on by the membership.

Day-to-day decisions are made by the national team, which consists of three persons working as equals, each with specific areas of responsibility: program coordination, financial and administrative work, and national coordination. The team meets weekly for self-evaluation and mutual accountability. The team and the board of directors (nineteen people, including the national team) meet three times a year to evaluate and plan, using a consensus model of decision making.[5]

Chicago Catholic Women is an independent feminist group that networks feminist activity in the Chicago area. It arose in 1974 out of the same dynamics that were to produce the Call to Action. It sought to prepare Chicago Catholic women for the 1976 bishops' Call to Action assembly in Detroit by holding hearings across the city on women's concerns. Although not accepted as official delegates, CCW took its findings to the Detroit conference as unofficial observers. It also has been a major actor in the formation of the Women's Ordination Conference and the Women-Church Convergence.

From 1975 to 1987 CCW was organized with a small staff (one full-time coordinator, one or two part-time workers and volunteers, together with a board of directors). In 1987 CCW moved to new space where they could create a women's center for small gatherings, group meals, and counseling. It was reorganized in a more participatory way, with a team of coordinators of different areas of activity. There are presently four major areas of activity, each with its coordinator and team of organizers.

These are (1) liturgical, including retreats and regular women's liturgies at the center and at other locations around the city; (2) education, which includes conferences, skills-training workshops, and lectures; (3) direct service, which includes both one-on-one counseling and support groups, such as those for lesbians and women in ministry; (4) networking, which includes the coffee house that meets monthly, providing a meal, poetry reading, music, and talk-back session where issues for networking and action can be raised; and (5) advocacy and solidarity work on such issues as the Equal Rights Amendment, abortion rights, and lesbian rights.

CCW also has sponsored an elder-care project, which networks elderly people, mostly women, in public housing and homeless women and children in a nearby shelter. The homeless women provide housekeeping and companionship, run errands, and do some nursing for the elderly, gaining skills for future employment, while the elderly parent and grandparent the women and children. CCW also has been a strong advocate for both women's ordination and women's reproductive rights. It conducts a yearly Mother's Day protest outside the Chicago Catholic cathedral, lifting up the grievances of Catholic women against the church. This protest is regularly attended and supported by other Catholic women's groups across the city.[6]

The fifth group to be profiled in this account is Mary's Pence. Mary's Pence arose as a direct response to the experience of lack of access to church funds by Catholic women's advocacy groups. Church women realized that they had always been the faithful fund raisers for the male clerical church, but they had virtually no access to such funds for ministries by and for women. The impetus for the project came at a prayer service in 1986 attended by several women who were doing counseling and support work for women in prison. They had raised 75 percent of the money they needed for their project, when they went to the cardinal to ask for financial help. While he praised their work and declared his full moral support for it, he declined to offer any financial aid.

At that same time Call to Action was calling for financial accountability in the church and for the boycott of the annual collection for the Vatican (Peter's Pence). Thus the idea was generated that what women in grassroots movements needed was a Mary's Pence, an alternative fund to which progressive Catholics could give to support the ministries of women to poor women and children. Catholic women also felt that they were wasting energy protesting against the hierarchical church. They needed to channel their rage positively by alternative organizing and fundraising.

All four of the other Chicago Catholic groups profiled here played a role in the genesis of Mary's Pence. Women leaders from Chicago Catholic Women, NARW, Eighth Day, and Call to Action gathered to give advice on setting up the funding organization, although none of them sought control over it. A board of directors was developed, about 50 percent laywomen and 50 percent from women's congregations. There is also an ongoing effort to draw in racial-ethnic diversity on the board. The organization is run with a salaried coordinator, part-time paid workers and volunteer help. The board meets three times a year for two and a half days as a working board to review past activities and plan fundraising and organizational development.

The board is divided into several working groups: (1) governance and administration; (2) education and public relations, (3) fundraising and finance. There is also a standing grants committee that reviews all the grant applications and decides on the grants to be awarded each year. The primary sources of funds for Mary's Pence are women's religious congregations and also many small donations from individuals. There also have been occasional opportunities to present the work of Mary's Pence to parishes and to take up an alternative collection. Funds have also been received from foundation grants and from a regular appeal letter sent out through mailing lists of progressive Catholics (such as the subscribers to the *National Catholic Reporter*).

By 1991 Mary's Pence had dispersed approximately $30,000 a year for three years in small grants of $500 to $2,000. Its guidelines call for grants to be considered only from Catholic women, both individuals and groups, who are in socially transforming ministry to poor women and children and who do not have large budgets and other major sources of income. Most applications come from women working in the United States, although some are received and have been funded internationally. One of the most gratifying aspects of the work of Mary's Pence is the identification of the extraordinary range of grassroots organizing going on among Catholic women.

In the first round of grants given in October of 1988, there were twenty-three projects funded in seven different areas: (1) pastoral ministry, (2) spirituality, (3) legal advocacy, (4) child care and head start, (5) education and literacy, (6) care for the elderly and housebound, and (7) shelters and housing.

In the area of pastoral ministry, four projects were given grants: (1) the Immigration and Naturalization Service Detention Center in Los Fresnos, Texas, to fund a woman ministering to the refugees, mostly women and children, fleeing from violence in their homelands in Central America; (2) the Basic Health and Nutrition Program in El Progreso, Honduras, to fund a woman working through a local parish to help women's groups develop health and nutrition programs for women and their families; (3) the Center for Enriched Communication of Grand Junction, Colorado, which does individual and family counseling, to pay for ten sessions for thirty women who are underemployed and have no insurance coverage; (4) New Ways Ministry in Mt. Rainier, Maryland, to provide seed money for organizing a support group for Catholic lesbians.

In the area of spirituality, there were two projects: (1) the Women's Spirituality Center in Santa Fe, New Mexico, to fund a spiritual and psychological support group for women facing burnout from work in human services; and (2) Let-It-Happen Retreats of Racine, Wisconsin, to help poor women and Witness for Peace Volunteers participate in retreats offered by the center.

In legal advocacy, there was one project, the Central American Refugee Center in Washington, D.C., to help fund counseling and clinical referral of women with war-related problems and traumas.

In child care and head start, three projects were funded: (1) Incarnation House in Minneapolis, Minnesota, a residential program for pregnant women and young mothers recovering from chemical dependency, mental illness, prostitution, and physical and sexual abuse, to provide child care so the mothers can attend therapeutic and support sessions; (2) St. Peter Claver Day Care Center in Lexington, Kentucky, to subsidize low-income mothers who qualify for state subsidy, but have to wait three to six months before receiving their monies; and (3) New Life Dwelling Place, in Thonotosassa, Florida, to help abusive and neglectful mothers to better care for their children, rather than putting them in foster care.

In literacy and education, there were five projects funded, including two grants to women to attend theological seminaries. The other projects were (1) the Mercy Learning Center of Bridgeport, Connecticut, to subsidize instruction for two low-income and illiterate women in math and language skills and improvement of self-image; (2) Stepping Stones of Immikalee, Florida, to expand their program of high school classes and living skills for pregnant teens; and (3) Harbor Me, Inc., of East Boston, Massachusetts, for an education program within a battered women's shelter.

In the area of help for the elderly and housebound, there were three projects funded: (1) Works of Mercy Advocacy Network of Far Rockaway, New York, to expand their program for frail, elderly, and economically poor housebound women and women with AIDS; (2) Holy Union Asian Center of Lowell, Massachusetts, for transportation for isolated refugee women to come to the center, and (3) Eldercare of Chicago (the project of Chicago Catholic Women, already described) to fund monthly gatherings for the elderly, hosted by the homeless women of the shelter, for conversation, celebration, and prayer.

In the area of shelter and housing, there were five projects: (1) the Coastal Women's Shelter Board of West Bern, North Carolina, for ongoing operation of a shelter for abused women and their children; (2) Jubilee Women's Center of Seattle, Washington, for food, emergency transportation, and materials for the resource library of a housing facility for single women in transition; (3) H. M. Life Housing Opportunity Services of Akron, Ohio, to help establish a women's resource center in a transitional housing program for homeless poor single mothers; (4) Magdalen House of Denver, Colorado, to help hire a counselor for an emergency shelter for women escaping prostitution; and (5) Genesis House in Chicago, Illinois, to help provide therapeutic recreational activities in a house of hospitality for women trying to get out of prostitution.

The range of grant proposals received in 1989 and 1990 represented a similarly stunning array of Catholic women's grassroots initiatives in service to the poor and needy. Mary's Pence receives an average of eighty to a hundred grant proposals a year, many of which do not meet its guidelines. It has been able to fund about one third of the proposals it has received, twenty-three projects in 1988, twenty-seven in 1989, and thirty in 1990. It hopes to be able to continually expand the number of projects it can fund and the money it can disperse.

Mary's Pence also hopes to encourage women in other parts of the

United States and other countries to develop their own Mary's Pence and to use their fundraising skills to raise money for their own ministries at the grassroots, rather than offering these skills to a male, clerical church that does not serve these needs. Ideally every diocese would have its own Mary's Pence that would gather funds from women of its area and fund its own local women's ministries. It is also hoped that when the male clerical church recognizes that it no longer controls the purse strings, it will have to become more responsive to women's needs.[7]

The five groups profiled in this essay represent a small but representative sample of the extraordinary proliferation of progressive grassroots U.S. Catholic organizations that have arisen in the last two decades following the Second Vatican Council. All are characterized by a high degree of commitment to social justice and a recognition of the interconnections of issues such as sexism, heterosexism, classism, racism, and militarism, as well as social violence, such as battering and drug abuse. All of them seek to serve concrete projects effectively, while doing so with a conscious social analysis that makes these interconnections.

All of these groups also practice a participatory rather than a hierarchical form of organization. Their immediate work groups and boards operate with a consensus model of decision making. They generate advice and feedback from their constituencies through surveys and, in some cases, give voting rights to this constituency. But most of the authority is given to the people working directly at the grassroots. Indirect control from those who are not participating is minimized, while maintaining clear structures of accountability.

There is continual evaluation and generation of new ideas by the working groups in an open process of self-development. Thus their model of organization might be called the functional "movement" type, in which the form of the organization continually adapts to the actual functions to be served. In addition, each organization also forms a local (or national) community of people who gather in mutual support, not only for work, but also for recreation and for prayer and spiritual renewal. Thus these groups function simultaneously as service organizations and, to some extent, as "base communities."

In relation to the Roman Catholic Church as an institution, they have discovered a remarkable way to be faithful to this church as a historical community, while being entirely free of its hierarchical control. They remain committed to Catholic Christianity, as reinterpreted by feminist and liberation perspectives, and they understand their work as a direct way of living out the gospel. They seek to witness to the clerical institution and urge it to ongoing reform of its own structures in order that it may more adequately serve the people in a similar way.

But, at the same time, they do not wait for this transformation to happen to others but become the living embodiment of that transformation themselves. They exist both within the Catholic Christian community and yet independently of its hierarchical system of control, becoming liberated zones of justice-seeking, participatory community in witness against the apostasy of segments of the larger institution and in direct ministry to the community. Most of all, they celebrate now the presence of the liberating Spirit in their midst.

Notes

1. See Rosemary Ruether, "Entering the Sanctuary: The Roman Catholic Story," in Rosemary Ruether and Eleanor McLaughlin, *Women of Spirit: Female Leadership in the Jewish and Christian Traditions* (New York: Simon and Schuster, 1979), 373–82.

2. See *Women and the Catholic Priesthood: An Expanded View: Proceedings of the Detroit Ordination Conference*, ed. Anne Marie Gardiner (New York: Paulist Press, 1976).

3. Information on Call to Action from interview with Sheila and Dan Daley, coordinators of CTA.

4. Information on the Eighth Day Center from interviews with its staff. For an example of the Good Friday March for Justice, see Rosemary Ruether, *Women-Church: Theology and Practice of Feminist Liturgical Communities* (San Francisco: Harper & Row, 1986), 251–59.

5. Information on the National Assembly of Religious Women from interview with Judy Vaughan, National Coordinator.

6. Information on Chicago Catholic Women from interview with Donna Quinn, Coordinator.

7. Information on Mary's Pence from Maureen Gallagher, National Coordinator. See also the article by Rosemary Ruether, "Promoting Women's Ministries," in *Cross Currents* (Spring 1989): 97–102.

E. DALE DUNLAP

– 12 –
The Protestant Experience
and Democratic Ecclesiology

Protestantism is marked by great diversity in both theology and doctrine and exhibits a remarkable variety of practices. As such it defies precise definition. Nevertheless, the Protestant experience is sufficiently articulate to afford commentary upon, if not guidelines for, a democratic ecclesiology. The perimeters of Protestantism make it impossible to cover the whole area in any kind of detail in an essay of this length. There are, however, identifiable common principles that are essential to an understanding of Protestant ecclesiology, as well as characteristic patterns of governance (polity) that speak to and illustrate what is involved in an ecclesiology that can be called democratic.

Central to most of Protestantism is the underlying principle affirming that God's grace is not and cannot be bound to any particular finite form. It rejects any human claim to the finality and absoluteness of any human construction. It requires a prophetic criticism of every human inclination to forget its finite and fallible nature. Since Protestants find no divinely created form of church governance mandated in Scripture, this principle applies as well to the structures of the church as to all other aspects of human endeavor, all of which are marked by finitude. The ecclesiastical landscape is strewn with the reminders of conflicts within Protestantism over matters of polity, indicative of the seriousness with which it is taken. While finding a given pattern of governance desirable for themselves, no truly Protestant body seriously contends that such a pattern is the divine will for all Christian bodies. John Dillenberger and Claude Welch, in their *Protestant Christianity*, remind us that Protestantism is "a spiritual attitude that recognizes that faith in the living God expresses itself in new ways of life and thought in response to new situations."[1] It is, they continue, "precisely the appearance of new and creative forms which demands the rejection of forms which have become irrelevant and therefore false and misleading."[2]

The classical and seminal doctrine of the Protestant Reformation was "justification by grace through faith," which held that Christ's self-offering is the sole and sufficient ground of salvation and can be accepted only through faith. The saving grace of God is mediated through Jesus Christ, to whom the believer has direct access in a personal encounter and relationship with God without the need of any intervening human or sacramental action. This doctrine is basic to and informs all other distinctive aspects of Protestantism.

An understanding of the nature of the church is basic to any discussion of the Protestant experience in democratic ecclesiology. The Reformation was a time of general renewal of both the church and its ministries. Much energy was expended on the issue of ecclesiology, resulting in a variety of ecclesiastical structures. There was a persistent concern to recover New Testament patterns of the church. The central clue was Jesus' own ministry in which he took the form of a servant. Taking the servant nature of Jesus' ministry as normative for the shape of his Body, the church, they held that its organized corporate and public life needed to be compatible with it. They saw there the church as a community of faith (*koinonia*) rather than an institution such as it had become over the centuries.

In the second century there already were signs that increasingly the church was ordering itself, and particularly its ministries, following the pattern of the Roman empire. By the third century it had completely taken on institutional forms patterned after the hierarchical forms and structures of its environment. This continued throughout the Middle Ages with increased rigidity until it was challenged in the sixteenth century by the Protestant Reformation.

Protestants recognize that the church is a creation of God and not a human contrivance, but understand that visible forms, which are the result of human creation, are essential to the life of the church. The Protestant principle, however, holds that no form is absolute and final. What was suitable for one place and time needs adapting to a new and different situation. It might even be allowed that the hierarchical form may have been effective and appropriate for its situation, but the situation changed and it could no longer be accepted as satisfactory. The issue is what form speaks to the needs of a new situation. There always has been and always will be a tension between tradition and its structures and experience arising out of new situations. This is what lies behind the Protestant insistence on *ecclesia semper reformanda* (the church reformed but always to be reformed): the constant necessity for re-evaluating and re-forming. If the church is to continue to be the church, it must be continuingly subject to reform. This is so not just because the members and officers of the church are human and fallible, subject to disobedience and to using the structures to serve their own interests. Another, and more basic, need for continuing reformation of the church's forms and structures is, as Colin Williams, in his *The Church*, points out, the fact that the church's living Lord is always "restlessly moving on and working with the changing shapes of human hope and need." This means that "yesterday's structures of obedience are today's barriers to new obedience" and that "obedience is an ever new event, not a changeless order of continuity."[3] Missional needs are always changing, which means that forms of ministry are always changing, which means that there have to be correlative changes in structure and authority patterns.

Classically and generally Protestants define the church as a congregation of faithful believers where the Word of God is truly preached and the sacraments are properly administered. The emphasis is primarily upon the church as a fellowship rather than an institution, upon evangelical mission rather than institutional forms. Increasingly the emphasis has moved toward understanding the church as mission, in which it has an "event character" that makes it open to the working of the Holy Spirit outside of any given patterns of tradition or institutional authority — an understanding that now has broad acceptance.

A corollary of this understanding of the church is the ministry of all Christians. The church is seen as a gathered community in which the laity is the essential, constituent part. In baptism all Christians are called and ordained to be God's ministers in the world, a "royal priesthood." By virtue of their faith in the Word of God, incarnate in Jesus Christ, all Christian believers are called to be priests to every other person.

By the second century the New Testament understanding of the whole Christian community as a "royal priesthood" was giving way to a separating of clergy and laity that, by the fifth century, construed the clerical status as a superior stage of Christian experience with complete control of the means of grace. During the Middle Ages this distinction between laity and clergy had hardened into a complete sacerdotalizing of the clergy. At the same time the monastic movement generated considerable inspiration and impetus for the increased role of the laity in the life of the church. The Waldensians in the twelfth century and the Lollards in the fourteenth century were movements of the laity stirring reform of the intransigent resistance of the clerically dominated official church. In this regard they were harbingers of things to come.

For Martin Luther and other sixteenth-century Reformers the "priesthood of all believers" was a corollary of justification by grace through faith and was a criterion of the true church that long had been subverted. The Reformers could find no scriptural grounds for what had come to be a radical distinction between laity and clergy. The New Testament word for clergy (*kleros*) refers to all Christians, not a special order that distributes the essential means of grace. The word for laity (*laos*) refers not to the receiving part of the congregation only, but to all Christians. Luther, in his *To the Christian Nobility*, held that "all Christians are truly priests and there is no distinction amongst them except as to office."[4] He recognized, however, that for the sake of order certain persons should be designated for responsibilities of preaching, teaching, and counseling, but these were offices whose nature was function rather than status. They were selected from among the community of faith, by the community of faith, and their priesthood was ministry of the community of faith.

Although it later was to be distorted by the impact of an exaggerated individualism which took it to mean that every person was his or her own priest, the priesthood of all believers has to be understood within its corporate and communal context: each one is called to be a priest to every other, often referred to as the mutual ministry of believers.

This new concept of ministry ultimately was to shape the history of Protestantism. It was a rejection of the control of the life of the church by a hierarchical clergy and the establishment of the laity as an essential, constitutive part of the community of faith and its governance. The work of the laity was at the core of the Protestant Reformation in all of its configurations, both established churches and free churches. The cruciality of this lay role in the American Great Awakening, the Wesleyan Revival in England, and continental Pietism is evident. The missionary movement was largely conceived and led by the laity. After a time of quiescence the recovery of the "ministry of the laity" was heralded and further enabled by Hendrik Kraemer in 1958 with his *A Theology of the Laity*. This revitalization became apparent in the Evangelical Academies in Europe, the German Evangelical Kirchentag, the Kerk en Wereed in Holland, and similar lay movements in all parts of Protestantism.

The modern ecumenical movement that eventuated in the World Council of Churches came from the impetus of the lay-led world missionary and student movements. A layman, John R. Mott, was a prime mover in the movement. At its second assembly in Evanston in 1954 the World Council established a Department of Laity as a part of its structure. But, as Kraemer wrote, "it is one thing to see and seize it [the ministry of the laity], it is another thing to give it shape and form in the reality of the church and to weave it as the basic pattern in the lives of the laity."[5] In mutuality laity and clergy are both part of the same *diakonia*, and a radical reshaping of the role of the laity in the church entails an equally radical reshaping of the role of the clergy and of the structure of the whole church. The renewal of the church in its apostolic character and mission is at stake here.

The attempt to classify ecclesiologies in Protestantism is problematical. There are reasonably clear basic types in general, but in both concept and historical development many communions reflect a "mixed" polity. The most common typology identifies four forms of Protestant organization. One type is the *episcopal*, or monarchical, form which tends to be governed clerically, with leadership being professional. This seldom is seen in Protestantism in a pure and unadulterated form. A second type is the *presbyterian*, or oligarchical, form. It is representative in nature with authority resting in representatives in council, clerical and lay, both of whom are chosen by the people to act in their name. All types of ordained leadership have the same status. A third type is the *congregational*, or democratic, form. Authority rests not in chosen representatives who act for the people but in the direct action of the people themselves. The church exists in the local congregation, which is united with other congregations, not organically but on the basis of voluntary fellowship in association. It has but one order of clergy. A fourth type has been given no particular name, but might be identified as *"pneumatic."* All fixed external form, including ministry, worship, and sacraments, is abandoned in the interests of giving free play to the immediate, direct, and unmediated guidance of the Holy Spirit.

Ernst Troeltsch, in his well-known ecclesiological typology, identifies two types: the church-type, which he associates with the episcopalian form, and the sect-type, which he associates with free churches. The problem with this typology is that it is inadequate and, with respect to the second type, is too imprecise to be useful. Troeltsch saw a third type to which he could not give a name. It was loose as to ecclesiastical forms and firm on the pragmatic nature of things, judging all form and organization, which were necessary, in the light of evangelical goals.

This type may be called an evangelical pragmatic approach that is rooted in the New Testament test, "By their fruits you will know them." Robert S. Paul, in his *The Church in Search of Itself*, suggests that this unnamed type is illustrated in the ecclesiology of Martin Luther and John Wesley. Both Luther and Wesley, he says, bring the authority of the Holy Spirit mediated through individual experience into relationship with the authority of the Spirit through received tradition and in Scripture. This differs from the fourth type above in that form and structure are essential, but are arrived at on a pragmatic basis and are adapted from time to time as the evangelical needs require.

John Wesley provides a clear example of this type. He was by nature and inclination a conservative and traditionalist priest of the Church of England. Satisfied that the Church of England polity was best for the English, he still thought that different churches in different places and including different people required different forms of polity. With respect to church practices and governance he turned out to be remarkably empirical and pragmatic. Wesley's passion was to save souls, and beyond anything else he felt the unquestionable commission of the Holy Spirit to "spread scriptural holiness throughout the land." The Church of England was not accepting of his efforts, and Wesley felt that he had no alternative but to take whatever steps were necessary to meet the spiritual needs of those whom the Holy Spirit had "called out of the world" through his preaching and given to his care. Three episodes will illustrate Wesley's views.

In 1739 John Wesley was astonished by the response of the people to whom he preached in the open air and became convinced that it was the work of the Holy Spirit and thus to be pursued. At the same time the pulpits of his own church were steadily being closed to him. Contrary to his own sense of propriety and the church's practice, Wesley was responsive to the Spirit's leading and took to "field preaching," since some new form was required to meet the evangelical demands of a new situation. Clearly Wesley could not evangelize the whole of England by himself with this method, but there was only half a handful of Anglican priests open to providing assistance. The usages of the church allowed only ordained clergy to preach, and Wesley felt bound by this. On one occasion when he was in Bristol word came to him that a young man he had left in charge of the Society in London was preaching. He hastened back to London intending to put a stop to this activity. Being warned on the way by his mother that he ought to listen to the young man before taking such drastic action, he did so, and acceded to what he recognized as the work of the Spirit. This led to his use of "lay assistants" as the core of the leadership of the movement.

The success of the field preaching created a new situation that called for a new response. The church could not accept the obvious success of his unconventional evangelism and failed to incorporate the people into its nurturing life. It became painfully evident to Wesley that these "babes in Christ" had to be sustained by nurturing groups that he called Societies and Class Meetings, which were connected with each other. They required organization and leadership, and he used the resources at hand: laypersons. The next step was the holding of conferences as a means of furthering the interests of the revival. Here was an embryonic polity developing in response to evangelical realities.

For John Wesley and the people in the Societies the Lord's Supper was a "chief means" of grace. Wesley admonished his people to avail themselves of it at every opportunity in the local parish. The parishes were not particularly hospitable and most of the Methodists felt "closed out." They urged Wesley to allow them to celebrate the Supper at the Society meetings, but he was adamant that an ordained person was required for this sacramental act. With the conclusion of the American Revolutionary War, however, a new situation arose with the Methodists in the new nation. The whole ecclesiastical situation had changed. The Methodist preachers there were not ordained, and Methodists did not have access to the sacraments through any other source.

Wesley's reading of Lord King's *Account of the Primitive Church* and Bishop Stillingfleet's *Irenicum* convinced him that in the New Testament *episkopos* and *presbyter* had the same meaning. He concluded that since he was a validly ordained presbyter/priest of the Church of England and was overseer (*episkopos*) of the Methodist Societies and of his "assistants" who were responsible to him, as he was for them to the Church of England, he had proper authority to ordain them — for the People Called Methodists, although not for the Church of England. The bishops of the Church of England rebuffed all of his entreaties for them to ordain persons for the Methodists in America. An evangelical and spiritual need clearly was present among the Methodists in America; he had authority to ordain, and he did just that.

It has to be acknowledged that Wesley's Societies were not a church in his time, at least not in England, although both in the United States and subsequently in England they became churches. Nonetheless what has been described illustrates an ecclesiological polity different from the traditionally identified types — one that develops pragmatically in response to the evangelical needs as new situations arise. John Wesley honored tradition and valued structure as being essential, but he also was an evangelical pragmatist regarding church order. No forms or practices were sacrosanct. The church had to be flexible enough to adapt to changing conditions, free enough to adapt itself in the service of the gospel.

No Protestant denomination exists as a pure example of a type of church organization. Elements of the various types are found in each one. Although the several types of church governance have their origins in Europe, the shape they have taken in the United States will be used for illustration.

Congregationalism is the type most generally associated with Protestant beginnings in the United States. Local church autonomy, the principle of covenanting, and the lay apostolate have been key marks of Congregationalism historically. A church is made up of a group of Christians uniting by voluntary agreement for worship and mutual advice, support, and edification. Each church is completely autonomous. It is governed by and for the people directly, not through representatives, with each member having an equal vote in management. The laity is sovereign, governing itself through a council or committee elected at a congregational meeting, using various boards and committees for specific activities. The pastor has only a consultative relation to this governing group and is without ecclesiastical authority. There is no religious or ecclesiastical differentiation between laity and pastor, who is elected and ordained by the local congregation.

Congregationalism laid great stress on independency, but also attached significance to the principle of fellowship, which held that local congregations had constantly to check their own conclusions by the experiences of others. This was implemented in the same way and for the same reason as the covenanting within the local congregation. This led to a series of supralocal church associations and conferences. These, however, were for counsel and cooperation in matters of common concern and had no binding ecclesiastical authority. At every level the membership was made up of ministerial and lay delegates elected by the relevant constituencies. This was the general pattern of governance characteristic of the Congregational Christian Church when it joined with the Evangelical and Reformed Church to form the United Church of Christ in 1957.

The congregationalism of the Evangelical and Reformed Church was modified by the presbyterial principle. Each local church was governed by a council elected by its own members. Local churches were organized into synods made up of the pastor and a lay member from each church. These territorial synods and the general synod, made up of equal numbers of clergy and laity elected from the territorial synods, had considerable authority over churches and pastors in their jurisdictions. Each synod was headed by an elected president, generally full-time and for a limited term with no possibility of reelection. That person was, in effect, an *episkopos* similar in many ways to a Methodist bishop, though with a wider range of authority and influence, having authority to "do whatsoever may be advisable under the circumstances." Here one finds a mixed polity that combines congregational, presbyterial, and episcopal elements.

The United Church of Christ came into existence in 1957 through a merger of the Congregational Christian and Evangelical and Reformed Churches. It was a union of churches with two different polities, one congregational and the other presbyterial. The result is a church that is locally congregational, administratively episcopal, and legislatively presbyterial. Broadly, the representative form of governance is used. Given the diversity of polity that has been merged, there is a measure of fuzziness and ambiguity still existent. What is manifested is a combination of unity and diversity with no great urgency to impose unity and resolve tensions by administrative fiat, whether by officialdom or commission. The local congregation is governed by a church meeting and usually is organized under a council composed of minister(s), deacons, and heads of the various organizations within the parish. Local churches are organized into conferences, associations, and a general synod with executives whose role in many respects is not very different from that of a bishop. The autonomy of the local church is modifiable by its own actions.

The family of Baptist churches, in its great variety, represents a variation on the theme of congregationalism. Traditionally Baptists have insisted on the principles of personal liberty and freedom of belief, which go along with the understanding of the church as a free association of believers functioning as a democracy in which the governing power of the church is vested in the people. Each local church is independent and congregational in form, controlling its own worship and discipline, electing all church officers, and calling and dismissing its pastors. It is governed by the pastor and other lay officers, sometimes with a standing advisory committee made up of the pastor and officials along with other members elected by the church. Ordination is congregational, initiated by a local church in requesting a person to be its pastor. If judged qualified by a committee from several neighboring Baptist churches selected by the candidate's church, that person is ordained by a presbytery of ordained pastors or a council composed of ordained pastors and unordained laypersons. The pastor's role is primarily that of teacher and administrator whose authority is moral suasion only.

Although local churches are independent, a true church cannot exist in isolation from other churches and must maintain fellowship with them, involving consultation with regard to matters affecting common interest, seeking and taking advice. This is achieved by associations of churches and national conventions. Typically associations have no binding authority and can only "determine" and "declare" by giving guidance and counsel, but not "impose." Local church authority remains inalienable and final in matters of ecclesiastical law and doctrine. Its power cannot be delegated. There may be "messengers" to associational bodies, but not delegates in the normal sense of that word. Ironically the Baptist family of churches, traditionally viewed as among the most democratic of Protestant churches, has experienced more fractures than any other. In response to the problems that have arisen as the result of radical individualism and extremes of local autonomy, many Baptist church have been moving in the direction of a stronger connectionalism.

Another example of democratic congregational ecclesiology is to be found in the Christian Church–Disciples of Christ. The movement began as two restorationalist efforts intent upon recovering the essential New Testament church, under the leadership of Barton Stone and Thomas Campbell respectively. These movements united in 1832. With freedom of association at the core of the movement, it began with a thoroughgoing congregational polity in which each church elected its own officers and had entire control over its own governance. There was a stress on the freedom of individual Christians to study Scripture for themselves, unbound by any human creeds or dogmas. No extracongregational or superimposed human ecclesiastical authority was recognized. Soon after the 1832 union they began to organize with associations and conventions, joining together to work through common agencies for various common purposes. Increasingly this called for organization and eventually led to a considerable bureaucracy. The common life of the church was expressed through three manifestations: congregational, regional, and general — all in covenant relationship. These extracongregational groups were for mutual help only and had no ecclesiastical authority.

For the Disciples of Christ the concept of covenanting was central in the life of the church: God covenanting with the people created the church; people covenanting with each other created the local church; local churches covenanting with each other created the denomination. In this tradition covenanting is not juridical, and authority is understood, as Michael Kinnamon explains in his *Disciples of Christ in the 21st Century*, "to be supporting, teaching, challenging, holding one another accountable, and caring and mediating for one another and all of God's creation."[6] He goes on to say that because the divine-human relationship is dynamic, all decisions and actions are provisional, and the life of the church is continuously being renewed.

Along with other Protestant churches the Christian Church–Disciples of Christ holds to the tenet of the priesthood of all believers. This corporate priesthood designates certain persons from within itself to be representative ministers charged with responsibilities not shared by others in order to be sure that specific responsibilities of service are fulfilled. The representative ministry includes full-time pastors and volunteer elders and deacons. All are ordained by the local church, which also has authority to call its pastor. Elders care for spiritual interests and deacons for financial interests and benevolence. The pastor has overall responsibilities for the life of the church, but is subject to the congregation's counsel and ultimate decisions about matters pertaining to the church. The Lord's Supper is central to the common worship of the church, but it is the elders, not the pastor, who offer the prayers, consecrate the elements, and deliver them to the deacons to be distributed among the people.

By the turn of the century many in the church were influenced by fresh biblical studies that demonstrated that there was no one New Testament divine constitution for Christ's church, but rather a diversity of forms. After a slow but steady movement from sect-type to church-type, by the 1960s the consensus was growing that regardless of how they started, they now were a church (denomination) and needed to act accordingly in "responsible fashion." This came to fruition in 1968 with the adoption of *A Provisional Design for the Christian Church–Disciples of Christ*. It reflected the tension between maintaining traditional essentials and the necessity of responding to a new situation. The *Design* defines the church in the traditional Christian–Disciples way, insisting that the nature of the church as given by Christ remains the same, but recognizing that faithfulness to its mission requires it to continuously adapt its structures to the needs and patterns of a changing world.

Building on a traditional base, the *Design* provided a structural balance between centralization and decentralization. Local churches no longer were totally independent, but were linked inextricably and irrevocably to the denomination. It introduced the representative principle into the structures beyond the local church. The articulation of the priesthood of all believers continues to underscore the corporate and collegial ministry that includes all Christians, and this finds expression in various manifestations of the church at local, regional, and general levels. Representative ministry continues to include pastors, elders, and deacons, but now clearly also includes department, auxiliary, and bureau appointments. Regional executives have become, in practice, something like "shepherding bishops." The local church's authority to ordain is now subject to extracongregational approval, and calling and dismissing a pastor requires consultation and advice from conference officials. Here is another example of a dynamic mixed polity, moving from a nearly pure independent and congregational pattern to one that is responsive to new situations, needs, and understandings.

The presbyterian type of church governance, followed by all Presbyterian bodies, is a representative conciliar government that is neither greatly diffused nor greatly concentrated and that provides a balance of powers between clergy and laity. Three main principles inform presbyterian polity: the right of the people to participate in the government of the church, the unity of the church maintained through the subjection of the part to the whole, and the parity of ministry. Presbyterian congregations are not autonomous, but are bound together in a hierarchical administrative system made up of sessions, which govern the local congregation, presbyteries, which govern a number of congregations within a limited district, synods, which govern the congregations of a larger district, and a General Assembly, which is the supreme judicatory body.

The session, usually moderated by the teaching elder (pastor), has authority over membership, spiritual affairs, and general discipline of the local congregation. Its membership is composed of the teaching elder(s) of the local congregation and ruling elders elected by the congregation. The presbytery, made up of all teaching elders and ruling elders from each session, has authority over teaching elders, supervises business common to all congregations, reviews all session reports, serves as an appeals court, and oversees general denominational matters. While technically amenable to two bodies of higher jurisdiction, the synod, for all practical purposes, is the basic governing body of Presbyterianism. The synod, made up of an equal number of teaching and ruling elders elected by the presbyteries, exercises general superintendence over the presbyteries and sessions and determines the number and makeup of presbyteries. The General Assembly is composed of teaching elders and ruling elders chosen by a formula and elected in equal numbers by the presbyteries. Being the highest juridical body in Presbyterianism, it legislates for the whole church, appoints general boards and commissions, determines the number of synods, settles all matters relating to doctrine and discipline, and is a court of final appeal.

The officers of a Presbyterian church are the teaching elders (ministers of the gospel), ruling elders (representatives of the people for the purpose of exercising government and discipline), and deacons. The teaching and ruling elders are the rulers of the local church. Deacons manage the temporal affairs of the church, but do not participate in governance. All three are ordained, the ruling elders and deacons being elected by the people and ordained by a teaching elder with the laying on of hands of the session, including laity. The teaching elder is ordained by the presbytery with the laying on of hands of the presbytery, including both clergy and laity. The presbytery has authority with respect to the selection, care, ordination, and call of teaching elders.

In a covenanting relationship between presbytery and local church, the presbytery must screen and approve all candidates for call before the interviewing process with the local church begins. While not opposed to episcopacy in principle, in the Presbyterian system the function of *episko-pos* is served through the hierarchical system of ecclesiastical judicatories. Judicatory executives, while having an administrative role only with no ecclesiastical or judicatory authority, by virtue of the encompassing nature of that role and its capacity for suasiveness, function as quasi-bishops. Governance in Presbyterian churches is also, in practice if not always juridically, becoming increasingly an instance of "mixed" polity.

Lutherans tend to be less pragmatic than many other Protestant churches in their polity, developing it more in terms of a basic theological rationale. They look upon the church as being constituted by the event of the preaching of the gospel. As such it is not a voluntary association of believing people, but a society of people whom God has chosen. While order is not to be belittled, no particular form or order is constitutive of the church, and uniformity of external organization is not and ought not be demanded.

It was a fundamental principle of the Protestant Reformation, and a corollary of the doctrine of the priesthood of all believers, that all ecclesiastical power inheres in the local church. It was in the interests of order, efficiency, Christian fellowship, and mission that supralocal church forms of organization developed. Lutheran churches in the United States fully accepted the autonomy of the local church and the control of the laity in all affairs of the church. Pastors may discuss, but usually have no vote at the local level. Even so, as clergy came from Europe they began to assert control, proceeding to appoint the elders. Although until the end of the colonial period the lay members of synods were consultants rather than voting members, the movement among the Lutherans was for more participation of the laity in governance.

Conditions in the colonies and then in the new nation required Lutheran congregations to organize as free churches. The general pattern of polity for Lutheranism is congregational at the local level and representative at synodical levels. The local church is autonomous, although under the general oversight of a bishop and amenable to synodical action in instances of serious breaches of the basic discipline of the church. The local church governs its affairs according to its own constitution, which must be consonant with that of the general church. The governing body is a church council made up of the pastor, who heads it, and church officers elected by the congregation, including elders, deacons, and sometimes trustees.

Most Lutheran churches are organized beyond the local level along synodical lines, usually with regional synods and the general Synod, which is the denomination in General Assembly, which has ultimate jurisdiction. Over the years the practical problems associated with training ministers, sending missionaries, education, etc. have led congregations to delegate power in such matters to the synods. Regional synods are made up of all ordained pastors and licentiates, with one lay delegate elected by the church council from each pastoral charge. Membership in the general Synod is determined by a representative formula.

The priesthood of all believers lies at the heart of Lutheran church life. Spiritual priesthood belongs to all Christians, conferred through baptism and the response of faith. The evangelical work of the church in the world is carried on by the laity for the most part, with the clergy existing to serve rather than rule. In the deepest sense there is no difference between laity and clergy, only a difference in office. Most Lutheran churches have but one order, that of pastor or presbyter, who is set apart by a rite of ordination by the laying on of hands by a bishop or the bishop's appointee. Laypersons may be invited to share in the laying on of hands. A candidate for ordination has to be approved by synodical action. Lutheran presidents or bishops are not in principle different from other clergy. Bishops have general oversight of the life of the church in the judicatory over which that officer presides. Local congregations call their own pastors from a list of synodically approved persons and with recommendation by the bishop. As with other Protestant churches, Lutheran church polity has been conditioned by and adapted in the face of the cultural climate and realities of its environment, which engenders a democratic approach to church governance.

The Episcopal Church probably is the clearest instance of episcopal polity among the major Protestant churches in the United States, although its polity is significantly modified in a democratic direction. The Episcopalians came to the North American colonies in 1607, the first Protestant church to be established. The name of the church originally contained the word "Protestant" to distinguish it from the Catholics, and the word "Episcopal" distinguished them from the Congregationalists and Presbyterians.

The governance pattern of the Episcopal Church is essentially hierarchical, but with a difference. It includes a large measure of lay participation in governance, providing good check and balance in relation to the clergy. Since 1789 no law can be enacted without the concurrence of the laity in council. Further, it maintains a balance of power between the executive and legislative branches.

The local parish is at the bottom of the organizational hierarchy in the Episcopal Church. It is headed by a rector who must be an ordained priest. Each parish has a board of officers called a vestry, made up of both men and women, charged with the administration of temporal affairs. The executive officers of the vestry are called wardens and are ex-officio delegates of the parish to the Diocesan Convention. The vestry elects the rector. They must give notice of election to the bishop who, if he or she finds no imperative reason to the contrary, will have the person instituted as the rector. The final decision, however, is with the bishop.

Each parish is an integral part of a diocese, which is the fundamental ecclesiastical unit of Episcopal organization. It is governed by the bishop in conjunction with a Diocesan Convention composed of all clergy and lay representatives from each parish. The Convention meets annually and regulates and administers the affairs of the church within its bounds. It annually appoints a Standing Committee, made up of both clergy and laity, as an advisory council to the bishop. Its advice may be proffered whether asked for or not. This committee exercises administrative authority in case of the absence or impairment of the bishop. The diocese elects its bishop, who must be approved by a majority of the bishops and Standing Committees of the denomination.

Dioceses are organized into provinces, which organizationally are patterned after the General Convention (see below). The Provincial Synod has very restricted legislative power and functions primarily as conferences to coordinate and increase the effectiveness of particular areas of the work of the church.

At the national level the Episcopal Church is governed by two executive-legislative bodies. One is the General Convention, which is the highest legislative body and ecclesiastical authority in the church. It is made up of a House of Deputies composed of lay and clergy delegates elected in equal numbers from the dioceses, and a House of Bishops composed of all of the bishops of the church. The houses deliberate separately, and both must approve a measure before it becomes law. The second body is the National Council, which acts as an executive body of the General Convention between its sessions. It has a fixed membership, made up of bishops, rectors, laymen, and laywomen, and it is presided over by the church's presiding bishop.

Candidates for ordination must be recommended by a majority of the vestry of the parish in which they hold membership. The candidacy is considered by the Standing Committee of the diocese who then recommend to the bishop. The bishop, after examination, may ordain, but he or she has the final decision and cannot be compelled to ordain. Bishops are elected by the Diocesan Convention, approved by the General Convention, and consecrated by not fewer than three bishops. The bishop, who must confirm new members in the church, has the supreme authority to receive or not receive candidates into membership.

The fact that the unifying principle of the Episcopal Church is comprehensiveness militates against extreme hierarchical patterns and encourages a basically democratic process in its governance.

The Methodist Church, a part of the United Methodist Church since 1968, provides an illuminating case study of the *process* of democratization in what in many ways is a representative Protestant denomination. Identifying itself as an "episcopal" church at its organization in 1784, the Methodist church has developed its polity pragmatically into a decidedly eclectic type. Originally it was episcopal with a monarchical episcopacy and governance by the clergy, both of which have been substantially modified through the process of democratization. It is congregational with respect to the basically democratic character of its procedures and to some extent in the required consultation process in the appointment of clergy to the churches. It is presbyterial in its conciliar approach through a hierarchy of conferences and way of selecting and ordaining clergy.

John Wesley, founder of Methodism in England, though pragmatic with respect to practices and government, was autocratic in his superintending administration. While laity exercised leadership in the Societies and Class Meetings, it was the lay traveling preachers (clergy in that context), a number of whom Wesley invited to join him in conference, who determined both doctrine and polity for the people called Methodists. Even so, they were entirely subordinate to Wesley, who at the close of the conference would tell them what the decisions had been. It was an amazing combination of lay involvement and clerical domination, of conciliarism and autocracy.

In the United States Francis Asbury was the counterpart of John Wesley in England, every bit as autocratic, but administratively under constitutional constraints. The rising influence of democracy was affecting all aspects of life in the new nation. This is to be seen in the event of Asbury's own ordination. In order to address the needs of the Methodists in the United States, John Wesley appointed Dr. Thomas Coke, already an ordained clergyman, and "set him aside" by either consecration or ordination (which it was being a moot matter) to be "general superintendent" (bishop, in effect) in America and to ordain Francis Asbury and make him a "joint superintendent." Asbury, sensing and sharing the rising republican sentiments abroad, refused ordination on Wesley's personal determination, insisting that he would submit to ordination only if elected by his peers. The preachers in conference did elect him, and he was ordained, with Philip Otterbein, a friend and United Brethren preacher, participating. Not only does one see the influence of democracy, but at the outset an episcopal form of government with ministers and bishops being selected and ordained presbyterially.

When the Methodist Episcopal Church was organized in 1784, provision was made for an annual Conference, composed of all the traveling preachers in "full connection," which had legislative authority. As the movement grew in numbers and spread geographically it was necessary to organize additional annual conferences. This led to a conciliar and hierarchical pattern of governing conferences, which included the General Conference, the Annual Conference, which became the functional governing body of the church, and the local Quarterly Conference. Local churches were not independent entities, but connected integrally and inextricably with all other churches in the denomination through this system of conferences, which is identified as connectionalism. Membership in the General Conference and annual conferences was limited to clergy. While laity did participate in the quarterly conference, it usually was dominated by clergy.

Probably more out of the influence of general democratic philosophy than through any clear theological conviction about the priesthood of all believers, the laity of the church began to insist that they had a right to participate in the "real" governance of the church in the annual conferences and the General Conference. The issue came to the fore as early as 1820, but the clergy resisted and responded by interposing a district conference between the quarterly conference and the annual conference in which laity could hold membership. This only added fuel to the fire since the action implicitly acknowledged that the laity had a proper role in governance beyond the local church. The issue came to a head in 1830 with the Methodist Protestant schism, in which laity (not including women or black persons) had equal representation with clergy in all conferences, a president replaced the bishop, and preachers were assigned to churches by a stationing committee made up of both laity and clergy.

The struggle continued, with the clergy resistingly giving ground only reluctantly. In 1866 the Methodist Episcopal Church, South, which had come into being through a break in the church largely over the slavery issue, although a kind of ecclesiastical "states rights" issue also was involved, introduced lay representation into the conferences and courts of the church. In 1872 the Methodist Episcopal Church allowed two lay delegates from each annual conference constituency to have membership in the General Conference. It was not until 1932, one hundred years after the struggle began, that the Methodist Episcopal Church gave laity representation in annual conferences. In 1939, when the Methodist Episcopal, Methodist Episcopal, South, and Methodist Protestant Churches reunited to form the Methodist Church, provision was made for equal representation of laity and clergy in the General, Jurisdictional and Central, and Annual Conferences. In the Annual Conference this included all traveling preachers in full connection and one layperson from each pastoral charge, with the provision that there could not be more clergy than lay members.

There was another facet of the issue of lay representation: the recognition of women as "laymen." This was raised by Sister Jenkins in 1852. The 1872 action giving limited representation to laity had said that "layman" referred to all members of the church who were not clergy, thus seemingly including women. Some subsequent arcane interpretation proved this not to be the case. In 1888 five different women from five different annual conferences (including Frances E. Willard, who probably was the most distinguished Methodist layperson at that time) were elected to be members of the General Conference, but were denied their seats. It was not until 1904, a half-century after the issue was first raised, that women were elected, present, and functioning as lay members of the conferences of the

Methodist Episcopal Church. It was 1922 before this place for women was realized in the Methodist Episcopal Church, South.

A further illustration of the process of democratization is seen in the matter of the ordination of clergy. For over 150 years only men were eligible for ordination in the Methodist churches (with the exception of the Methodist Protestant Church). In 1876 a petition went to General Conference proposing the ordination of women, beginning a seventy-five-year struggle. Finally the ordination of women was provided by the uniting conference of the Methodist Episcopal, Methodist Episcopal, South, and Methodist Protestant Churches in 1939, but women still were not permitted to be full clergy members of the annual conference (except those who already were members of conference in the Methodist Protestant Church). It was not until 1956 that full membership was granted. Both ordination and annual conference membership were incorporated into the discipline of the United Methodist Church in 1968. This movement reached its zenith in 1980 when Marjorie Matthews was elected and consecrated a bishop.

The itinerancy of clergy has been a distinctive and essential aspect of Methodism's system since the time of John Wesley. It is the way Methodism has deployed its clergy resources in its strategy of mission, putting the right person in the right place at the right time. It gives the bishop authority and responsibility to appoint, requires the preacher to go where appointed, and requires the congregation to receive and recompense the person appointed. Almost immediately after the 1784 conference some local congregations began to object to and some preachers to resist the absolute authority of the bishop to appoint without any appeal to conference. This practice has been conditioned over the years by several factors: the development of the bishop's cabinet for consultation, the lengthening of the limits of time for a pastor to stay in one place, and the requirement of consultation with the pastor and local church in the process of appointment making.

The movement to require consultation with the local church in the appointment process failed in 1940, but in 1972 action was taken to require consultation by the district superintendent with the pastor and the local pastor-parish relations committee concerning their specific appointment before any announcement of appointment was made. The failure to implement this by some bishops and cabinets resulted in a fairly dramatic restriction of the power, if not the authority, of both bishop and cabinet in 1976 with a broadening of the participation of both pastor and local church in the decision-making process of appointment making.

There are several other instances of democratization in Methodism. In the beginning the episcopacy was strongly monarchical and fairly autocratic. Very early there were signs among both clergy and churches of chafing under this kind of episcopal authority. Technically the episcopacy still is monarchical, but as a result of two centuries of the process of democratization few bishops are able to and most do not desire to exercise this kind of autocracy. The development of conferences, boards, councils, and committees has effectively reduced the bishop's role in the program decisions of the church. The heavy workload of the bishop led to the melding of the several district superintendents into a cabinet, collegially shaping the work of the bishop. While technically the bishop alone is given authority to appoint pastors to churches, in 1939 the bishop was required to consult with the district superintendents and announce to them openly the appointments before the official declaration. In fact these and similar kinds of decisions now are participated in by the cabinets.

During most of the history of Methodism the laity have played no part in the authorization and ordination of clergy, except at the beginning of the process when a candidate has to be recommended by the local church in which she or he holds membership. Only clergy can vote on the ordination and character of the clergy. For some time, beginning in the 1970s, some Boards of Ordained Ministry in annual conferences had, without specific authority, included lay members who voted on all board business, even the interviewing of candidates, with the exception of action on ordination and character. In 1988 this practice was regularized, and there is continuing pressure to allow laity to vote on ordination and character matters also. In ordination bishops ordain, with the assistance of other clergy, persons who have first been elected by the clergy. As of 1988 a bishop may invite a layperson to participate in the laying on of hands in ordination. Since laypersons are members of the Jurisdictional Conference, which elects bishops, they participate on equal terms with the clergy in that election. The democratizing process, with a tension between form and freedom, continues in the United Methodist Church.

The Protestant experience of democratization has to be seen in the context of the churches' astonishing resistance to change and the clergy's sturdy resistance to the loss of power. Democratization, even though it has been integral to a developing Protestantism, has been and continues to be a long and often agonizingly frustrating process. It does not happen in a moment.

What can be learned from the Protestant experience with democratic ecclesiology?

1. The basic lesson is that given the radical sovereignty of God, it has to be recognized that all forms and structures are finite, and all claim for the finality and absoluteness of any human construction rejected.

2. There is a necessary tension between the church as mission-event and the church as institution, but the church is to be understood primarily in terms of mission rather than institution, with its form and ministries centrally defined as *diakonia*. The dynamic of the gospel always expresses itself in new ways in response to new situations, requiring constant reformation of the forms in order to faithfully fulfill the mission to which it calls.

3. The priesthood of all believers is a central, seminal, and crucial factor

in defining the nature of the church and shaping the church. Renewal in the church characteristically has come through essentially lay movements.

4. Diversity and what Colin Williams calls a pluriform church structure are essential. COCU (Churches of Christ Uniting), made up of nine major Protestant denominations, has, after three decades of wrestling with the shape that unity in the church should take, shifted from a dominant emphasis on the permanent, historic, and given structures of the church, turning, as Robert S. Paul summarizes it, to "the Spirit as its ultimate authority, which finds its justification neither primarily in historic traditions nor in its appeal to a scriptural pattern, but in an evangelical outreach."[7] This means an openness to experimental and plural forms in which ministry and governance can be expressed, a stress called for by the World Council Study Commission on "The Missionary Stance of the Congregation."

5. Faithful apostolicity and the democratic process necessarily involve checks and balances: between autonomy and conciliarism, between continuity and diversity, and between laity and clergy.

6. Democratization of the church, particularly in nondelegated forms of governance, inherently runs the danger of inauthentic and destructive individualism, the tyranny of majority rule, and oligarchy of the elite who know how and have the power to manipulate the system.

7. The "evangelical-pragmatic" approach to governance runs the danger of becoming an end in itself, subjectively mistaking its own objectives for those of the gospel and of being unduly shaped by culture.

Protestantism has to acknowledge that its affirmation of *semper reformanda* applies to itself. Its understanding of the church and the priesthood of all believers has been realized only by fits and starts, and probably nowhere finds complete fulfillment. Nonetheless, its experience with a democratized ecclesiology speaks to these kinds of issues in the whole of Christendom.

Notes

1. John Dillenberger and Claude Welch, *Protestant Christianity* (New York: Charles Scribner's Sons, 1954), 315.

2. Ibid.

3. Colin Williams, *The Church* (Philadelphia: Westminster Press, 1968), 146.

4. Hendrik Kraemer, *A Theology of the Laity* (Philadelphia: Westminster Press, 1958), 61.

5. Ibid., 136.

6. Michael Kinnamon, *Disciples of Christ in the 21st Century* (St. Louis: CBP Press, 1988), 17.

7. Robert Paul, *The Church in Search of Itself* (Grand Rapids, Mich.: William B. Eerdmans Publishing Co., 1972), 331.

JOHN A. COLEMAN, S.J.

– 13 –
Not Democracy but Democratization

How does a sociologist look at efforts to achieve greater democratization in the church? What secular movements might provide clues for devising effective strategies for achieving a greater degree of participative governance in the church? My remarks in this essay will congeal around three major themes: (1) The church is not, in any formal sense, a democracy since ultimate sovereignty does not rest with the people, expressed through majority vote and/or representative organs of government accountable, in the final analysis, to majoritarian scrutiny and control. Nevertheless, in democratic societies, the church, like other institutions, willy-nilly, will become subject to pressures toward greater democratization.

The church's own theological self-understanding contains strong analogues to crucial elements in a democratic ethos. Since the church has, in the past, adopted structures from forms of governance that differ from its own theological self-understanding (e.g., monarchy, the military, the formal bureaucracies of Renaissance states), nothing, in principle, impedes its adopting democratic forms of governance that it then tailors and transmutes to fit its own unique theological self-understanding.[1] That theological understanding sees the constitution of the church as a hierarchical communion instituted by the will of Christ and governed by norms of *collegiality, subsidiarity,* and *justice as participation.*

(2) A *reformist* program for improving participative governance in the church would look to improving already existing forms of participative governance in the world church, in national churches, and in dioceses and parishes. The 1983 revised Code of Canon Law either mandates or allows many new forms of participative governance in the church.[2] Ultimately, however, a reformist program will run up against several impediments toward a genuinely participative governance structure in the church: true access of the laity to the governing function in the church; the absence of a genuine system of accountability based on checks and balances built into a tripartite system of government: executive, judicial, and legislative.

(3) A more *radical* program for improving participative governance in the church will build on strategies for improving public opinion in the church and use freedom of association in the church to create *in the community* models of alternative structures of participative governance that might put pressure on *organizational structures in the church*. In this, a radical movement for reform can look to and learn from Eastern European dissidents' attempts to create *in civil society* freedoms denied by the state. To be successful, *communitarian* movements to reform participative governance in the church must garner the support of diverse elements in the church: hierarchy, clergy, laity.

Not Democracy but Democratization

In *Ecclesiam Suam*, his first major encyclical upon assuming the papacy, Pope Paul VI stated flatly: "The church is not a democratic association established by human will."[3] Several elements of church structure, usually seen as essential to the very nature of the church, contrast profoundly with democratic legal forms. The church's innermost authority structure includes hierarchy.

To be sure, the sources of legitimacy for authority in the church are multiple: Scripture, the binding decisions of the *magisterium*, the testimony and lives of saints and prophets and human experience filtered through prayer and discernment in a mature *sensus fidelium*. Thus, authority in the church is not, totally, hierarchical. But ultimate legislative, executive, and judicial authority rests in the college of the world episcopacy, presided over by the pope, who exercises, within this college, primacy.[4]

Popes, bishops, priests, deacons, and other ministerial offices or charisms in the church derive their legitimacy not from the people expressed by the electoral will of the majority, as in a democracy. Rather, their legitimacy derives from a perceived and tested call from God (vocation) and from the mandate of Christ, who left the church the mission and power to continue his sanctifying work.[5]

In a democracy, every kind of qualification to hold office ultimately derives, through constitutional structure and representative organs, *from below*, from the inalienable sovereignty of the people. Indeed, as sovereign, the people invest authority in a democracy (and can freely transmute its forms through legislative action or constitutional reform) wholly from below. On the contrary, as German theologian Karl Lehmann notes: "In the church, every kind of basic qualification to hold office ultimately derives from the authority of Jesus Christ. Now, if this is true, then it follows with regard to the question of what the basis for this authority is that it can never, formally as such, be transmitted wholly 'from below.'"[6] Lehmann adds, in commentary: "A community which has a genuine spirit of obedience to Jesus Christ will not even wish its leader to be in a position of *total* dependence upon the community and only able to 'reproduce' that which is already a living force" within the community.[7]

In Lehmann's view, while every exercise of official authority in the church "must remain constantly rooted in the soil of a community conceived in terms of brotherhood [and sisterhood] and collegiality," nevertheless, officers in the church, at root, remain as much responsible to their mandate to maintain fidelity to the gospel (as bottom-line unnormed norm for all church governance) as to reflect the current will of the majority.[8] Officers in the church (resting their legitimacy on office) as well as prophets (whose authority flows from charism) can and must resist majoritarian opinion when it lacks a full sense of fidelity to the received faith (*sensus fidelium*).

Democracies do not entail — as in the church — any deep sense of a corporate *magisterium* that, by sacred mandate, "traditions" the founding and grounding act of the church, i.e., "hands-over" faithfully and adapts to new circumstances the normative content of Jesus' message and saving activity.

To be sure, the essential definition of democracy itself remains contested.[9] Democracy involves an interrelated set of principles, attitudes, patterns of behavior, and legal forms. Democratic principles espouse (1) equality before the law; (2) the freedom of individuals and corporate groups as a presumptive rule against absolutism; (3) constitutionality, and (4) open public opinion formation, a dialogue that is free, undistorted, and open to all. The forms of democracy entail universal suffrage, representative organs for legislation, accountability structures for judges and executives, a division of powers, and a set of basic rights (such as the rights to free speech, freedom of the press and assembly) enshrined in law and enactable through a court system.

In democracies, legitimate government rests on the consensus of the ruled. Citizens in a democracy always retain their basic power, as the foundational trustees of the state, to serve as the ultimate source of legitimacy and direction for the state. This grounding notion of the inalienable sovereignty of the people, at root, distinguishes church structure from democracy.[10] Most modern democracies, moreover, rest on a competition of parties: a governing faction and an organized, if loyal, opposition. There is no "organized opposition" in the church, nor — given the theological notion of the church as a *communion* — should one expect any ready acceptance in the church for a notion of a permanently given structure of "organized opposition" to the party that rules.

An Ethos of Democracy

Therefore, we must carefully distinguish between democracy as a formal system of governance (which the church, in its constitution, is not) and an ethos of democracy. The ethos of democracy espouses "mutual respect, a readiness of members to make the common interest one's own and to listen to one another, a discussion in which all who are affected by a given decision are accorded a hearing."[11] Nondemocratic forms of organization (e.g., economic corporations, bureaucracies based on competency rather than election) can be held to the spirit or ethos of democracy, even if they are not formally democratic in governance. The demand is for a participatory, "dialogical," and expressive style of communication rather than for majoritarian rule as such.

Democracy is as much an ideal, a spirit or ethos, as a formally constituted principle and form of governance. Thus, for example, since the 1960s in advanced industrial democracies, movements for democratization have attempted to apply the ethos of democracy to forms of governance, e.g., universities, corporate economic structures, which are not and are unlikely to become formal democracies as such: they are not ruled by the principle of "one person, one vote" or by majority rule. Democratization, in forms of governance that are not democracies, envisions the formal enactment of norms of consultation, collaboration, accountability and due process, even in the absence of a mechanism of elections.

Churches, in democratic societies, can expect to experience similar pressures toward democratization. Indeed, this has occurred. Hence, the strongest demands of the American Catholic laity urge greater democratization of church governance structures. A representative sample of American Catholic laity, for example, shows that a majority (in each age, gender, or socioeconomic category almost always a two-thirds majority) "of those under 55 years of age favor the idea that the church should have more democratic decision-making at the local parish, diocesan and Vatican levels."[12] Moreover, as Patrick Granfield and others have persuasively argued, when the church exists as a voluntary organization within a democracy, its very credibility as an authority depends on its responding to calls for democratization.[13]

Absent democratization, churches suffer a crisis of legitimation. As Granfield notes,

> On a practical level, the bureaucratic system of the church diminishes its legitimation when it neglects consultation, collaboration, accountability and due process and when it assumes an adversarial and negative attitude. An overly monarchical and centralized bureaucracy distances itself from the faithful and loses its contact with urgent pastoral needs. Administrative procedures and management styles have to be critically assessed, in order to avoid the undesirable aspects of bureaucracy such as inflexibility, cumbersomeness, inefficiency and unfairness.[14]

Collegiality as the Primary Constitutional Principle

Even if the church is not, formally, a democracy, its theological self-understanding, especially since Vatican II, encourages a deep-going application of the democratic ethos to its structures and behavior. The church, too, has its own theory of equality, rooted in the notion of a universal priesthood of all believers. At Vatican II, in the document on the constitution of the church, *Lumen Gentium*, the council fathers argue that this fundamental equality of all believers takes precedence over hierarchy as a grounding belief about the church. They preface their treatment of hierarchy by a more encompassing claim about the universal call of all in the church to holiness, rooted in baptism: "All share a true equality with regard to the dignity and to the activity common to all the faithful" (*Lumen Gentium*, no. 32c). "There is in Christ and in the church no inequality on the basis of race or nationality, social condition or sex" (*Lumen Gentium*, no. 32b). Vatican II chooses an inclusive rather than a hierarchical metaphor, "the people of God," as its primary model for understanding the church.

Democracy's concern for freedom is echoed in Vatican II's insistence in its Declaration on Religious Freedom (*Dignitatis Humanae*) on the essential freedom of the act of faith. Vatican II also affirms an essential diversity within the church: "By divine institution, the Holy Church is structured and governed with a wonderful diversity.... This diversity among its members arises by reason of their duties" (*Lumen Gentium*, nos. 32a; 13c). The major impetus for democratization in the church derives from Vatican II's definition of the church as a collegial communion.

Collegiality: Papacy and Episcopacy

The church as collegial communion means that the church is also not an absolute monarchy. When Pope Paul VI requested that the council fathers insert into their schema on the church that the pope was answerable to God alone, they refused. The pope is not an absolute monarch. "The pope is the head of the episcopal college as 'successor' in the apostolic ministry to Peter, who is head of the college of apostles. As head of the college, he is relative to the other bishops who are members of the same college."[15] The pope may not abrogate the rightful ordinary authority of bishops in their dioceses. Neither does he bestow nor take away their rightful succession to the apostles in the college of world bishops. Bishops remain coresponsible, with the pope, for the unity, legitimate diversity, and freedom of the world church.

Karl Rahner puts this point succinctly:

1. The pope is not an absolute monarch in the political sense;

2. The episcopate exists always by divine right;

3. The papal primacy juridically constitutes the church only when conjoined with this episcopate; and

4. Bishops have episcopal power distinct from the pope and not as delegated by the pope.[16]

Hans Küng concurs. The power of the pope is neither absolute, arbitrary, nor without limits. It is limited by Christ, by the apostles and their successors, and by both natural and divine law. It is limited by the existence of the episcopacy, which the pope can neither abolish nor dissolve. It is further limited by the ordinary exercise of office by the bishops (the pope cannot intervene in the daily exercise of office by the bishops). It is qualified by the ultimate purpose of the Petrine ministry, which is the edification and unity of the whole church. It is limited, finally, by the manner in which the pope must exercise his office, i.e., it must not be arbitrary, inopportune, or exaggerated but must be dictated by the needs and welfare of the church.[17]

Collegiality: Episcopacy and the Presbyterate

In the Vatican II document on the presbyterate, collegiality is extended to apply to the relation of bishops to ordained priests. Priests carry out their ministry in the name of Christ (see *Presbyterorum Ordinis*, no. 2). Their office is bestowed on them through the sacrament of orders whereby they are able to act "in the person of Christ." Through their ordination they receive the gift of the Holy Spirit. Bishops are instructed to listen to their priests, to ask their advice, to consult with them. Priests are called the bishops' friends and brothers (*Presbyterorum Ordinis*, no. 7). Peter Huizing captures the independent collegial role of priests (and all ministers in the church) in the following way:

> The priest's independent role — and that of deacons and laypeople in pastoral ministry — is determined by their direct link with the local communities in which they work. The bishop's role is clearly different from this. The idea that the pastoral care of parishes and groups of people is entrusted to pastoral workers alone because the bishop himself cannot be everywhere at once and do everything himself, though this should be the ideal, is absurd not only as a matter of obvious practical experience but also as a matter of principle: the diocesan church too only exists "in" and "out of" local churches with their own life, and the existence of these demands that they independently have at their disposal the pastoral ministries they need under the coordination of the bishop.[18]

Collegiality: The Laity

Collegiality applies also to the laity in the church. The Second Vatican Council stresses the rightful autonomy of the laity in the secular order. The hierarchy has neither the ability nor mandate to take upon itself the church's entire mission. Its task is to provide a ministry of leadership and inspiration for the individual mission of every one of the faithful with his or her abilities and charisms (*Lumen Gentium*, no. 30). Lay apostolate is an independent participation in the mission of the church in which the laity's mission comes from the Lord himself through baptism and confirmation (*Lumen Gentium*, no. 33). Laypersons have the right and often the duty to give their judgment on the church's internal affairs (*Lumen Gentium*, no. 37).

The revised Code of Canon Law notes that the laity share also in the governing office of Christ. The Christian faithful "have become sharers in Christ's priestly, prophetic and royal office and are called to exercise the mission which God has entrusted to the church to fulfill in the world, in accord with the condition proper to each one" (can. 204, no. 1). Vatican II's decree on the lay apostolate points to the freedom of association of the laity in the church, even for directly apostolic enterprises (*Apostolicam Actuositatem*, no. 19). At root, as Dom O. Rousseau has argued, the idea of the church as a *communion*, above all, signifies *koinonia*, a free circulation of the same spiritual goods between Christian brothers and sisters.[19]

Subsidiarity

The principle of *subsidiarity*, first enunciated by Pius XI in his social encyclical *Quadragesimo Anno*, assumes that good order, in any society, depends on preserving the diversity and vitality of local subunits and genuine communities in that society. As stated by Pius XI, subsidiarity insists that "that which individual men and women can accomplish by their own initiative and their own industry cannot be taken away from them and assigned to the community; in the same way, that which minor or lesser communities can do should not be assigned to a greater or higher community. To do so is a grave injury and disturbance of the social order; for social activity by its nature should supply help to the members of the social body, never destroy or absorb them."[20]

Subsidiarity favors intermediate associations between the individual and the highest organs of governance in a society. It represents a bias about where real societal creativity is to be found. It assumes that problems are best formulated and solved by those who feel them most acutely. Subsidiarity enhances a principle of local freedom and initiative in society. Catholic social theory favors, without absolutizing them, decentralized forms of authority.

But does subsidiarity apply to the church? The answer is a decided yes for several reasons. First, what holds true for all and every healthy human community must hold also for that special community called the church. Moreover, the church's authorities themselves have pronounced in favor of an application of subsidiarity to its own structures. In 1946, when addressing the newly appointed members of the college of cardinals, Pius XII noted that the principle of subsidiarity "is valid for social life in all of its organizations and also for the life of the church."[21] The Vatican commission entrusted with revising the Code of Canon Law was instructed by church authorities to take subsidiarity as a guiding principle for devising law in the church.[22]

Subsidiarity follows necessarily from truly understanding the universal church as a communion of local churches, a communion of communions. This understanding of the church receives a strong endorsement from Vatican Council II: "The church of Christ is truly present in all legitimate local congregations of the faithful which united in their pastors, are themselves called churches of the New Testament. For in their locality these are the new people called by God, in the Holy Spirit and in much fullness (cf. 1 Thess. 1:5)" (*Lumen Gentium,* no. 26).

Social ethicist Johannes Messner sums up the root meaning of subsidiarity: "No social authority, therefore, has a right to interfere with activities for individual and social ends as long as those responsible for those ends are able and willing to cope with them."[23] In church, no less than society, the role of social authority exists as an instrument to guarantee freedom and the finality of Christian freedom itself.

Messner connects subsidiarity with the common good: "The laws of subsidiary function and the law of the common good are in substance identical."[24] They are identical because in Catholic thought the common good envisions not only the good of the whole but the good of individuals who comprise that whole as well. In this sense, authority does not replace nor should it interfere with the rights of persons and their legitimate intermediary groups. Authority's function is subsidiary: to help the individual and intermediary groups to help themselves. The law of subsidiary function prescribes that authority act for the common good in accord with the dignity of the human person by allowing men and women and lesser societies through social action to freely pursue their own perfection, diversity, and creativity. The freedom and dignity of human persons sets constitutional limits on the powers of authority, even within the church.[25]

Justice as Participation

If subsidiarity links up with the great Catholic notion of the common good, it joins, as well, the newer insistence in Catholic social thought on justice as participation.[26] In this view, it is not enough for individuals to be passive recipients of justice. As Vatican II insists in the document on the Church in the Modern World, individuals are also active subjects of history, codeterminants of their social structures and "conscious that they are themselves artisans and the authors of the culture of their community. Throughout the world there is a similar growth in the combined sense of independence and responsibility. Such a development is of paramount importance for the spiritual and moral maturity of the human race" (*Gaudium et Spes,* no. 55)

Collegiality and subsidiarity, then, link up with a larger sense of justice as participation in any community, even the church. Some might argue that the church is exempt from the norms it proclaims in its social teaching for a just society since it was set up for a supernatural end that transcends the dimensions of this world. This type of argument is not valid. The church, which sees itself as "the sign and sacrament of the unity of the human race" (*Lumen Gentium,* no. 1), claims thereby to be that earthly community that is overcoming the divisions that impair human unity in the world. Precisely as sacramental sign, the church must visibly embody what it means to be a just society.[27] Just societies enable and invite the mature participation of all its adult members in the goods of that society, spiritual as well as temporal.

All three of these central themes for the constitution of the church (collegiality, subsidiarity, and justice as participation) reinforce an "elective affinity" between the theological self-understanding of the church and secular movements for democratization of structures in our world. Just as, in earlier periods, the church adopted to its own needs structures taken from aristocracy, state bureaucracies, and monarchy, it is free today to adopt structures of democratization.

A Note on Language Usage

As we have seen, the notion of democracy is itself a controverted concept. Moreover, the church is not simply a democracy. It might be better to speak of democratization in the church than of democracy as such. We point out, thereby, the ways in which even structures that are not formally democracies must be subject to norms of participation, accountability, and due process. Moreover, even when we use the language of democratization, we do well to specify its theological content by referring back to the three root concepts of collegiality, subsidiarity, and participation in a genuine community.

Church reform movements have usually succeeded only when they were allied to wider secular pressures for change. In this case, the work for church reform benefits from a larger cultural movement for democratization. Nevertheless, church reform movements are constrained to make their case for reform also by referring to the language of the church, to theology, linking the secular movement's language to the normative language of the tradition.[28] The church, in this, is no different from other communities of tradition and memory as bearers of a unique language. Indeed, in the long run, one is probably more likely to evoke, if not consensus, minimally genuine engagement with a discussion about how we can best structure the church as a genuine communion and as collegial than in conversations linked only to the more secular notion of applying the norms of democracy to the church. But are there different strategies for democratization in the church?

Reformist Options for Democratization

Since Vatican Council II, diverse organizations have been introduced into the structures of the church to embody collegiality, subsidiarity, and justice as participation. A reformist option for democratization in the church looks to these new openings to fine-tune them, improve their functioning, or open them wider. Reformists sometimes say that we do not need to devise new structures or totally reform the canon law but to use more judiciously and wisely the opportunities in the participative structures that already exist to achieve more democratization. There is some truth to this account but it avoids, too simply, the difficulty of lay voice gaining true access to governance in the church and the strange anomaly that in the church there is no system of checks and balances between the legislative, judicial, and executive functions. The same people and bodies fill all three functions.

Postconciliar writings about collegiality between the pope and bishops mention, especially, the following structures: the synod of bishops; the college of cardinals; the conferences of bishops in each nation or region; the particular councils or synods in nations; the Roman curia; pastoral visits of the pope to a country; *ad limina* visits.[29] Let us look at two of these in terms of reformist options: the synod of bishops and the conferences of bishops.

The Synod of Bishops

The singular lack of success in improving the mechanisms for the collegial functioning of the synod of bishops can be seen starkly in the introductory report to the 1985 Extraordinary Synod by Belgium's Cardinal Godfried Danneels: "Theological questions remain to be resolved: what is the relationship between the universal church and particular churches? How is collegiality to be promoted? ...Moreover, the respondents mention their desire to see a marked improvement in relationships between the particular churches and the Roman Curia. Finally, the reports stress the need for information, mutual consultation and intensified communication." These lines from the 1969 Extraordinary Synod faithfully summed up for Danneels what remained the agenda for the synod of 1985![30]

From the beginning the synod has been awash in ambiguity. Is it — as in a council — a deliberative or merely an advisory body? Because of the overriding emphasis on the primatial principle, synods have been viewed by the various popes as merely instruments for offering advice. Yet, as the Polish canon lawyer Remigiusz Sobanski forcefully argues: "However important advice may be, the meaning of collegiality does not lie here."

Rather, in Sobanski's view, the collegiality of the bishops at the synod derives from their root participation in the worldwide episcopal college. Their participation in the mission of the whole church and in coresponsibility for the whole church "does not allow us to dismiss the bishops' contribution as mere advice." Sobanski appeals to the rich notion of ecclesial *testimony:* "Here we have the legal claim which is contained in the witness 'among colleagues.' The claim is based on the obligation of the teacher of faith to the truth and to the hearers of the word. This obligation is borne by all bishops and, therefore, the claim cannot be separated from the obligation of a sharing in the formation of a common testimony which is ready to listen and to learn, a testimony which would correspond to the truth and to the needs of the time (both in formulation and in practical effects). That is what the exercise of collegiality is all about."[31]

It became clear at the 1985 synod of bishops that what mainly distinguished the bulk of the participating bishops and the writers of the final report of the synod was "the wish to relativize the importance of the structures and the distribution of powers" in determining collegiality between pope and bishops.[32] The writers of the final report of the synod, bypassing many voices of the synod bishops, inordinately stressed the notion of *affectus collegialis* (affective collegiality) but shied away from any attention to structures that might more appropriately embody and guarantee a genuine collegiality.

Structural Reforms of the Synod of Bishops

Reformist voices, then, have suggested various structural changes to increase the effectiveness of the synod of bishops as an instrument for accountability and democratization in the church:

1. There have been calls to open the synod up more — as at the council — to the presence of *periti*, theologians chosen by the member bishops for advice and consultation.

2. There have also been proposals to invite observer representatives from other churches, again following the example of the council, to widen the consultation among Christian voices. Both of these two reforms can be rooted in the initial inspiration for institutionalizing the synod of bishops at the Second Vatican Council. There the new structure was seen as a periodic prolongation of the council.

3. A third reform envisions the restructuring of the present Council for the Secretariat of the Synod. This council — made up of diocesan ordinaries — at present only serves between the gatherings of the synod. It has some say on the choice of themes and on the preparation of documents that serve as consultation papers or questionnaires (*lineamenta*) sent out to the world bishops. It also has input into the final working paper for the synod (the *instrumentum laboris*), which is based, in principle, on the answers from the conferences of bishops to the *lineamenta*. Yet, at present, as soon as the plenary session of the synod begins, the Council for the Secretariat of the Synod dissolves and disappears.

One reform argues that the council should continue throughout the life of a synod session, present and explain its work, and give an account of it at the first plenary session as well as help oversee the winnowing of propositions into the final report from the deliberations of the synod. These propositions are winnowed from the various reports from the *circuli minores* (discussion groups by language areas) and then are presented for a synod vote. Importantly, the Council for the Synod (made up of episcopal ordinaries) would help draft the final report of the synod.

Since the groundbreaking 1971 synod report *Justice in the World*, the synod has not controlled its final reports, with the result that the curial redactors of the synod reports frequently neutralize what has been said and proposed by the groups into an innocuous and harmless document that does not faithfully report the discussions. This reform would make the Council for the Synod truly accountable both to the synod's bishops for overseeing the reports and votes at the synod. It would allow greater episcopal control over the agenda and procedures of the synods.

4. A fourth reform of procedures for furthering democratization of the synod of bishops entails the freedom for bishops' conferences to publish their responses to the *lineamenta* in their respective national journals such as *The Tablet* in England and *Origins* in the United States. This would enhance horizontal collegiality among bishops of different countries, elicit informed response from the clergy and laity of each nation to their bishops' input at the synod, and open up through the organs of public opinion in the church serious discussion and consultation about synodal topics that have impact on the life of the entire church.

These suggested reforms might go some way toward mitigating the very pessimistic judgment of Ludwig Kaufmann of *Orienterung* on the democratic nature of the present synodal process:

> The name synod is misleading if it is supposed to mean that both delegate bishops and the pope and his staff are involved, in a partnership of equal rights, in finding the way to truth and forming opinion. But the body cannot perform a real advisory function, either, because the procedure is hardly aimed at leading to a decision between alternatives. The malaise which repeatedly develops, time and again, that "the mountain brings forth a mouse" also has a paralyzing and disillusioning effect on other bodies within the church.

Kaufmann ends with a very pessimistic diagnosis of the will toward democratization at the core of Rome: "Unfortunately, I can see no sign of the pope and the curial apparatus wanting to change anything in it."[33]

Episcopal Conferences

At the synod of bishops in 1985 the question of the meaning and theological status of episcopal conferences came under close scrutiny. That synod endorsed what an earlier theologian, Joseph Ratzinger, rightly saw as the deepest theological meaning of conferences of bishops. The younger Ratzinger claimed that they are "one of the possible variants of collegiality which experience partial realizations that, in turn, point to the whole."[34]

In the revised Code of Canon Law, episcopal conferences appear as a legal institution, a legal subject — a "middle authority" or a "hierarchical intermediate authority" — which represent an authentic hierarchical and collegial authority. They enjoy a genuine, if limited, jurisdiction in the church (in questions of the disposal of ecclesial property and above all in liturgical renewal).

Debates about the precise theological status of episcopal conferences have continued since the 1985 synod. Minimally, as John Paul II has described them, conferences are an instrument "in accord with the needs of our time, effective in ensuring the necessary unity of action by the bishops."[35] However, in a 1987 draft document from the Congregation of Bishops, episcopal conferences were viewed as "a non-necessary structure," needing regulation by law, which lack the dogmatic foundation enjoyed by structures that are divinely appointed.[36]

Karl Rahner, for his part, argued that "the idea of the conference of bishops arises out of the nature of the church itself." Rahner sees it as an absolutely necessary form of an element of the church's being. In his view, the conference of bishops is "a mediation in human law of that for which the foundation is laid by divine law."[37]

The legal status and competency of episcopal conferences is important for applying subsidiarity to the church. Rahner, indeed, grounded them in the structural principle of subsidiarity. The competence of episcopal conferences in his view, vis-à-vis the Roman curia and the pope, was a "natural competence" "for the group of responsibilities which, on the one hand, appertain to the individual bishop who is part of the national conference of bishops, by reason of his office and ordinary power of jurisdiction, but which, on the other hand, cannot in practice be assumed by him except by agreement and in collaboration with the rest of the bishops of the same nation or region."[38]

What holds good for national episcopal conferences would hold as well for regional groupings of bishops such as the Federation of Asian Bishops' Conferences, African regional conferences of bishops for Francophone or Anglophone or geographic areas, e.g., the Association of Member Episcopal Conferences of East Africa, the Inter-Regional Meeting of the Bishops of South Africa, the Association of the Episcopal Conferences of Anglophone West Africa, and the Regional Episcopal Conference of Francophone West Africa. Important continental-wide bodies of bishops exist for Africa (SCEAM), Latin America (CELAM), and Europe (CCEE). In the near future regional synods of bishops will be held for Africa and Europe.

Reformists argue that strengthening the organizational unity, communication, competence, and procedures for these national, regional, and continental bodies will further democratization in the church by furthering collegiality, subsidiarity, and participation in the world church. Moreover, within these bodies themselves, as the American experience of wide consultation process at the United States Catholic Conference has shown, procedures for democratization can be institutionalized. Attention to episcopal conferences at the national and regional level might heed Alexis de Tocqueville's insistence that the most effective institutional guarantee for democratic freedom consists in local freedoms embodied in intermediate bodies, the sort of intermediate hierarchical authority the canon law speaks of when it refers to the episcopal conferences.[39]

Collegial Reforms at National and Diocesan Levels

The Second Vatican Council also envisioned structural embodiments to further collegial coresponsibility between local bishops and their priests and between both groups and people. It mandates a presbyterial senate in each diocese. Indeed, the senate can serve as the canonical board of consulters in each diocese (see *Presbyterorum Ordinis*, no. 7; canons 495–501). The decrees on the pastoral office of the bishops in the church (*Christus Dominus*, no. 27) and on the lay apostolate (*Apostolicam Actuositatem*, nos. 24–26) express the council's wish for pastoral councils of priests, religious, and above all laity to be set up in dioceses and at other levels in the local churches (see canons 511–14).

Most Catholics encounter the church through and in their parish. Canon law has mandated serious changes in the way we think more democratically about the parish. The parish itself is dealt with as a community of persons before any mention is made of the pastor. The revised law envisions parish pastoral councils (but leaves their implementation to the discretion of local bishops [canon 536]). Where they are absent, it is quite clear who has power and is responsible to mandate them.

What is not optional is a finance council for each parish in which members of the parish assist in the financial administration of the parish (can. 536). Generally speaking, the law does not grant this finance council true decision making or executive jurisdiction, but "the bishop could establish instances where the council's deliberative vote would be necessary, e.g., approval of the annual budget, exceeding limits for extraordinary expenditures, establishing salaries for lay employees not subject to diocesan norms." [40] Other elements in the revised Code of Canon Law that further the democratization process at the parish level are the acknowledgement of parish team ministry (can. 517), the provision for roles of deacon, laypersons, or community sharing in true pastoral care within the parish (can. 517, no. 2), and in provisions for a fixed term for the pastor and a fixed age of mandatory retirement. In most American dioceses diocesan personnel boards have removed some of the earlier arbitrariness in appointment of pastors and try to tailor appointment to competency and the desires of both parish groups and candidates for pastor. The shrinking number of competent priests, however, sometimes make this "fit" less than ideal.[41]

Episcopal and Pastoral Appointments

Quite clearly, there is widespread dissatisfaction in many parts of the church about the method of appointment of bishops and, perhaps less so, pastors. There is also some debate about the legitimacy of electing bishops (and, if so, by what appropriate body). Clear antecedents exist for the election of bishops by people or by the lower clergy. Pope Celestine I stated baldly: "Let a bishop not be imposed upon the people whom they do not want."[42] Pope Leo I put it this way: "He who has to preside over all must be elected by all. Let a person not be ordained against the wish of the Christians and whom they have not explicitly asked for."[43] In his great twelfth-century compilation of canon law, Gratian notes that "the election of the bishops belongs to the bishops and the consensus to the people."[44] The first three bishops in the United States were elected by the lower clergy.

There is room for serious discussion and debate about whether we want to reintroduce a direct election of bishops and pastors by the people. Interestingly, a national sample of American Catholics that showed, generally, overwhelming majorities of Catholics favoring further procedures for democratization in the church shied away from asking for a direct election of their pastors. Perhaps they feared the introduction of factions into the local church or learned from ecclesial polities that embody the election of pastors that this can, sometimes, minimize or reduce the authority of the pastor.[45] Few would desire electoral factions around the appointment of bishops or pastors. By and large, in the American church the new form of a diocesan personnel board for the appointment of pastors has reduced greatly strains between pastor and people.

Nevertheless, deep strains also exist about the current way in which bishops are appointed, subject to the unfettered nomination of the pope. As one author notes, "Roman centralization excludes the local churches and the faithful, even at the phase of consultation, and is carried forward in open dissension or without taking any account of the proposals formulated by the organs of the local churches by choosing candidates either directly or above all in contradiction to all the indications of the nuncios."[46] The Cologne Manifesto in Germany, the Manifesto of Italian Theologians and People, and deep conflicts about the appointment of bishops in Switzerland, the Netherlands, and Austria in the last few years have shown that the present process of choosing bishops violates accountability, participation, and anything akin to the ethos of democratization.

Reform of the means of choosing bishops — a reform that respects true collegiality, subsidiarity, and participation — would need, minimally, to poll the people of a diocese in terms of their profile for an ideal bishop (even if they are not the direct electorate) and consult them, the presbyterate, and neighboring bishops. One suggestion might return to a variation of an earlier form of nomination of bishops by the cathedral chapter, but with some variations. The cathedral chapter (or its equivalent, e.g., the senate of priests) might nominate two people for the list of nominees. This local nominating committee could be bound by canon law to consult the faithful before their deliberation.[47]

The bishops of the metropolitan area might nominate two more names (with the possibility of endorsing in these two votes the same nominees as the cathedral chapter or senate of priests). A committee of an entire national body of bishops might add one other name. The list of five nominees would be sent to the pope, who would then choose (with the advice of the *nuncio*) one from this list. The pope might have the privilege of returning the list for a second or, if necessary, third round of nominations from these local bodies. Obviously, canon lawyers and others will be more competent than I to address the issue of a precise form to improve the procedures to further collegiality, subsidiarity, and participation in the selection of bishops. What is obvious is that the present system violates all three central church values and flows against the stream of any ethos of democratization. But all such reformist speculations fly in the face of clear evidence that important elements in the Roman curia resist *any* serious reforms toward greater democratization in the church. Hence, we need to look at a more radical option for democratization.

Radical Options for Democratization: Coalitions, Lobbying Power, and Public Opinion in the Church

In my view, the most radical strategies toward democratization in the church will rest on that freedom proclaimed by the Vatican Decree on the Lay Apostolate concerning freedom of association in the church (*Apostolicam Actuositatem*, no. 19) and the freedom for public opinion in the church professed in canon 212, no. 3, of the revised code, which reads: "The faithful have the right and even at times a duty to manifest to the sacred pastors their opinion on matters which pertain to the good of the church and they have a right to make their opinion known to the other Christian faithful, with due regard for the integrity of the faith and morals and reverence toward their pastors."

We have heard repeated claims that true freedom of expression often gets squelched or subtly subverted in the participative structures that already exist *de facto* in the church (e.g., synods of bishops, episcopal conferences, presbyterial senates, diocesan and parish councils). A rich associational life in the community of the church will be indispensable to breathe the spirit of democratization into these already existing forms of participation.

The church is not unique in facing the dilemma of participative structures that do not work in the absence of a real will toward genuine democratization. Even in democratic societies, the rule by experts, bureaucracy, and the closure of elective office to a wider variety of representatives (because of cost in elections or the role of the party apparatus in screening candidates) makes imperative a greater democratization of public opinion formation by multiplying the communication channels in society (newspapers, media, organizations in the public interest).

Democracy also entails the forging of effective coalitions. Some have even argued that lobbying, coalition-building, and effective access to public opinion are more important for democracy in modern societies than the mere exercise of the vote.[48] Indeed, some feel that modern Western democracies have much to learn from the Eastern European opposition during the period of communist rule.[49]

This opposition appealed to the notion of *civil society* (the zone of freedom between the citizen and the state, the place of intermediate associations in the sense of Alexis de Tocqueville) as the privileged locus (rather than the state, as such) where democratization has to begin. Civil society, moreover, remains the ultimate locus for the guarantee of the continuation of democracy, even when formal participative structures have been put into place.

What would be the main role of associational life and public opinion formation in the church vis-à-vis the process of democratization? I see it as threefold: (1) promoting public opinion in the church and discussing issues that a systematic communication distortion in the church will not allow to be freely discussed; (2) effective "lobbying" (making one's will present to office holders in the church) for needed actions, pastoral priorities, or structural reforms; and (3) building coalitions around important issues that might further democratization in the church. As in modern democracies, social movements outside the direct sphere of governance are the radical first source of renewal and reform of laws and structures. Legislatures respond to these movements, in time, and translate their desires into law and policy.

Let me give two examples of what I have in mind through my appeal to public opinion formation, "lobbying," and coalition-building around an agenda of greater democratization. I serve as a member of the national board of directors of one association in the church: the Association for Rights in the Catholic Church (ARCC). As a body, ARCC promulgates a charter of rights for Catholics in the church. This set of rights is based on Scripture, natural human dignity, and canon law. The charter rights are not arbitrary nor are they the mere adoption of a purely secular agenda, but rather they are theologically grounded.[50]

ARCC sponsors yearly conferences in different areas of the country to bring together activists and scholars to further discussion about participative government in the church: how to improve the forms that already exist; what new forms need to be championed. It dreams of a possible large "constitutional convention" in the American church to brainstorm about structural renewal. Through its national board, ARCC takes action, periodically in the course of the year, to commend or protest agencies or individuals in the church (bishops, the episcopal conference, local groupings) that further or impede respect for the fundamental rights of Catholics in the church.

Thus, for example, if a speaker is banned from a diocese on arbitrary grounds, ARCC contacts the bishop, university, or other organization involved to protest this violation of freedom of expression in the church. If the American bishops take a stand in support of more collegial forms of governance (e.g., the decision to hold a series of open hearings among Catholics with the American bishops attending the synod of bishops), ARCC writes to show its appreciation and approbation. Like Amnesty International, ARCC keeps itself to a short list of essential rights and only takes action based on this mandate.

ARCC publishes a newsletter that disseminates information on issues where participative principles are violated (e.g., the decision to consolidate parishes in the archdiocese of Detroit without any real consultation process) and reprints articles that further democratization in the church. ARCC maintains links with cognate organizations in the European church.

Through its concrete networking and a representative board membership, ARCC tries to build new coalitions or foster relations with other groups working for democratization in the church, e.g., the Canon Law Society of America, the Call to Action, the Leadership Conference of Religious Women. To be sure, ARCC is only one finite group in the American church, representing about a thousand members.

But each such group needs to ask, on any given issue concerning the collegial nature of decisions in a diocese or in the national church: (1) Where does decision making truly lie? In a pastoral planning commission? In a committee of the United States Catholic Conference? In a parish council? In a diocesan or national committee serving the bishops? In a committee of bishops? When power is identified, it can be spoken to and held accountable. (2) What action can we take to call these decision makers to accountability? Minimally, as in any public opinion formation, we can do something as pedestrian as writing a letter. More strongly, we can write an article or take the issue to Catholic news media asking them to address a noncollegial procedure or process. Even more strongly, we may choose to try to build or join a larger coalition to improve or change present procedures of accountability in a diocese or national church.

ARCC's board consists of representatives of the laity (the board president is almost always a layperson), the clergy, and religious of both sexes. We try to involve bishops in our programs and actions. It is our conviction that only when all elements in the church (bishops, clergy, laity, religious) are united in concerted actions for more participative structures in the church will we succeed in furthering democratization. In this sense, we honor the unique nature of the church as a *hierarchical communion* by insisting on seeing the church as a community of communication of spiritual goods, a circulation of saving truths, actions, and behavior among brothers and sisters.

A second example may clarify how the freedom of associational life and public opinion formation in the church enunciated in canon law can be drawn upon to further democratization in the church. Many Catholics feel that the American bishops' letter on women, despite many good intentions and an attempt at wide consultation, is so deeply flawed that it must be abandoned. Each new draft became more difficult to accept as reflective of the church's understanding of basic equality in Christ. A free association of Catholics in the American church, Priests for Equality, has suggested gathering people to lobby the bishops to table the document. They also suggest that the bishops inaugurate some other action, besides a document, to further the reflection in the church on the role of women.

One recognizes the many good efforts in trying to bring the document together and the sincere will of many bishops to be more participative and open in the American church. One applauds the collegial effort to involve many women and men in the discussion of the various drafts. But, ultimately, the process failed.

Subsidiarity in this issue will not win out, nor will a genuine collegiality because of pressures on the bishops from Rome. Perhaps, even, a case can be made for Rome's fear that a local document will not remain merely local. In any event, the original purposes of the letter have been now subverted.

Success in an attempt to use public opinion and free association in the church to exert leverage on the bishops would depend on coalition building between Priests for Equality and other groups in the church: organs of opinion formation such as *America, Commonweal*, the *National Catholic Reporter;* other associations in the church such as ARCC, the Leadership Conference of Religious Women, priests' senates, diocesan and parish councils. Ultimately, it will involve a serious dialogue with our bishops.

In the final analysis, as de Tocqueville so strongly argued, free association and free speech are the major bulwarks of the spirit of democracy. This is no less true in church than in society. They remain the most radical weapon to further democratization in the church and they do not depend on the permission of office holders in the church for their exercise.

I want to end with some words of the Dutch canon lawyer Peter Huizing, which capture well my sentiments about democratization in the church:

> The Catholic church's legal structure can be neither monarchic nor democratic. Thanks to its nature as a community or fellowship of local churches, its legal structure can only be that of a community in which the mission and equal dignity of everyone is respected and protected by everyone. Every distortion of this balance necessarily upsets the mission of the church itself. The church does indeed remain a fellowship of earthly men and women and disturbances will thus always occur, but it remains necessary to anticipate them as much as possible and to repair the damage. It is finally the legal structure of a fellowship which would abandon its mission if it did not continue to strive for the fulfillment of the prayer: that they may all be one. (John 17:11)[51]

Notes

1. For the introduction of secular political structures into the church, see John Lynch, "Power in the Church: An Historico-Critical Survey," in James Provost and Knut Walf, eds., *Power in the Church*, Concilium 197 (Edinburgh: T. & T. Clark, 1988), 13–22.

2. For an extensive discussion of the new Code of Canon Law, see James Provost and Knut Walf, eds., *Canon Law–Church Reality*, Concilium 183 (Edinburgh: T. & T. Clark, 1986), 121.

3. *Acta Apostolicae Sedis*, August 6, 1964.

4. Donato Valentini, "An Overview of Theologians' Positions on Collegiality," in James Provost and Knut Walf, eds., *Collegiality Put to the Test*, Concilium 1990/4 (London: SCM Press, 1990), 37.

5. For an argument that orders and office in the church do not derive "from below" by community appointment, see Kenan Osborne, O.F.M., *Priesthood: A History of the Ordained Ministry in the Roman Catholic Church* (New York: Paulist Press, 1988), 84.

6. Karl Lehmann, "On the Dogmatic Justification for a Process of Democratization in the Church," in Alois Muller, ed., *Democratization of the Church*, Concilium 63 (New York: Herder and Herder, 1971), 80.

7. Ibid., 82.

8. Ibid., 84.

9. See G. Satori, "Democracy," *International Encyclopedia of the Social Sciences* 4 (1968).

10. Lehmann, "On the Dogmatic Justification for a Process of Democratization in the Church," 74.

11. Heinrich Schneider, "Democracy: The Idea and the Reality" in Alois Muller, ed., *Democratization of the Church*.

12. William D'Antonio et al., *American Catholic Laity in a Changing Church* (Kansas City, Mo.: Sheed and Ward, 1989), 109–11.

13. Patrick Granfield, *The Limits of the Papacy: Authority and Autonomy in the Church* (New York: Crossroad, 1987).

14. Patrick Granfield, "Legitimation and Bureaucratization of Ecclesial Power," in Provost and Walf, eds., *Power in the Church*, 92.

15. Richard McBrien, "Collegiality: State of the Question," in James Coriden, ed., *The Once and Future Church: A Communion of Freedom* (Staten Island, N.Y.: Alba House, 1971), 16.

16. Karl Rahner, *The Episcopate and the Primacy* (New York: Herder and Herder, 1962), 64.

17. Hans Küng, *The Church* (New York: Herder and Herder, 1967), 444–80.

18. Peter Huizing, "The Central Legal System and Autonomous Churches," in Provost and Walf, eds., *Canon Law–Church Reality*, 29.

19. Don Olivier Rousseau, "Le deuxième synode des evêques: collegialité et communion," *Irenikon* 42 (1969): 467–71.

20. *Quadragesimo Anno*, no. 23.

21. *Acta Apostolicae Sedis* 38 (February 20, 1946): 145.

22. See Provost and Walf, eds., *Canon Law–Church Reality*, 67.

23. Johannes Messner, *Social Ethics* (St. Louis: Benzinger Brothers, 1949), 196.

24. Ibid., 196.

25. On the issue of constitutional limits on the power of authority in the church see William Bassett, "Subsidiarity, Order and Freedom in the Church," in James Coriden, ed., *The Once and Future Church*, 205–74.

26. For justice as participation see David Hollenbach, *Justice, Peace and Human Rights* (New York: Crossroad, 1988), 87–99.

27. For this argument see Gregory Baum, "Structures of Sin," in Gregory Baum and Robert Ellsberg, eds., *The Logic of Solidarity* (Maryknoll, N.Y.: Orbis Press, 1989), 123–24.

28. See the argument of political scientist Scott Mainwaring about the need to use explicitly religious language to be effective in religious reform movements in Scott Mainwaring, "Grassroots Catholic Groups and Catholicism in Brazil: 1964–1985," Kellogg Center for International Studies, University of Notre Dame, *Working Paper no. 98*, 16–17.

29. For this list see Remigiusz Sobanski, "Implications for Church Law of the Use of the Term Collegiality in the Theological Context of Official Church Statements," in Provost and Walf, eds., *Collegiality Put to the Test*, 46.

30. Cited in Jan Grootaers, "The Collegiality of the Synod of Bishops: An Unresolved Problem," in Provost and Walf, eds., *Collegiality Put to the Test*, 20.

31. Sobanski, "Implications for Church Law," 50–51.

32. Grootaers, "The Collegiality of the Synod of Bishops," 25.

33. Ludwig Kaufmann, "Synods of Bishops: Neither *Concilium* nor *Synodus*," in Provost and Walf, eds., *Collegiality Put to the Test*, 76.

34. Josef Ratzinger, *Das Neue Volk Gottes* (Düsseldorf, 1969), 23.

35. Cited in Peter Leisching, "Conferences of Bishops," in Provost and Walf, eds., *Collegiality Put to the Test*, 81.

36. Ibid., 82.

37. Cited in Leisching, "Conferences of Bishops," 86.

38. Ibid., 87.

39. For Alexis de Tocqueville's classic argument on the essential role of free intermediate associations for democracy, see *Democracy in America*, vol. 2, book 2, chap. 4.

40. John Huels, "Parish Life and the New Code," in Provost and Walf, eds., *Canon Law–Church Reality*, 66.

41. A diocesan personnel manager of my local diocese told a parish that he could find for them only a "marginally competent" pastor to fit their needs for a new pastor, given the shrinking pool of priests in the diocese!

42. *EP.* 4, 5 in J. B. Migne, *Patrologia Latina*, 50, 434.

43. *Ad. Anast.*, in J. B. Migne, *Patrologia Latina*, 54, 634.

44. Cited in Pasquale Collela, "Considerations on the Nomination of Bishops in Current Canon Law," in Provost and Walf, eds., *Collegiality Put to the Test*, 101.

45. William D'Antonio, et al., *American Catholic Laity in a Changing Church*, 118.

46. Pasquale Collela, "Considerations on the Nomination of Bishops in Current Canon Law," 101.

47. For the story of an attempt to implement a variant of this nomination structure in the Dutch church see my *The Evolution of Dutch Catholicism* (Berkeley: University of California Press, 1978), 184ff.

48. See Robert Bellah, et al., *The Good Society* (New York: Alfred Knopf, 1991), 111–44.

49. Jeffrey Goldfarb, *The Cynical Society: The Culture of Politics and the Politics of Culture in American Life* (Chicago: University of Chicago Press, 1991), makes the case for our learning from the Eastern European democratic opposition.

50. See Leonard Swindler, ed., *Charter of Rights for Catholics in the Church* (Kansas City, Mo.: Sheed and Ward, 1989).

51. Peter Huizing, "The Central Legal System and Autonomous Churches," 30–31.

EUGENE C. BIANCHI and
ROSEMARY RADFORD RUETHER

– Conclusion –
Toward a Democratic Catholic Church

More than a quarter of a century has passed since the end of Vatican Council II. An overriding lesson of this period is that the promise of continuing reform in the Catholic world has been stymied because the structure of the church still concentrates decision-making power in a paternalistic, monarchical hierarchy, culminating in a divine-right-of-kings papacy. The main obstacle to continuing reform is not lack of piety or of charismatic leaders or of good will among Catholics. It is rather a problem of structure or church polity that cuts off the avenues of participation, deliberation, and decision making for all but a few men in the monarchical hierarchy. This structural system must be changed. The centuries-old call for real reform *in capite et membris*, in head and members, has been too long delayed. It must take place now for the sake of the church's gospel ministry as the Catholic community enters its third millennium. From the standpoints of theology, history, canon law, social teaching, and current movements in the church, a firm basis is already in place for building a structurally participational *ecclesia* at every level.

Vatican II enunciated themes from the New Testament and from later theology that undergird the fashioning of a multifaceted democratic church. Collegiality, people of God, pilgrim people, and many other terms from the council denote an egalitarian and communal church. The council wanted to draw the laity into joint responsibility with clergy in shaping church ministry, although the council was timid in providing instruments for such participation. The leading thinkers of Vatican II knew that there was no one determined polity structure in the churches of the New Testament. Rather it was pastoral service of the gospel, in keeping with the faith of the Apostles, that called for diverse joint ministries of leaders and communities, and eventually of clergy and laity.

Biblical theology provides many supports for building democratic church structures. In earliest Christianity, decentralized and pluralistic community networks were held together by a common faith and similar practices. In this period, a powerful egalitarian dynamic was at work, a "discipleship of equals," based on a common baptism. Underlying these participational dimensions was a profound theology of the Holy Spirit that militates against the sacralizing and fixing of any form of governance.

As Elizabeth Schüssler Fiorenza makes clear in her chapter, "A Discipleship of Equals," the democratic construction of the Christian church was not so much a complete or perfect reality in the earliest church as it was a partial reality, present here and there and expressed as a vision that provides an enduring inspiration for continuing efforts to realize this vision throughout the church's history. It is not just an unrealized ideal but an active process that is an integral part of the church's processes of expressing the reality of redemptive relations between persons in community.

The history of the Catholic institution from the Constantinian era to the present manifests, for the most part, a growing centralization of control in monarchical forms. Such developments were understandable and even useful in those early historical contexts. The church is a human institution that adapted itself to given forms of imperial and monarchical government in various periods of history. It is not a matter of condemning these vertical structures of the past. Rather, what counts is understanding their historical relativity. The order of clerical kings and princes is not divinely ordained once and for all. What was created in history can be changed in history. Catholics today are most familiar with a church directed materially and spiritually by a complete papal monarch and his princely vassals, the bishops. Without deeper biblical and historical reflection, it is easy to conclude that since this is the way it is, this is the way it must always be.

But the egalitarian and communal structures of the New Testament church were never completely suppressed or driven underground. They surface again and again in the spiritualities of Pachomius and Francis, in the rule of Dominic, in the theology of Aquinas. Thomas stressed the community of believers as the bedrock of the church, and he relativized institutional forms by subordinating them to the evangelical mission of the church. New Testament collegiality rose again in the conciliarists whose democratizing work was betrayed by the resurgence of centralized papal monarchy.

The Protestant Reformation struggled in various ways to recapture something of the early Christian *koinonia*. In light of the mystery and sovereignty of God, no institution was to be absolutized. Across the Protestant spectrum, polity was meant to serve evangelical function and to adapt itself to the needs of fellowship for mission. The clergy-laity distinction was one of function, not status. The reassertion of the priesthood of all believers led to lay participation at all levels. The Protestant experience also allows us to see the gradual process of democratization as in Methodism. These sister churches, moreover, point out the pitfalls and shortcomings attendant on democratic polities.

The Catholic experience in the United States was deeply influenced by republican democracy. The controversy over lay trustees in parishes stressed the role of the laity in decision making, not just in consultation. In the new American climate of populism, Catholic leaders came to respect the principles of republicanism: trust in the people, open elections, religious freedom, and written constitutions that clarify democratic rights and duties. Vatican strictures on Americanism and Modernism suppressed the nascent appreciation for democratic structures, and the Irish-led hierarchy became more subservient to papal monarchy. Yet John Courtney Murray was able to articulate the American Catholic respect for religious freedom in ways that turned it into official church teaching at Vatican II. Murray also pointed to the still unfinished task of orchestrating such freedom in the life of the church itself.

Another area of great inconsistency between Catholic teaching and its intrachurch application is that of papal social encyclicals. For a century from Leo XIII to John Paul II, the church has preached to the nations the democratizing doctrines of subsidiarity and structural change in society. But the church has failed to apply these teachings to its own structures. Subsidiarity implies participation of the people in decision making from the grassroot levels. The principle of subsidiarity stressed popular participation in economic, political, and social life. It was a reapplication of the ancient dictum, cited especially in the first millennium of church history: that which affects the whole people should be decided by the people. Papal social encyclicals showed increasing support for human rights and for subordinating institutional concerns to the demands of truth and justice. To avoid hypocrisy, the hierarchy needs to take to heart the old advice: physician, heal yourself. This healing would consist in substituting the social encyclical themes of freedom, participation, and equality for secrecy, manipulation, and dominance. The arena for such renewal is the democratizing of church structures.

The Dutch church, more than any other national church, offers an example in the last quarter century of steps toward internal democratization and their repression by the Vatican. The movement for lay participation in decision making among the Dutch goes back to the 1950s. Progressives in the Netherlands became champions of collegiality and respect for pluralism at Vatican II. After the council, the Dutch church instituted "an ordered process of democratization" through an extensive development of pastoral councils in which clergy and laity had a voice. A dialogical approach toward authority meant widespread involvement in decision making with a sense of reviewing and changing decisions when needed. As early as 1970 the Dutch were ready for a married priesthood and women ministers. The Vatican, mainly by appointing very conservative bishops in Holland without popular consultation, stopped this democratization of church structures. The Dutch experience of stymied hopes for a democratic church underscores the problems of bringing about structural change in Catholicism.

In the present monarchical church system, ultimate and absolute power resides in the papacy. Countervailing checks and balances have not been established. The agony of the Dutch church invites reformers to create effective strategies and tactics to bring about successful democratization of Catholic structures.

Religious orders of women have been in the forefront of spiritual and structural renewal since Vatican II. The general guiding principle of change within the lives of these groups has been that mission determines form. Joined to this insight about the relativity of structure is the democratic conviction of the need for community participation in decision making. In the spiritual search to discover God's dynamic will, nuns moved away from the vertical model of equating the superior's command with divine desire. The voice of God was sought in community and in the agenda presented by the poor and deprived of the world. For these religious women, the time of exaggerated dependency and infantilization by a patriarchal hierarchy was over. In addition to the ethos of Vatican II, the sisterhoods have been deeply influenced by the modern women's movement. The feminist themes of dialogical communication and the importance of relationship blended well with Vatican II's teaching of collegiality. The renewal experiences within these religious orders offer helpful models and insights for democratization of structures in the wider church.

The history of canon law, at first blush an unlikely source for democratic thinking in the church, surprises us with a rich vein of democratizing legislation. Medieval canonists saw the church as a network of communities. They struggled with concrete problems of authority on local, regional and international levels. In this process, canonists elaborated principles of consultation and consent, representation and participation. The democratic potential of these themes awaits fruition today. Post–Vatican II canonists are called to take up again, in light of the underlying theology of church as communion of the faithful, the democratizing enterprise of their medieval forbears.

Perhaps the most important awareness of contemporary ecclesiology concerns the laity. We have come to see how excluded lay persons have been from their rightful place in church decision making and mission. The church has been so thoroughly clericalized that most lay persons fail to understand their own key role in the "apostolic succession." They need to take back their key functions in the leadership of the church at every level. We are still very far from concretely realizing the vocation of Catholic men and women, based on their fundamental baptismal reality of *laos,* that community of faithful that constitutes church.

Since Vatican II a number of popular movements for spirituality and social justice give promise for an eventual democratizing of structures in the institutional church. The original 1975 Call to Action assembly in Detroit was remarkable both in its organization and its proposals. Before this national meeting, issues were discussed at local levels. Delegates were sent to Detroit in representational ways. The process involved lay and clerical participation. Again, however, the hierarchy balked at proposals for change that were not favorable in Rome. The Call to Action movement continues as a potentially important vehicle for renewal. Still other grassroots organizations, such as Women-Church, Chicago Catholic Women, and Mary's Pence, demonstrate the self-starting vitality of groups that claim their Catholic heritage but are free from hierarchical control. The goals of such movements focus principally on social justice, while their internal operating procedures emphasize lay participation. Similar groups like Corpus, Association for the Rights of Catholics in the Church, Federation of Christian Ministries, and Women's Ordination Conference witness new possibilities for ministry and church life to the clerical institution without waiting for the latter's approval or transformation. These groups, with their international counterparts, are continuing signs of hope among Catholic progressives for democratic renewal in the church.

Through liberation theology and the base ecclesial community movement, the churches of Latin America have fashioned important theory and practice for democratizing the church. Although liberation theology is not intrachurch in its orientation, its themes of consciousness-raising, option for the poor, grassroots participation, and structural change toward justice are eminently applicable to democratic reform of church institutions. In Brazil and elsewhere, the older territorial parish model with its clerical sacramentalism has been challenged and complemented by biblically oriented base communities with covenanted, face-to-face lay involvement in small groupings. In some ways, the unresolved relationships between base communities and the official church mirror those of similar progressive movements in the wider church. Involved are issues of identity, belonging, class, decision making, and institutional control. Although the base community movement is still numerically modest, its renewal potential is significant. In a dramatic way, it brings into the church the powerful leaven of biblically motivated grassroots lay participation. In this sense, it is an essentially democratic, populist movement. It will be interesting to observe how base communities relate toward the broader movement in Latin American society toward gradual democratic change instead of revolutionary overthrow.

Twentieth-century Catholic teaching on collegiality, subsidiarity, and justice as participation provides ample theory for democratization of church structures. But the Vatican bureaucracy has successfully prevented such teachings from taking concrete and effective form in such structures as the synod of bishops, episcopal conferences, or a democratized method of electing bishops. Greater hope for democratic reform may lie in forging effective coalitions beyond hierarchical control. These movements would be strongly influenced by lay participation. They could employ the strategies of molding free public opinion in the church, lobby for change, and focus energy on specific issues toward democratization.

In light of these themes and movements toward a democratic Catholic Church, what is to be done? In answer to that question, we can explore five principles for a democratic restructuring of the church. It is important in these early stages of imagining and shaping a democratic church not to impose a single template of democracy on the whole church, as the monastic model was imposed on the whole clergy in the twelfth century. Such a method would be presumptuous and foredoomed. For no one has "the" democratic answer for Catholicism. Moreover, such a method would belie a number of principles discussed below, such as respect for pluralism, subsidiarity, and decentralization. We should examine these democratic principles as they apply in various ways to the needs of national and regional churches. We will discuss the five principles in general, followed by some concrete suggestions for reform.

An essential preamble to these principles is that they must be based on solid theological reflection. It is not a matter of merely imitating the structures of post-Enlightenment democracies in the secular world. Such secular patterns can profitably inform Catholic rethinking. For Vatican II reminds us that we are a learning as well as a teaching church. But the principles for restructuring the church must flow primarily from the gospel as understood in a continuing reflection on the lived faith of believing communities. This vision of a multifaceted Christian people moving through history underscores the need for a theology of the Holy Spirit as the foundation for Catholic democratic reforms. For it is the Spirit who manifests God in the evolution of history. And it is the Paraclete who brings alive the spirit of Christ in a developing world. Thus, the questions to be asked of the following principles is not how well they copy American or European democracies, but rather how faithfully they orchestrate a gospel ethos in our own time.

Yet who is to interpret the theological viability of these democratic principles? A full discussion of this query goes beyond the scope of this book. But the interpreters must not be confined to the magisterium in the narrowly understood meaning of contemporary Vatican officials and other bishops. The interpreters of the future will need to include a much more broad-based grouping of laity and theologians from the world church. These interpreters should be convinced that the church is primarily a congregation of faith, or, in the phrase of Vatican II, a people of God, and not primarily a hierarchy. The interpreters would understand that the institutional structure of the church must not be absolutized. The institutional church has a functional purpose. It does not exist for itself, but to facilitate the pastoral mission of the gospel. If the structure is an encumbrance to that mission, it needs to be changed. A number of suggestions for reform under the five principles correlate with the significant

Call to Action statement of 1990: "A Call for Reform in the Catholic Church."

Participation

The theological underpinning for the principle of participation is that through faith and baptism, all Christians, not only the hierarchy, constitute the church. Through the gifts of the Spirit, all Christians are called to represent Christ in the assembly and in the world. And according to the centuries-old dictum, what concerns all should be adjudicated by all in a representational way. If this principle were truly implemented today, major groupings of Catholic Christians would not be excluded from the decision-making process. For example, it is all too clear that women do not participate at every level of the Catholic Church. The wider community of the laity has little or no voice in shaping the future church, even though many of the best younger theologians today are laypeople. Nor is that group, once referred to as the "lower clergy," well represented in decision making.

Participation in choosing church leaders and exercising a shared ministry is an important example of the principle. Since Vatican Council I, the pope has appropriated almost total control in selecting bishops, and this control has been reenforced under Pope John Paul II. In a restructured church, wider participation in selecting leaders would be implemented from parish to papacy. On the parish level, elected representatives and the parish assembly as a whole would participate in calling the pastor, in administration of resources of the parish, and in planning ministerial programs. On the diocesan level, elected representatives of parish councils would collaborate in a deliberative way in the calling of a bishop, as well as in the accountability of funds and in program and policy development in the diocese.

On a national level, the present National Council of Catholic Bishops would be complemented by a national assembly of representatives of priest and lay councils. These representatives would meet with the bishops at stated times to vote on areas such as budget and program for the national church. This body would also propose and vote on candidates for episcopal office who would, in turn, be called by dioceses. On the international level, the pope might continue to be elected by a college of electors, but this body would be much more representative of national churches than the present college of cardinals. The papacy would lose the right to appoint bishops; the pope would confirm those elected by representative assemblies of national churches. All offices from pastor to pope would have a limited tenure determined by assemblies at the proper level.

To foster such participation, a draft plan envisioning the democratic reorganization of the Catholic Church should be drawn up on a national level. Once a draft plan is developed, it would be circulated to a range of representative groups, encompassing all constituencies in the church. A constitutional convention would be announced and each of the groups invited to send delegates in proportion to the group's size. The constitutional convention would revise and vote on the draft polity. When the draft is voted on and thus claimed by a representative array of Catholic groups in the United States, it would be presented to the American bishops. At the same time, there would be efforts to encourage other national churches throughout the world to take up the discussion and hold similar constitutional conventions.

Conciliarity

A key thread running through Catholic history is the conciliar process of dealing with issues of doctrine, structure, and practice. Just as a sense of covenant is more prominent in the Protestant tradition, so the conciliar heritage is more indigenous to Catholicism. The theological roots of conciliarism go back into the collegial dimensions of New Testament Christianity. This can be seen in the collaborative ministry of Jesus and his disciples. Its echoes resonate all the way back to the Council of Jerusalem in Acts. The church continued this tradition in the doctrine of the apostolic college. Even the symbolism of Trinity reflects a "conciliarity" of sorts in God. Local, regional, and universal councils were called throughout history. But some of the best and most explicit theological reflection on conciliarity can be found among the thinkers of the conciliar movement in the fourteenth and fifteenth centuries. The crisis of papal schism awakened new thought on the nature of councils. The present crisis of a major council denied stimulates us to these democratic and conciliar proposals today.

The conciliar style of regional and global decision making is as old as the church. Matters of faith, morals, and discipline were decided by councils. This tradition is already a form of ecclesial democracy, although it was more or less controlled by a monarchical papacy or a monarchical metropolitan bishop or by secular princes. For instance, Vatican I was tightly orchestrated by Pope Pius IX, in contrast to the more collegial exchanges of Vatican II under John XXIII and Paul VI. In our present moment of authoritarian retrenchment in Rome, we might forget that conciliarism is a very traditional form of Catholic democracy. The councils themselves, as made up of only voting bishops, need to be expanded to include representatives of the laity and of other religious professionals. Women, especially, must be included in the ranks of decision makers. But the theory and the history of the councils remains profoundly democratic. Observe, for example, the democratic dimensions of Vatican II: worldwide representation, public debate and dialogue, examination of issues in light of the church's first "constitution," the gospel, and decision making through election and consensus from committee to general assembly.

We have already alluded to conciliarity in the shared ministry of diocesan and national bodies. In a future democratic church, the papacy would lose the right to define doctrine, theological and moral, from above. These functions would belong to representative gatherings of global councils including episcopal, sacerdotal, and lay representatives from national churches. The pope would become a titular head of the church, *primus inter pares*, as bishop of Rome, but he would not be a universal monarch with divine-right-of-kings power. His primary ministry would be that of spiritual and moral leader, witnessing to the Christian vision of life on earth.

The conciliar principle needs to be implemented in an ecumenical way. Just as we can learn a great deal from secular experiences in democracy, so too various Protestant churches offer important historical experiments. For example, the Episcopal model of a House of Bishops and a House of Delegates (laity) can be a source for learning lessons through trial and error. The democratic traditions of other churches also teach us checks and balances in the use of power. If such terminology seems too secular, think of it in the light of mutual stewardship in churches that are also made up of sinners.

The Protestant experience with democracy can also teach us about the negative possibilities in what we see as a very positive enterprise. Excessive individualism can militate against the common good. Majorities can tyrannize minorities in the name of electoral politics. Elites can learn to subtly manipulate the system to their own advantage. And without constant reflection on gospel values, democratic structures might be too easily shaped by the surrounding culture. In light of these dangers, Catholics would do well to consult with Protestant observers throughout the democratizing process. In this way, the new Catholic conciliarism would carry forward the tradition of Vatican II that encouraged Protestant observers.

Pluralism

The theological basis for the principle of pluralism in restructuring the church resides in the freedom of God's leadership as well as in respect for the diversity of the Holy Spirit's gifts. By honoring a plurality of myths, rituals, and institutions in the church, we confess to the splendid freedom of God expressed in wonderful multiplicity. A theological problem with present Vatican control over the whole church is the identification of God's will with the will of John Paul II or of Cardinal Ratzinger. The freedom of God and the gifts of the Spirit would be more truly respected in a decentralized and pluralistic church.

The basic church community movement (or base ecclesial community) represents a powerful contemporary example not only of subsidiarity but also of pluralism. These examples of church from the bottom up, in Latin America and elsewhere, offer a horizontal variety of church structures instead of the vertical, monarchical, clerical model now in control of the church. These decentralized communities encourage lay participation and decision making as a counterbalance to the long-prevalent clerical control. Base communities foster the Christian communitarian spirit by direct relationships, reciprocity, and communal aid. These groups help the whole church rethink its structures in more communal, diversified, and democratic ways. Base communities must be adapted to the spirit and needs of different national and regional churches.

But it would be naive to advocate pluralism and decentralization in the reshaping of the Catholic Church without considering the dangers of fragmentation and factionalism. Communities do not exist in some tensionless, pure state. There are always conflicts over theory and practice, based on the convictions of different interest groups. Some fear that a pluralist, decentralized church structure will maximize human tendencies toward conflict, resulting in alienation and disunity.

Yet these dangers are no more endemic to democratic than to totalitarian systems. Moreover, within democratic societies the tendencies to alienation and disintegration can be more favorably mitigated by the many networks of dialogue and representation that are lacking in authoritarian, vertical systems of control. If the centralized authority of the Vatican monarchy were structurally changed, the result could be an even greater sense of unity in the church. Individuals and groups at various levels would feel responsible for the welfare of the church. They would experience the unitive thrust of upholding an institution that maximizes their freedoms. The polarity of resolving conflicts is necessary and beneficial. It pushes us to overcome barriers between persons and groups.

An example of pluralistic decentralization in the world church might be a moveable center for Catholicism. The tasks for a worldwide administrative and interconnectional center would be considerably reduced in a truly decentralized church, as these functions will have been largely accomplished at local, national, and regional levels. The pope would remain at his or her Roman see. But what is now referred to as the Vatican (another name is not beyond our imaginations) could move every ten years to a different country. In an expanding age of cybernetics and rapid communication, requisite information for such a world center could be easily moved and accessed. A democratic Vatican as a moveable feast would testify to the universality and diversity of the gospel.

Still another aspect of pluralism is respect for diversity in lifestyle and close attention to the worthy demands of minorities. A democratic church would find a balanced way of incorporating gays and lesbians into its structures. Women would be incorporated into all levels of ministry and decision making. This means abandoning the medieval discipline of mandatory celibacy and opening the priesthood to women and married people, including resigned priests. A decentralized and democratic Catholicism would also foster diversity in worship and sacramental life in keeping with the needs of different peoples. Such a church would also abandon its resistance on the remaining differences that separate Christian churches and translate the many results of their ecumenical dialogue commissions into serious concrete plans for reunion.

Accountability

The principle of accountability rests on the theological doctrine of stewardship for the gifts God has given us. It reflects the New Testament attitude that to whom much has been given, much will be required. Accountability also manifests charity in a community where all are equal brothers and sisters in Christ. The church in its present monarchical form is especially negligent of this principle. One can point to the Vatican bank scandals a few years ago or to the cover-up of pederasty in St. Johns, Newfoundland. In both cases, secrecy and nondisclosure ruled the day. Tragic events came to light only after years of hidden abuse. Full accountability concerning the use of money and property on all levels of the church does not obtain. This or that church leader may be accountable to the people, but specific structures of accountability are lacking. Catholic monarchy lends itself to secrecy and nondisclosure. Hierarchical "royalty" owns the church, as it were, in a vertical line of authority. The wider community of the laity is to pay and obey, but not be privy to the inner sanctum of church finances and decisions about property.

It is interesting that in the reams of literature about reforming the church after Vatican II, little or nothing is written about who "owns" church property and wealth. This is almost a form of modern gnosticism, ignoring our physicality and the stubborn reality of things. This amnesia of the concrete, however, sustains the present monarchical authority, which will be very reluctant to change as long as it can exclusively control church wealth. Unlike business owners, however, bishops are not majority stockholders in the church. Unlike secular corporations, the church belongs to all of us. We are the church. Our leaders should be accountable to us, not according to their whims, but according to definite structures of accountability. Catholics should explore all legal means for restoring effective lay participation in the disposition of church assets at every level. For example, the legal status of many bishops in the United States as "corporation sole" could be challenged in court. Such a legal fiction no longer fits the collegial theology of Vatican II. As the church democratizes, it needs to work out written procedures of financial disclosure and accountability from parish structure to the papacy.

Dialogue

The democratic church principle of dialogue flows from a theology of the freedom and mystery of God. Dogmatic closure of discussion among theologians today and sanctioned suppression of dissent negate the quest for the truth that shall make us free. A telling example of this scandal in modern Catholicism concerns the whole area of human sexuality. Even moderate theologians are sacked or harassed over their positions on sexual issues. Men who are experientially and intellectually out of touch with questions of sexuality parrot dead-end answers in the name of the magisterium. This continuing travesty stems from a structural problem in the church. For a divine-right-of-kings monarchy knows truth and error, that is, knows the mind of God.

In contrast, we need a dialogical church. Such a church is able to admit its past mistakes, because it is made up at every level of fallible sinners. This church will be sensitive to structures of due process as admirably expressed by leading contemporary canon lawyers. It is a learning church in dialogue about the real experiences of its people. A dialogical church does not mean a debating society in which everything goes and nothing is decided or acted upon. Here the principle of conciliarity offers forums for agreement and disagreement among Christians of good will. Decisions for action are made and periodically reviewed for adequacy and emendation. In complex matters, the principle of pluralism calls for respecting diverse consciences. Thus one democratic church principle is complemented by another. All these principles sustain dialogue in communities of pilgrims on their way to understanding and living the gospel more fully.

Yet the implementation of these principles toward a democratic Catholic Church demands strategies for bringing about change. Agreement with the principles is not enough. New strategies for action must be imagined and tried. Two types of strategy drawn from modern experiences of institutional change can be helpful. The first derives from the civil rights movement, the strategy of nonviolent resistance. If enough Catholics were convinced that the monarchical structures of the church were ill-adapted for the pastoral mission of the gospel, they could resist authority in various ways. A whole panoply of resistance strategies might be imagined from financial boycotts to demonstrations. A second type of strategy could be called proactive. These tactics range from educational programs to experimenting with alternative ministries within the church. Perhaps the bravest experimenters with diverse strategies for change today are groups of women religious. The issue of strategies for change from a monarchical to a democratic Catholic Church deserves careful study and elaboration.

As we stand on the brink of the twenty-first century, a major task for the Catholic Church is inner reform toward democratic structures. The success of other reforms in teaching and practice depends to a large extent on the structural changes we have reviewed. The history of the church from its inception offers many *loci* for reflection on horizontal, participational movements. The seeds of a democratic church are not foreign to it; they are rooted in its historical ground. They need to be cultivated by investigation, education, and action. People within the church need to use their imagination and creativity in pushing forward a grand design of democratic reform.

Our focus has been mainly on the inner reform of Catholic ecclesial structures. Yet the church does not exist for itself, but rather for the welfare of the world. This was the overriding vision of Vatican II, especially in its document on the Church and the Modern World. When John XXIII launched the council, he warned us about the prophets of doom, those afraid of change within and condemnatory of change without. They are still with us, even in the highest places. But it was hope, not fear, that inspired the pope of Vatican II. For him, a truly renewed church could be a catalyst for other great reforms toward social justice and peace amid an ecologically enlightened humanity. May this vision prevail.

Contributors

John Beal is a Canon Lawyer with the Diocese of Erie, Pennsylvania.

Philip Berryman is a former pastoral worker in Panama and Latin American representative for the American Friends Service Committee in Philadelphia. Among his books is *The Religious Roots of Rebellion: Christians in the Central American Revolution*.

Eugene C. Bianchi is a Professor of Religious Studies at Emory University in Atlanta, Georgia. Among his books is *Aging as a Spiritual Journey*.

John Coleman, S.J., is Professor of Religion and Society at the Jesuit School of Theology in Berkeley, California. His most recent book is *One Hundred Years of Catholic Social Thought*.

Charles Curran is a diocesan Catholic priest and the Elizabeth Scurlock University Professor in Human Values at Southern Methodist University in Dallas, Texas. Among his many books is *Toward an American Catholic Moral Theology*.

Jay P. Dolan is the Director of the Cushwa Center for the Study of American Catholicism at the University of Notre Dame in Notre Dame, Indiana. Among his publications is *The American Catholic Experience: A History from Colonial Times to the Present*.

E. Dale Dunlap is a Methodist minister, former Dean and Emeritus Professor of Theology at the Saint Paul School of Theology in Kansas City, Kansas.

Elisabeth Schüssler Fiorenza is the Stendahl Professor of Divinity at the Divinity School of Harvard University in Cambridge, Massachusetts. Her most recent book is *But She Said: Feminist Practices of Biblical Interpretation*.

Walter Goddijn, O.F.M., is Emeritus Professor of Sociology of Religion at the Catholic University of Tilburg in the Netherlands and author of *The Deferred Revolution: A Social Experiment in Church Innovation in Holland, 1960–1970*.

Hans Küng is a Catholic priest and one of the foremost European Catholic theologians. His most recent book is *Judaism: Between Yesterday and Tomorrow*.

261

Marie Augusta Neal, S.N.D., is Emerita Professor of Sociology at Emmanuel College in Boston, Massachusetts. Among her publications is *From Nuns to Sisters: An Expanding Vocation.*

Pedro A. Ribeiro de Oliveira is a research scholar with the Instituto de Estudo da Religião in Rio de Janeiro, Brazil. Among his publications is *Religião e dominação de classe.*

Rosemary Radford Ruether is Georgia Harkness Professor of Theology at the Garrett-Evangelical Theological Seminary and member of the graduate faculty of Northwestern University in Evanston, Illinois. Her most recent book is *Gaia and God: An Ecofeminist Theology of Earth-Healing.*